Praise for The Secrets of Ordinary Heroes

"A timely and timeless masterpiece, this book is a must-read that enriches our understanding of personal and geopolitical struggles of the Jewish people in the Islamic Republic of Iran."
—**Nilofar Niazi**, Founder & CEO of Nextherapy

"This is a remarkable story about a father. It is a story that needed to be told! It is both touching and inspirational!"
—**John Maraganore, Ph.D.** Founding CEO, Alnylam Pharmaceuticals, Inc, Previous Chair of the Biotechnology Innovation Organization, Mentor to many biotech entrepreneurs

"Ray tells a timely, poignant and essential story about the exodus of Jews from revolutionary Iran that invokes universal experiences. The Secrets of Ordinary Heroes is beautifully written and expertly crafted, a must-read!"
—**Lauren Pearle,** former Senior Producer, ABC News

"A compelling and inspirational story that takes readers through a relatable journey of self-discovery and perseverance. In dark times that test our identity, we are reminded about the strength of the human spirit and foundation of family."
—**Mikhail Keyserman,** Managing Director, Healthcare Investment Banking

"Ray's story is heartbreaking, inspiring and ultimately it is an American story. Immigration the way it should work. America and the world can learn a lot from Ray's story!"
—**Abraham Paul Sarkis,** Ordinary American

THE SECRETS OF ORDINARY HEROES

THE SECRETS OF ORDINARY HEROES

The Multi-generational Odyssey of an
Iranian-Jewish Family and Their Escape
from Khomeini's Revolution to Israel and
Redemption in America

DR. RAY TABIBIAZAR

KERAL
Publishing
Wholly owned by Five2Six Ventures

The Secrets of Ordinary Heroes: *The Multi-generational Odyssey of an Iranian-Jewish Family and Their Escape from Khomeini's Revolution to Israel and Redemption in America*

Copyright © 2024 Dr. Ray Tabibiazar

First Edition

ISBN: 979-8-9899200-0-6 (Hardcover)
ISBN: 979-8-9899200-2-0 (Paperback)
ISBN: 979-8-9899200-1-3 (eBook)

Editing by Kevin Anderson & Associates

Cover illustration by Rob Duckwall

Cover layout and interior formatting by Becky's Graphic Design®, LLC
www.BeckysGraphicDesign.com

A memoir

Dedicated to Baba and Fafa,
And to all the ordinary heroes who shape
our lives with their personal sacrifices
to make the world a better place for us all.

CONTENTS

DISCLAIMER

This is a memoir. It is therefore subject to the vagaries of human recollection. Dialogue has been reconstructed through conversations held with my parents and other family members over the years. Some names, dates, and places have been changed to protect people's privacy.

The story in this book touches on many historical events, which are multifaceted. Please keep in mind that this memoir only attempts to portray events as my family understood them at a particular time.

If you, the reader, have any interest at all in Middle Eastern or Jewish history and culture, I encourage you to conduct your own research on these topics and draw your own conclusions.

"To laugh often and much; To win the respect of intelligent people and the affection of children; To earn the approbation of honest critics and endure the betrayal of false friends; To appreciate beauty; To find the best in others; To give of one's self; To leave the world a bit better, whether by a healthy child, a garden patch, or a redeemed social condition; To have played and laughed with enthusiasm and sung with exultation; To know even one life has breathed easier because you have lived – This is to have succeeded."

—*Ralph Waldo Emerson*

THE ART OF LEADING
TWO LIVES AT ONCE

A RIVERBOAT RESTS IN its dock at Ross Landing by the Tennessee River in Chattanooga. Boxy as a store-bought swan and old-timey as a glass of hand-pressed lemonade, the riverboat sports three open decks. Each is loaded with people gripping boat drinks, smoking cigarettes, taking in the warm summer air and the sunset. The bow of the ship has two tall smokestacks, white-washed, one to each gunwale, port and starboard. And somewhere aboard her, even from where I stand by the shoreline, I hear a banjo-piano duet as it leaps through a sprawling Dixie-time tune.

Another riverboat glides up the river and passes the one at the dock. It blasts its horn. Beside me, a shoreline dotted with scurrying children whose parents run after them cheers back while a flurry of hands rocket into the air.

I stop breathing. Because, just for a moment, I thought those hands were not waving hello. They were tightly clenched fists, which the radicals punched at the sky as the revolution exploded.

"Irane ma daryaye khun ast, hukumate khodkame shah sarnegun shode ast!"

Our Iran is a sea of blood, the tyrannical regime of the shah has been overthrown!

I gasp, coming back to myself. It takes me a second to realize it's happened again.

As a doctor I understand that, medically speaking, my amygdala just hijacked my thoughts, which, in turn, assumed control of my physicality, hunching my shoulders, shunting the bulk of my blood to my core, preparing my body for fight or flight. Some memories are like puppet masters, pulling our strings, getting us to act in certain ways unconsciously. I notice my guts have contracted. I slam my eyes shut. I have never enjoyed big crowds. Part of me feels desperate to escape this one. But where would I go?

Easy, Ray. Take it easy. This is Chattanooga, not Khorramshahr. The two cities may look alike physically, but they are in different times, different places. Come back to reality.

Inhale. Exhale.

Better. But try it again.

Inhale and exhale.

Good.

Okay, open your eyes. Look again. What do you see?

What at first I'd taken for fists are actually palms held aloft in happy salutes. The frowns I noticed turn out to be smiles.

Why? I wonder. Why does this still happen? It has been decades.

My father's voice speaks in my head, which is very unusual. My father is not a loquacious man. Most often, his language is silence.

Ray, he says. *Be calm. You are no longer up on the mountain. This river is not the Karun in Khorramshahr.*

For one thing, the Tennessee River is cleaner.

Again, the riverboat blasts its horn and I will myself to enjoy it. I tell myself, *Relax. You are no longer in danger. Your family is safe. You all made it out.*

This is how a man lives when he is alive in two places at once. He keeps one foot moored in the past while the other has anchored here, in the present. One foot in the affluent suburbs and lush front yards of beautiful Chattanooga while the other, sandaled and covered in dust, pounds the turbulent, shriek-laced streets of Khorramshahr near the oil fields of Abadan in southern Iran.

When you live this sort of life, the sky can be cloudless and sunny one moment, strangled with smoke and pregnant black clouds the next. The darkness does not ask permission to come. It appears when it wants to, crushing you, blotting out light, bearing hurricane winds whose hammer blows push me backward, into the past.

When I blink my eyes again, I am back in the Zagros mountains. The sun has gone down. It is night. It is cold. The valley crouches below us, dark and silent. Beautiful. Treacherous. Waiting.

Above me, the black velvet sky is pinpricked by ten million shimmering stars. There is no moonlight or we'd be able to see Turkey from here, as we have on so many previous nights when that bright silver coin gazed down on us, beautiful, peaceful. I learned to despise it.

For ten days, that moon has held us frozen up on this mountain, waiting for a night dark enough that we could cross the border into Turkey. We were not prepared for this. We did not bring enough food or water or other necessities. Toilet paper. We were not prepared emotionally for the toll such a torturous journey would take. Or the metaphor, I think. The fact that light, that magnificent symbol of all that is good and right in the world, should now make our passage to freedom impossible.

The smugglers have told us this time and again. We cannot travel by moonlight. Someone will see us if we do—the border Pasdaran or the Revolutionary Guards. If they catch us, no matter which side they are on, they will drag my family out to the nearest ravine and shoot us. As a punishment, yes, certainly, but really more to deter others from trying to do what we're doing: escape our war-ridden country.

We have waited ten days but tonight is the crossing.

My father stands beside me with my little brother, Ramin. Even in darkness, I note how pensive my Baba is. Silent, he stares at the mountains as if he envisions our fate just beyond them.

"Baba, what are you thinking about?" I ask.

At first, he does not respond. Then he says: "Your great-great-grandfather Avram was a *Roossy*." In Farsi, this word means "Russian." "He walked over these mountains once, into Iran. That's how our family came to be here, did you know that?"

"Yes."

"Now we flee by the same path." Baba chuckles sadly, shaking his head, like he's saying, *The irony.*

Behind us, my mother hisses in the dark. "You all get over here now. The smugglers are saying the time has come!"

We arrive to find that an argument has broken out. The smugglers are waving their arms like men trying to land a plane. They all wear traditional Kurdish attire—the *ank-o-chokha* they call it, layers of caftan worn under short-waisted jackets—with weapons slung over their shoulders: Kalashnikov rifles, jeweled ceremonial daggers, and pouches of ammunition.

Agitated, the men bark at my father in Kurdish, while my brother, Ramin, age nine, grabs my arm and presses his lips to my ear. "What are they saying?" Ramin whispers.

I don't catch it all. They are talking too fast. But I understand a word in Kurdish, which I hear over and over again. *Dokhtar bache. Little girl*, the smugglers are saying. The girl is the issue. They are talking about my sister, little Romina. She just turned four about a month ago. *How can* she *be the problem?* I wonder.

The lead smuggler keeps repeating himself. He is a big man whose thick black beard merges seamlessly with the darkness, making his face seem part of the night. He is agitated and very determined. "The *dokhtar bache* must come with us now," he insists. "Only her. She is slowing you down. We cannot miss our car."

I watch tension warp my father's face. Despite the cold mountain air, fat crystals of sweat have broken out on his forehead. I imagine the anxiety he must be feeling. Could it be worse than my own? These smugglers—human traffickers—want to take little Romina with them. . . alone. What will happen if we do that? Will we ever see her again?

"No," my father says, waving his arms at his children, his wife. "We do not separate."

"There is no other way!" The smuggler is now emphatic. "The little girl comes with us or all will be lost. The rest of you must go by a different path."

"What are you talking about? What different path?" my father says.

The smuggler gestures. Like some kind of magic trick, one of his colleagues slips from behind some trees and walks quickly into the headlights, gripping a short hank of rope. My mother inhales sharply and moans as hooves *clip-clop* on the hard-packed earth.

The man who walked out of the trees is leading a "ghost" horse.

It is later that afternoon. I am no longer at the Chattanooga Riverbend Festival. I sit in the bleachers beside a pool surrounded by parents watching a swim meet. In the background, like supernumeraries on a movie set, everyone wishes their children good luck, then turns and moves to the bleachers, joining the backdrop of parents who all know the drill. When a new heat begins, we all cheer. When a heat is finished, we relax, make a few jokes, and talk to each other.

In intimate settings like these, my dark features and foreign accent raise certain questions. I am often asked: "Where are you from?"

I've been in the States a long time now and I've learned how to handle this question. Mostly, I just reply, "Israel." A half-truth.

When we first moved to Chattanooga, I tried out a joke. I said, "I'm from the south." Big pause, then I'd smile and I'd clarify. "Southern Iran."

But whenever I made this joke, I got crickets. Dull or blank looks. Was it something about my delivery?

"Wait," a person once said to me. "You said that you're Jewish?"

"That's right."

"A Jew from Iran?"

I nodded again.

"But how can that be? Aren't Iranians Muslims?"

Where to begin?

Should I tell them the history of Jews in Iran dates back more than three thousand years, long before the country became Muslim? Is this the appropriate tack to take when your kid is about to compete in the 200-meter freestyle?

"Yes," I answered this person. "The vast majority are Muslims. But there are a few Jewish people left in Iran even today, after the revolution."

Just thinking these thoughts pulls me backward again, into memory.

My mother steps up to the smugglers and flatly refuses to mount the eerie-looking albino mules they have brought. "We cannot ride those animals. They are ghost horses," she says.

The head smuggler is losing his patience. "Call them whatever you want, Khanoom," he says. *Khanoom* means "lady" in Farsi. "These beasts are the best choice for walking the trail that crosses the border. You *have* to get on!"

"I will not." My mother turns to my father. "I had a dream last night. My dead father came to me and told me clearly, 'Do not ride the ghost horse. The ghost horse is death!'" She points to one of the bone-white mules. "Now what does that look like? Huh? I would call that a ghost horse, wouldn't you?"

"I cannot believe this!" Pointing at my mother, the smuggler turns, addressing his fellow smuggler. "*Khanoom* is so superstitious, she will not ride the horses!"

The smuggler turns back to her, waving his hands. I can see he is torn between the deep respect he has for my father, whom he knows is a doctor, and my mother's unyielding demands. "*Khanoom*, I am trying to save your life. I tell you, you *have* to get up on these horses right now. Either get on your horse or let go of your *dokhtar bache*."

I look at Romina. Her little face is paralyzed with fear. Not a peep comes out of her.

What should we do?

I blink and am back at the swim meet again.

The girl who stands before me isn't my sister. She is my oldest child, my daughter, Eliana. Not a four-year old *dokhtar bache* but an athletic teenager closing fast on sixteen.

I watch her walk toward me wrapped in a towel with her hair dripping wet and her eyes on the scoreboard. "I came in second." She says the word *second* like it's some kind of curse. She is competitive, hardworking. "I could have done better."

"I think you did great," I say. "Don't compare yourself to others, you beat your own time. That's progress. Keep up the hard work for next time."

Then I think, *There are so many worse things than coming in second for my* dokhtar bache.

My parents are now arguing with each other in the dark using broken and rudimentary Hebrew so the smugglers won't know what they're saying. Like anyone could doubt; their body language gives them away. They are animated, furious with each other. I can tell by the smugglers' faces: they get it. This is a marital spat. Or, to those in our family, just another day in my parents' relationship.

The tension of all that we've been through has exacerbated my parents' age-old animosity. They have never been what I would describe as tender toward one another. Their love is fiercer than that. It crushes and grinds. Sometimes it stabs. It heals by wounding. Cherishes as it disdains.

"Did you not hear me?" my mother is shouting. "I said, I will *not* get onto that ghost horse! I tell you, my father came to my dreams last night and he told me—!"

"I don't care about your crazy dreams!" my father replies. "I care about getting us over the border without losing our daughter or dying!"

My mother points at the beasts. "Those horses are death!"

The lead smuggler finally snaps. "Doctor, our window is closing, we need to move."

It is at this very moment, with the mountain wind whistling soft in my ears, that I first understand the stakes we are dealing with. Certain death lies on one side of the mountain pass, possible death on the other. Which do we choose?

My poor parents. They have fled their native country so their children could be safe. . . only to find that placing us in jeopardy is the only way to survive.

My mother turns to a smuggler and says, very clearly, "Take my daughter. The rest of us walk. We will see her on the other side."

Back home, after the swim meet, our house phone rings the moment we key through the front door and enter our foyer. I already know who it is so I hustle to grab the receiver, leaving my wife, Kelly, to organize our children like some immensely compassionate drill sergeant.

"Hello?" I say.

My mother's voice answers. "Farzin?" My childhood nickname. To my mother and a few select others in our family, I will always be Farzin, not Raymond.

"How is he?" I say.

"Not well." Mom's silence tells me how bad things are. "He says the Nazis are coming."

"The what?"

"The Nazis. Your father says they are on the way now. We must hide, he says. They're coming to take all of us to the ovens. He isn't speaking Farsi, he's speaking in Turkish."

This all makes a terrible kind of sense. Turkish was the language my father grew up with, a tongue he speaks only to his brothers and sister.

"He's hallucinating," I say.

I can feel my mother nodding. "He developed. . . some psychiatric illness. They gave it a name. It was. . . oh. . . wait. I have to think what it is. . ."

"What, Mom?" I said. "What did the doctors call it?"

". . . late onset schizo-something. . ."

It's so funny, I almost laugh.

"Maman," I say. "It's not schizophrenia. People don't develop that when they're eighty. Something else is going on."

"Well, then I don't know what to tell you, Farzin. The doctors here have given your father a lot of medicine but he is still getting worse. He keeps saying the house is on fire, that his skin is falling off. He says he is worried about you, Ramin, and Romina. That we need to keep you all safe from the Nazis."

Quickly, I take stock of what my father could be suffering from. Two years earlier, he developed lung cancer, which recently metastasized to his brain. Doctors started him on a treatment of chemo and brain radiation. *Think, Ray, think. What, given that course of treatment, might be causing my father to hallucinate?*

"Maman, Baba probably has encephalitis."

"En-sipp-a. . . no. That wasn't what they told me. . . what did you call it?"

"Encephalitis." In cases such as my father's, autoimmune or infectious encephalitis is a very real threat with very real side effects. But hallucinations brought on by encephalitis need something to root themselves in. Like trauma. Terrible memories. It turns out my father has plenty of those.

"What are you saying?" I hear my mother's voice cracking, growing soggy with tears. "What is happening to him?"

"His brain is on fire. Inflamed," I say.

"But why is he talking about Nazis?" my mother asks, puzzled.

"I don't know. Let me talk to Ramin and his doctors. We'll figure something out. Just don't worry. We will take care of him." With that, I hang up.

Dear God, I think. *It must be all still in his head. Every awful thing that happened to him, which he never talks about, and all the people he has loved.*

The same way it's all still in mine.

"Pappy," my son says. "Is everything alright?"

His voice snaps me back to myself. Only then do I realize I have been standing there, staring at the phone like it might ring again.

"You look upset," Liam says. Good Liam. He has the cunning ability to read people's emotions. Gifted with empathy, he is sensitive to people's feelings.

"Fafa just called," I say. "Baba is sick."

"I know. He has cancer."

"Right," I say. "It's more than that now."

"How is it more?"

"Well, there is a problem," I say—and then realize I just used the same words the smuggler uttered, high up on that mountaintop in the Zagros chain, forty-odd years ago.

Liam takes a seat at the kitchen table, his face growing far too serious for most eleven-year-old boys in Chattanooga. Not even bar mitzvah age. "Tell me what's happened," he says.

Quickly, I tell him about encephalitis. Why Baba has it. Why it inflames his brain and the impact that has on his mind.

Liam listens carefully. When I finish my brief explanation, he looks at me sagely. "The Nazis from World War II?"

He reads a lot of books. Some of his favorites are about World War II. I nod.

"But why would Baba think they were coming to get him *now*?" Liam asks.

"Because," I tell him, "the memories of what happened to him. . . to us. . . they are still in his brain, and they are alive in there. At the moment, he cannot tell the difference between what is real and what he remembers."

Liam ponders this. "So the Nazis. . . they really came for him? I mean sometime back in the past?" I nod and watch him make a decision. "Tell me," he says.

"Tell you what?"

He folds his hands, sitting back and preparing himself. "Everything. Tell me what happened."

"Liam—"

Can he take this? I wonder. Will he understand if I tell him the perilous twists that allowed him to sit right here, right now, feeling safe, loved, and happy in our Tennessee home?

He and his sisters have never known hunger or fear, true deprivation, or homelessness. To them, heroes wear capes and have extraordinary powers while the world's worst villains are played by Hollywood stars outfitted with makeup and eye-popping CGI effects. If my children bother to ponder the past, I suppose they think about the black-and-white images printed in history books. They know their Baba as a kind man, very gentle, who barely speaks. He is not a large man, undersized in the height and weight departments. At boisterous family gatherings, he often sits quietly off in a corner, asking for nothing. Fafa is just a sweet grandma who barely speaks English but makes the best food in the world. How do I possibly explain the decisions they made many years ago? The little secrets that have motivated Baba and Fafa all these years. . .

How do I tell the why and how of their lives?

"Pappy?" Liam says.

I was drifting again. Sighing, I pull a chair out from the table and sit down. "Are you sure you want to hear this?"

"I'm sure," he says.

"This could take a long time."

"Anything worthwhile takes time. Isn't that what you tell us?"

He got me on that one. "Yes, this is true."

"Then where do we start?"

That's a very good question, I think.

"We could start this story going back nearly two hundred years," I tell him. "To Baba's great-great-grandfather, the one you got your blond genes from. His name was Avram. He was the first of many ordinary heroes and heroines in our family story. Heroes and heroines with extraordinary secrets."

And so I begin.

CHAPTER ONE

AVRAM WALKS OVER THE MOUNTAINS

Kiev, Ukraine, and Northern Iran | 1815–1882

LONG BEFORE RUSSIA ROLLED tanks through its beautiful valleys in the winter of 2022, before it declared independence from Russia, before the War to End All Wars gave way to an even bloodier conflict, Ukraine became the stage upon my which family history started.

I say this with tongue pressed firmly in cheek. Beginnings, as I tried to explain to Liam, are notorious as moving targets. Where does anything truly begin? Most history books will tell you that the Jews showed up in the region of modern Ukraine region during the late ninth century. Others would say they came even earlier, during the days of the Roman Empire.

My father's family tells its own story about how our ancestors ended up in Ukraine—*Roos* as they called it. They say it is likely our ancestors wandered out of Israel to Egypt first, then continued west on a detour through northern Africa to settle in Spain. But with all the religious prosecution during early Christianity, they drifted eastward again until, over time, they reached Italy. Generations later, they somehow wound up in eastern Europe.

Yes, ancient Jews experienced halcyon days. Life in the diaspora has always been defined by its ebbs and flows. Good times follow bad times followed by good times and bad times. Repeat, repeat. Just like is written in the Book of Ecclesiastes: There is nothing new under the sun.

By the early part of the nineteenth century, my father's ancestors were living in what was then southwestern Russia. They'd made their home in the city of Kiev where, for the most part, Jews were welcomed. Life was good for the Jews between 1801 and 1825. Throughout the nineteenth century, Czar Aleksandr the First worked to ease certain restrictions on Jews that his father, Paul the First, put in place. Aleksandr decreed that Jews should be able to travel more freely. He let them enroll their children in schools. Importantly, he twisted the faucet shut on anti-Jewish propaganda. For long stretches, conditions for Jews would improve. They might flourish, becoming the center of attention—until things changed and they became scapegoats again.

Aleksandr's death in the late 1880s sealed the fate of the Jews in Ukraine. Their lives turned miserable. Suddenly, Jews were being persecuted to dizzying heights. New laws were put into place forcing Jews to compulsory military services. Without question, the plight of the Jews in Ukraine reached a sort of precipice during the lifetime of my great-great-grandfather Avram.

According to family lore, Avram was born in the mid-1800s. No photos of him survive. I have only vague descriptions that say he was tall, blond, blue-eyed, and very handsome. Even today, anyone with good looks in our family credits Avram with their genetics.

In the late 1800s another pogrom—read: an organized massacre of helpless Jews—broke out in Odesa on the northern shore of the Black Sea. Such an occurrence was not uncommon. The justification for violence was that Jews had vandalized a church in a predominately Greek community. For Avram, this triggered a personal decision. He decided that too many Jews had already died in the pogroms. He was not alone in this assessment. When the killings began in earnest, thousands of Russian Jews packed their trunks and hustled their families to the nearest port to book passage abroad. The bulk of this exodus made its way to America. But my great-great-grandfather Avram had a different plan.

Avram would have been about seventeen years old, in the prime of his life. Perhaps goaded by the impulsiveness of youth, he left everything he had known and set out on foot. Likely, he carried nothing but a blanket and the clothes on his back. Likely, he went south following the east bank of the Dnipro River. And when he reached the coast of the Black Sea, Avram turned east. Crossing the snow-capped peaks of the Caucasus, he put Europe behind him and continued south across lands burned gold by the sun, past old roads left by Emperor Xerxes when he sought to bend Greece to his will.

Finally, great-great-grandfather Avram stopped on the northern spur of the Elburz, which borders Iraq, on Iran's western flank. He had walked nearly 1,200 miles over lands most men at that time had never heard of, let alone seen. Common sense says he was tired and hungry. Above all, he must have realized that his life had changed forever.

Descending the mountain, he came upon a little town called Miandoab. In the local tongue, the name means "between two rivers." Our family history says that, like any good Jewish boy crossing a border into territories unknown, Avram sought out a synagogue. But in those days, a synagogue was not some vast and illustrious temple, especially out in the hinterlands. It was a small house created by a local rabbi or a cohen who'd gathered a minyan, the traditional quorum of ten worshippers over the age of thirteen, to celebrate Shabbat prayers and high holidays. This temple would pull double duty as the rabbi's family dwelling.

I have often wondered what the local rabbi thought when he saw this pious if deeply bedraggled young man enter his temple and lay himself out like a corpse on his flagstones. Here again, I draw from our family lore. The rabbi noted my great-great-grandfather Avram's tall, blond, blue-eyed good looks, his Russian savvy, his charms—so inherently Jewish. I imagine he took an instant liking to Avram. How could he not? This rabbi had no son of his own, a condition that riles the spirits when even the calmest of men have reached late middle age. So he offered Avram some food. He gave him some water. He gave him new clothes. When Avram's mouth opened and tales spilled forth, the old rabbi sat back and listened.

Doubtless, Avram recounted his travels without guile. Doubtless, too, the rabbi must have understood this young man had just made an incredible journey. He was truly grateful for life, for food, for shelter, for water, for clothes, as well as the milk of human kindness. Perhaps this accounts for why, not long afterwards, the rabbi offered Avram the hand of his twelve-year-old daughter in marriage.

The girl's age was not so uncommon. In those days, many Iranian Jews promised their young daughters in marriage, or *aroosi*, "engaged to be wed." The predominant fear at that time was that young Jewish girls could be lured away or abducted by men from other religions. That would have been a tragedy. At best, the child would immediately be disowned. At worst, her family's bloodline would be lost. Pledging a daughter in marriage while they were still young was a way of "reserving" them until such time as they came of age.

This rabbi must have been worldly, I think. He knew that merely offering his young daughter as a future bride would not sate an ambitious man like Avram. So the rabbi also offered his orchard as prepayment on his daughter's dowry.

The worth of this gift was beyond calculation. Persia in those days produced some of the best fruit found anywhere in the world. Fat-waisted oranges. Low-drooping grapes. Soft peaches whose soft down awakens each morning glistening with nectar and dew. Sweet dates, shriveled and brown in ancient clusters lowing from palm trees. Melons and tangerines. Cherries and walnuts. The list of this bounty goes on and on.

The rabbi's orchards must have been particularly. . . well, fruitful. I say this because the soil upon which Miandoab rests is highly prized to this day. They don't call this the Fertile Crescent for nothing. The mountains rising on all sides grind their stones over hundreds of thousands of years. A local river, the Zarriné-Rūd, picks these minerals up and scatters them into its floodplains, feeding the water with dust that can make a crop leap toward the sky.

Thus did my great-great-grandfather, Avram the Wanderer, trade in his patched set of clothes and his torn-soled shoes for his new role as Avram the Farmer. Russia was now but a memory. Kiev and Ukraine had passed like a nightmare at dawn. For the first time in his life, Avram was prosperous. He had food in his belly, warm blankets to cover his body at night, clean water to drink, and new friends. Best of all, he had a new purpose. This alone has been known to rejuvenate even a man who lies at death's door.

Avram also had a new identity. His poor, illiterate family had no surname. Perhaps it was the rabbi who picked one out for him. "You are Jewish," the rabbi may have told him. "The son of Avraham, Itzhak, and Yaakov. And so we will call you Avram Ben-Israel. Ben-Israel, meaning 'Son of Israel.'"

My great-great-grandfather Avram accepted this name, plus all the fruits that came with it.

Years passed. Under Avram's steady hand, the orchard business thrived and spread. He enjoyed his newfound freedom, plus all the peace and prosperity growing like fruit vines in little Miandoab.

In the fullness of time, Avram was given a firstborn son, whom he named Nisan. In Hebrew, the word Nisan refers to the first month of the Jewish new year, which is also the time of harvest.

And Nisan, who was my great-grandfather, had a son of his own, called Ahron. And Ahron, my grandfather, had six children of his own: five sons, as well as a daughter.

The youngest son of this brood was named Yeshayahu.

He would later become my father.

CHAPTER TWO

JOHOUDKOSHAN

Tabriz | 1937–1941

MY FATHER, YESHAYAHU BEN-ISRAEL, was born in the summer of 1937. I envision his first few years of life as idyllic. How could they not be, growing up as he did in an orchard, safe in the picturesque town of Miandoab in northwestern Persia? (The country had changed its name to Iran in 1935 but my father's family still thought of it as Persia.)

The family plantation would have been a wonderful home for a child. I imagine my father as a two-year-old. Picture him, with his milk-toothed smile while wobbling this way and that, pointing delightedly at everything that interested him. His first words would have been mixtures of Turkish, his father's language, and Kurdish, the native tongue of his mother. Later, he picked up Farsi, Hebrew, and probably some Arabic, plus a smattering of local dialects. And, although he was never really the mischievous type, even then, I suspect, he found trouble. Blame it on the stars he was born under or the family and religion he was born to. From his earliest days, these seemed to throw trouble at my father the way clouds throw rain at a coastline. Or blame geography. Because, as it turns out, in Miandoab, when my father was growing up, big trouble was practically everywhere.

This was the run-up to World War II. My father recalled to me once how the tensions began when he was quite young. Persia at that time was ruled by Reza Shah Pahlavi, a career politician who'd been a decorated officer in the imperial army. Reza was no ordinary soldier. Back in 1921, guided by British intelligence, and with an eye toward stifling Russian meddling in Persia, he led a contingent of some four thousand troops from the Cossack Brigade to Tehran and captured the city. The British claimed they were helping Reza centralize power for the good of all Persians. It went without saying that they were also hoping to protect their vital trade routes to India.

Reza Pahlavi helped oust the then prime minister. He also played a key role in appointing a new one. From that point on, he rose quickly in the new regime. First, he became the Sardar Sepal, or commander in chief of the army. Two years later, the Persian Parliament granted him dictatorial powers. He exiled the man who was then Persia's Shah—one Ahmad Shah Qajar—and set himself up in his place as the new king, which began the Pahlavi dynasty.

The term "Shah" is a Persian word deriving from the court of Cyrus the Great in sixth-century BCE. It hearkens back to the term *shāhanshāh*, which means "emperor" or "king of kings." Being a *shāhanshāh* carried sweeping powers, most of which Reza Shah Pahlavi used rather wisely. He had a vision of steering Persia away from hardline theological influences and modernizing the country under a gentler, secular society. Under his leadership, the Persian government showed a greater acceptance of Jews. Unlike under the Qajar rule, Jews had rights in the Pahlavi regime. They were free to practice their religion without fear of recrimination, free to openly call themselves Jewish and to practice Jewish culture, albeit quite cautiously.

Reza Shah had been responsible for changing the country's name from Persia to Iran back in 1935. He thought the new name would better accompany the new nationalistic sentiment he was promoting. The name Iran means "Land of Aryans." The Aryans were a people of antiquity who had lived in Persia centuries before. It was never a term that meant race. Being Aryan was a religious, cultural, and linguistic identifier. Knowing this, Reza Shah thought he could rebrand his nation to gently separate it from its Arab neighbors while integrating its multiple, fragmented ethnic groups.

But his vision of a fast-paced modernization was complicated by three key factors. First, his subjects were illiterate. Second, the specter of war had again raised its ugly head through the Nazis up north in Germany. Third, his country had no infrastructure to speak of.

With so many foreign powers vying for Iran's oil wealth, the shah decided his best course of action was to keep Iran neutral. He refused to take sides in the coming war. Rather, he would pursue the economic and social programs he'd envisioned for his country. For no better reason than this, he partnered with Germany on projects such as the Trans-Iranian Railroad. A priceless public asset, the railroad linked Tehran to the Caspian Sea before continuing south to the Persian Gulf. The entire project was planned and constructed by German engineers, most of whom were lodged in a neighborhood of Tehran that soon got a funny name. People called it "Nazi-abad."

The relationship between Germany and Iran grew even closer in 1936. The Nazis classified Iranian Persians as "pure blood Aryans." Iranian Jews were very negatively impacted by this relationship. The company that built the Trans-Iranian railroad was specifically told not to hire any Jews. Because of such discrimination, many Iranian Jews feared they would suffer a similar fate to the Jews in Europe.

By most accounts, Reza Shah was not happy with these circumstances. He recognized the limits of Nazi race-based agendas. But leaders must make hard decisions, some of which have bad or unintended consequences. Iran's economic alliance with the Nazis created a prosperous economic partnership. So that's what the shah pursued.

I pause, looking at Liam. "Are you with me so far?"

He nods. "I never knew any of this. It's so. . ."

"Don't worry," I assure him. "History's complicated, a subject with many layers. In fact, one of the ways I think of history is like an onion."

"What do you mean?" Liam says.

I chuckle. "The more you peel, the more complex it gets. And the more it makes you cry."

We have to consider that these were strange times, full of propaganda and outright lies crafted to serve political agendas. My father once told me the story of a radio announcer whom the Germans employed to perform anti-Jewish tirades during the war. In the spring of 1941, when my father was only four years old, this anti-Jewish radio announcer began promoting a rather incendiary idea during the celebration of Purim. Muslims should take revenge on the Jews for the ancient Purim massacre that killed an ancient Persian prime minister named Haman and all his sons.

The choice to recall Haman's murder was wickedly calculated. Though it likely happened back in the fourth century BCE, this event was one of those cultural wounds that never quite heals. It was thus the perfect pressure point to elicit ancient anti-Jewish hatred in the Middle East.

The biblical story of Purim is one that every Jewish family knows well. The emperor of Persia once married a beautiful woman named Esther. His prime minister was a man named Haman, who hated the Jews. And Esther was Jewish. Her cousin, Mordechai, leader of their community, was Haman's archenemy. Not wanting to cause trouble in her marriage or for the country, Esther kept her Judaism a secret.

At one point, Haman became so inflamed, he pushed for every single Jew throughout the empire to be slaughtered. He kept goading the emperor to choose a date upon which all Jews would be put to the sword. There is even a term for this in old Persian: *Johoudkoshan*, "Massacre of the Jews."

Horrified, Esther took matters into her own hands. She invited her husband, the emperor, and Haman to attend a feast she held in their honor. During this feast, lovely Esther revealed that she herself was a Jew.

The shah must have been surprised when he found out the love of his life was a Jew. Haman was probably more surprised when Esther turned to him and noted calmly that any plot to kill Jews was therefore a plot to kill the emperor's wife. On which point, the law was quite clear. This was an act of treason, the punishment for which was death. Haman was taken outside and hanged at once. Some versions of the legend say that his ten sons were hanged alongside him. The shah then appointed Mordechai his new prime minister. Together, they created some of the first pro-Jewish laws in the region. At least one of these laws allowed Jews the right to defend themselves.

It was this event which, centuries later, the Nazi propaganda machine leveraged to galvanize Iranian radio listeners toward attacking Jews. The traditional anti-Semitism propaganda that worked in Europe didn't translate well to Iran and the Middle East in general. There were too many cultural differences. The Nazis therefore had to conjure anything they could from local history to fuel their anti-Jewish propaganda machine. They picked at an old wound, the subsequent furor over which would catch my father, his family, and all other Jews throughout Iran in the crossfire.

Hoping to stave off the Nazis, Reza Pahlavi declared all Jews to have been fully assimilated. This didn't work so well. Despite the shah's desire to create a more secular Iran, anti-Semitism ran deep in the citizenry. At that time, a substantial part of the population was poor and uneducated—read: susceptible to having their opinions swayed by loud voices. Then, too, the path of neutrality Pahlavi had chosen was practically doomed from the start. His kingdom was quickly overrun by agents of foreign governments representing both Axis and Allied forces. They roamed unchecked all over the country. Wherever they went, outbreaks of partisan thuggery bloomed. Things only got worse when Hitler's forces invaded the Soviet Union in June 1941. The Allies watched the Nazis closing in on Moscow. They knew what this meant and they feared it.

Everyone seemed aware of the Nazis' plan. While Stalin's forces flailed through their death throes, Hitler's armies would use the distraction, push over the Caucasus, and roll right down into Georgia. Their thrust would not stop at Iran's northern border. Having almost no one to stop them, the Germans would seize Iran's oil fields while commandeering the priceless Trans-Iranian Railroad. Which, in turn, would cut off vital supply arteries leading from British-controlled India to where the Allied war effort needed them most.

If the Nazis cut that supply line, the Soviets, already half-beaten, would starve to death. Everyone saw the writing on the wall. And everyone blamed Reza Shah. Because of his neutral stance, the alliance would topple, the war would be over, and Hitler would win.

Knowing this, the Allies altered course. Citing the shah's refusal to expel German spies from Iran, they mounted a staggering all-out assault on the country. History books call this the Anglo-Soviet Invasion of Iran. The British and the Soviets simply rolled in and started shooting. Their attack overwhelmed the Iranian military. Within two short days, the Allied powers were clearly in charge. It was a crushing defeat for the throne.

In August 1941, the Red Army began occupying most of northwest Iran, all the way south to the city of Tabriz. Uneasy with the Soviets being so close, Great Britain and the United States announced they would stay in the region until six months after the end of the war with Germany. Then, hoping to find a more tractable ruler, the same Western powers that helped Reza Shah rise to power replaced him with his son, the crown prince.

The new Shah, Muhammed Reza Pahlavi, loved the West. In all things, he tended to side with the British, and later with the Americans. His father's official exchange, or abdication, took place the following month, on September 16, 1941. From that point forward this pliable youth, Muhammed Reza Pahlavi, ruled Iran.

My father was four years old when all this happened. He remembers the upheaval. Fear had poisoned the spiritual wells of the country. Violence erupted in the cities but spread quickly to the hinterlands where, like a predator, it began to feast. At times, it even crossed the border into places like Iraq, where a bunch of pogroms broke out. Quiet little Miandoab, seated in its green bucolic space between all those lovely Iranian mountains, found itself suddenly under attack. Hell had come to paradise, you might say. One moment, my father was running through fields full of flowers and fruit, laughing his four-year-old head off, infatuated with the world. The next moment, partisans sympathetic to Axis racial agendas rode in on horseback, barreled through mountain towns, and set fire to Jewish businesses and homes.

If this wasn't a full-out pogrom, it was close. Along with the torch-bearing riders, an old Persian word came racing through the green fertile valleys of northern Iran: *Johoudkoshan.* "Massacre of the Jews." Gleefully, the terror riders told every Jew they encountered they would be tortured or killed if they didn't uproot themselves at once and move on. Some even hinted that room could be made for them in the Third Reich's concentration camps. Even the Jews of Miandoab understood what that meant. Nobody wanted to be gassed or shoved in the ovens or made to work until they dropped. Heeding these warnings, many Jews packed their valises and disappeared.

With the mob and partisan horsemen coming closer by the hour, my grandfather Ahron came up with a plan. The women and children of his family would depart at once while Ahron and his two oldest sons stayed to pack up the house. They would rejoin their loved ones later.

Picture little four-year-old Yeshayahu being told to pack his whole life in a bag. It's hard to imagine how he must have felt when he learned he could only take clothes, no toys or books. Such things weren't essential to where he was going. To leaving the orchard alive.

"Hurry!" my grandfather Ahron told him. "You have to be quick now! Please move faster, Yeshayahu!"

Questions must have abounded at once. Where would the exiles go? Where on earth would they find themselves safe in such turbulent times? My family decided to go to Tabriz, the capital city of Azerbaijan province, some forty miles north of Miandoab. Picture a little enclave nestled snugly between the tall cones of two dead volcanoes, Mount Eynali and Mount Sahand. Back in those days, the bustling streets of Tabriz played home to a large population. Merchants and messengers, students and pilgrims, workers and hirers—everyone came to Tabriz. Since people were always moving about there, it would be an easy place for refugees to blend in without being noticed. And my family had friends in Tabriz, trading partners from the Bahá'í faith who would give them shelter at time of need.

There was only one problem. All roads leading into and out of the mountains were blocked by partisan forces. How would the women and children get to Tabriz? My grandfather Ahron concocted a bold scheme. He told his wife, "Go to the train station."

"Why bother?" my grandmother said. "That station is guarded by partisans loyal to Nazis."

Ahron told her not to worry, he'd take care of everything. So it was that, with his bag clutched tightly in his pink little hand, my father left the family orchard with his mother, his grandmother, the youngest of his older brothers, and his very young sister. Following Grandfather Ahron's instructions, this group of aspiring evacuees went to a particular depot at the Miandoab train station. Rolling back the massive doors of a wheel house, they looked inside and saw several oil tanks lined up on flatbed trollies.

Grandfather Ahron had told them which tank they should use. "It is that one," my grandmother pointed. "Number Five. You see it there? Good. Now climb up the ladder. I want you all in there at once. *Yallah yallah!*"

The women and older children helped the smaller kids up the ladder. Carefully, using ropes, I imagine, they lowered themselves into that cavernous belly of steel. It stank of petrol and it was pitch dark, my father recalled to me later.

This tank had been left empty on purpose, of course. Windowless, lightless, airless, it was a perfect vessel for smuggling Jews, a metal womb that, God willing, would birth strange offspring when it at last arrived in Tabriz.

The Nazi sympathizers showed little inclination to check yet another oil tanker leaving the depot. My father, his brother and sister, my grandmother, and great-grandmother made it past barricades and checkpoints, over the city borders, and disembarked in Tabriz like passengers riding in Pullman cars, albeit a bit less comfortably.

"It's still in my mind, that claustrophobic, dark space," my father once told me. He shook his head. "I still remember the gasoline smell."

My father has always been a man of few words. The fact that he was speaking so much on this subject struck me as odd and somehow important, and so I pursued the matter with gusto.

"When you get to be my age, Farzin," my father said, "you begin to see how much of what we consider the truth is really just a bad memory."

He never went back to Miandoab. From that day forward—until he'd graduated medical school and joined the Iranian army—he lived out his life in Tabriz.

CHAPTER THREE

DOCTOR FIRE

Tabriz and Tehran | *1941 to 1950s*

IN 1941, THE YEAR that my father was forced off his family's home and fled in an empty oil tanker to Tabriz, my mother had not yet been born. Later, however, her own mother, Sara—whom I knew as Maman Bozorg—recounted to her what conditions were like in their home city of Tehran.

Years before the war, when my maternal grandmother was still just a girl, her family lived in one of Tehran's Jewish ghettos, a bad place to be. Ghetto dwellers routinely endured poverty, hardships, and discrimination against both women and Jews. For instance, during this time in Tehran, Jews were ordered not to walk outside when it rained. The local Muslims imagined their water supply would be contaminated if it touched Jewish skin. Such water would become *najes*, they said, impure. To drink such water or come into contact with it in any way would make a Muslim untouchable for their daily prayers.

"Jews have no rights in our country!" these religious Muslims argued. As did so many others.

Anti-Jewish sentiments reached a fervor during the war. Even in Tehran, Jews feared that, eventually, the Nazis would take over Iran and ship them to European concentration camps. Years later, my grandmother Sara would experience her fears anew each time she told tales of how she and her fellow women said prayers. These women alone, she maintained, were responsible for foiling the Nazis' plans for Iranian Jews.

"It was incredible!" Maman Bozorg said. "We women heard that the shah was planning to join the Allies. So all of us went to the temple, where we fasted for two days. The whole time, we prayed that God would save us Jews in Tehran from the threat of the Nazis and their evil camps. And wouldn't you know it? God heard us! From genocide and annihilation, He delivered us into the hands of the Allies!"

With the Allied powers rising, Reza Shah's abdication, and a new monarch sitting on the throne, a new era began in Iran. Or did it? Muhammed Reza Pahlavi was then only twenty-two years old. Word had it, his Western counterparts sort of sidelined him during the war. The new Shah could run his own country, they told him, so long as he didn't deviate much from the Western powers' playbook. Any tensions that may have arisen from this relationship were soothed when, in January 1942, Great Britain and the Soviet Union signed a treaty recognizing Iran's independence and sovereignty. As part of this treaty, the Allied powers pledged to shield Iran's economy from the ravages of war. They also promised to withdraw their troops from Iranian soil within six months of the war's conclusion.

Obviously, this had nothing to do with generosity. As in all matters political, the decision was centered on resources, money, and power. Stalin, Churchill, and Roosevelt may have been allies, but just for the moment. Each leader was deeply aware that, if they succeeded in winning the war, a new war would begin where they fought one another. What actions could they take then to gain an upper hand in that conflict?

There exists a famous black-and-white photo of these three men sitting in chairs, looking exhausted. They met in Tehran for a brief summit during which they signed an official document called "The Declaration of the Three Powers Regarding Iran." While the title might sound pro-Iranian, the true intent of that document was to keep this trio of tired old men from fighting one another. At issue was the following: Should the Allies split Iran, north to south? That would give Abadan's oil fields to the Brits and Americans while the Soviets got nothing. What about splitting the country east to west? That wouldn't work either. It gave the Russians access to the warm waters of the Persian Gulf, increasing their shipping capabilities.

In the end, the Three Powers decided to not split the country. Far better to simply leave Muhammad Reza Pahlavi on the throne. The young king was fiercely pro-Western. He liked the wealth and prestige that the West could offer him. It is rumored that, despite the war, the shah acquired no less than twenty-five custom-built cars: Buicks, Cadillacs, a Mercedes, and six Rolls-Royces.

As a result of all this, by the spring of 1942, Shah Muhammed Pahlavi had severed all ties with the Axis powers and kicked out all their spies who lived and worked in the country. While my father and his family were setting up their new life in Tabriz, Iran had basically joined the Allies.

It was an uncomfortable situation. Tabriz had been occupied by the Red Army since the Anglo-Soviet Invasion. The city remained under Soviet control until May 1946, by which point my father was nine years old. Regardless of which power occupied the city, my family were still Jews. No matter where you lived in Iran, things had not yet reached a point where Jews could afford to stop looking over their shoulders.

In Miandoab, my father's family had been openly Jewish. They spoke the local languages—Turkish, Kurdish, Farsi, and so on—but kept Jewish customs, which included learning Hebrew. All this became increasingly more difficult in Tabriz, where Muslims predominated and business opportunities diminished. At least in Tabriz, a larger, more bustling town, they could keep a low profile. Distracted by the war and its aftermath, nobody cared to bother them much. Besides, they had arrived in Tabriz as refugees with nothing but the clothes on their backs and a bag or two for each of them. My father's life had changed literally overnight. Now everything was a struggle. The entire family, including my father's brothers' wives and all of their children, had taken up residence in a single, tiny home where privacy was obliterated. They became dependent upon one another as never before.

"For the first time, we started to see the benefits of getting a formal education," my father recalls. "When you live in a city, the dynamics are different. Education becomes your only ticket to gain some control over your life."

His older brothers got busy helping their father and grandfather cobble together enough business to keep the family afloat. They were merchants now, making their living by trading in goods. It therefore fell to my father to help his cousins, nieces, and nephews master their schoolwork. His childhood was over; his new life as teacher and truant officer had begun. Who else could handle those jobs? The women in his family were illiterate. Most of the men were effectively so. The most educated person among them had very little formal education. Most everyone left school early to work in the family business. That is how people survived in those days.

When the war ended in September 1945, my family celebrated, albeit with reservations. Victory or no victory, they had already lost so much. And of course, no matter how anyone sliced it, things were still pretty difficult for the Jews. Wise people didn't assume that anti-Semitism would simply halt when Hitler was found dead in his private bunker ten stories below the Reich Chancellery in Berlin. Things got a little bit better when, on May 14, 1948, David Ben-Gurion, then head of the Jewish Agency, proclaimed that Jews would establish their own state. He called the new nation Israel. Later that day, American President Harry Truman announced that the United States would recognize the proclamation. Soon after that, the United Nations passed a resolution, upholding Ben-Gurion's move. Iran and the Arab world voted against the resolution. Shortly afterwards, war erupted again.

Countries like Syria, Egypt, Jordan, and Iraq sent fighters who entered the new land of Israel, seized control of its edges, and, as if the new country were a fine Persian rug, tried yanking it out from under Jewish feet. They attacked Israeli forces but they also attacked Jewish settlements, killing innocent women and children. If you look up this fight in the history books, people call it the 1948 Arab-Israeli War. My father was eleven years old when this happened. My mother was seven.

I can imagine that my family, like Jewish families across the world, followed the war very closely. Luckily, events swung in their favor. Eighteen months after the war began, Jews not only controlled the lands proposed by the UN resolution, but they had seized nearly 60 percent of lands guaranteed for an Arab state. The Arab-Israeli War so completely remodeled the region that, eventually, Shah Muhammad Reza Pahlavi forged close ties with Israel. In fact, Iran became the second Muslim-majority country to recognize Israel as a sovereign state (Turkey was the first). In almost no time at all, the two nations became close. Israel saw Iran as its vital ally, a diverse and therefore ultimately non-Arab country embedded in the Arab world. Iran reciprocated by letting Israel set up a permanent presence in Tehran long before ambassadors were officially exchanged in the 1970s.

But this new relationship kicked off internal struggles between the young monarch, Shah Muhammad Reza Pahlavi, and his new prime minister. Mohammad Mosaddegh was a seasoned politician who was then in his seventies. In word, attitude, or deed, Mosaddegh represented the national interests in a country with deep Muslim traditions, which had held sway since the 1500s. His stances on practically every issue put him at odds with the West, and therefore at odds with the shah, who was wary of Mosaddegh's increasing popularity. Mosaddegh was steadfast in achieving economic and political independence for Iran.

In every photograph ever taken of him during this period, Mosaddegh looks like a skeletal, brooding bald eagle dressed in a suit. He was not a man to be underestimated. He had a new vision for his country as a secular nation that could forge its own path forward, devoid of external interference. Mosaddegh believed that all Iranians, regardless of ethnic or religious background, should have a voice in their own affairs. This, of course, would diminish the power of the monarchy. Mosaddegh's bold vision caused a lot of Iranian Jews to support him while simultaneously placing them at odds with the new Shah, and therefore the West.

And so, like his father before him, Muhammad Reza Pahlavi found himself caught between a rock and a hard place. In the end, he chose to retain the trust and backing of his Western partners, the better to retain the powers of his monarchy.

Ultimately, it was Mosaddegh's attempted nationalization of Iranian oil that led to his downfall. In the coup of 1953, orchestrated by the CIA and MI6, those groups most negatively affected by loss of access to Iranian oil branded Mosaddegh a Russian Communist puppet and overthrew him. The shah was reinstated as the country's ultimate ruler with the West controlling Iran's oil. To cement his grasp of the country, the shah—again with the help of the CIA, MI6, and, this time, Mossad—created a brand-new secret service called SAVAK, an acronym for *Sazeman-e Ettela'at va Amniyat-e Keshvar*. In English: "Intelligence and Security Organization of the Country."

Like many Iranian Jews, my parents found the Iranian postwar economy deeply challenging. Many were pulling up stakes and heading for Israel, the first country to be sanctified under Jewish rule. My father's second-oldest brother, Elyahu, left for Israel in 1950 at age seventeen. His father—my grandfather—went with him, along with Elyahu's father and brothers.

Once they got there, they found the new country too young and too poor for them to prosper in. My father and uncles moved back to Iran. Elyahu chose to stay. He had met his extended family in Israel. His mother's brothers and sisters had lived in the vicinity of Jerusalem since before the country formed.

They were a close family and they welcomed my uncle Elyahu with open arms. Elyahu fell in love with one of his distant cousins and married her. As of the writing of this book, they are still soulmates, happily married and just as in love as if they'd met yesterday.

Meanwhile, back in Tabriz, my father, Yeshayahu, was finishing high school. And he had a plan. "My grades are good enough," he told his parents. "I want to go to medical school."

In Iran, in those days, students could attend a seven-year medical school right after high school. But there wasn't a single person in the family who'd graduated high school, let alone university. The men were all merchants and entrepreneurs who'd created businesses and worked hard to make them profitable. If Yeshayahu followed his plan, he would not only become the first Ben-Israel to graduate high school but the first to become a doctor.

"First, we lose Elyahu to Israel, now we lose Yeshayahu to university," my uncle Rabbi joked. "An educated man in this family? What are things coming to?" He turned to my father. "Tell me, oh Learned One, which pitiful school would accept such a lamebrain as you?"

"That's easy." My father smiled. "The University of Tabriz."

Founded just a few years earlier in 1947, the University of Tabriz is the second-oldest university in Iran. The oldest is the University of Tehran, which was officially founded in 1934. Both universities were created as arms of the Iranian government. But even back then, the University of Tabriz had a certain reputation. Its administrators and professors were exceedingly strict. They followed their own set of rules when doling out grades rather than using academic standards practiced all over the world at other institutions for higher learning. Accordingly, most grade point averages for students at the University of Tabriz were lower than anywhere else. This continues even today. It is still quite common for students at the University of Tabriz to insist that their grades should be higher than they are. My father once told me he found medical school so challenging that, on more than one occasion, he thought about chucking his plan, moving back with his parents, and going into business alongside his uncles and brothers.

One of the biggest hurdles my father faced was financial. His family eventually blessed his career decision, but money was tight and a college education costs money. Yeshayahu was not the type of man who begged people to help him.

He'd been raised to pull his own weight. And so, to meet his living expenses, he took a job as a projector operator at the local movie theater.

I can picture my father as a young man sitting up in the tiny projection booth. I see him trying to recline in the uncomfortable, rickety wooden chair they inevitably gave every projector operator back then. He told me he'd use that time alone to puff on cigarettes, aping the heroes whose flickering images he hurled at the silver screen three times a night. He'd picked up the cigarette habit from watching Humphrey Bogart films. (I'm pleased to say that he put it back down almost as quickly.) And that strange little mustache he grew at the time? He borrowed that from another of his heroes, Clark Gable.

As the first Ben-Israel to attend university, he became a curiosity at family events. Whenever he visited home, everyone would ask him, "How are your studies going, Yeshayahu?"

"Oh. Quite well. Thanks for asking."

That was the end of that conversation. What else could he tell them? They could barely read.

My father used his movie money to buy a pale green Volkswagen Beetle, of which he became enormously proud. His Beetle let him commute to school and allowed him to impress women. The latter part was especially helpful since my father was short, not particularly attractive, and shy in proximity to the opposite sex. Clark Gable might have been suave and composed but his alter ego, Yeshayahu Ben-Israel, was a clumsy, stammering rube.

Right around this point, and in defiance of nearly every tradition his people had ever devised, Yeshayahu Ben-Israel started to show interest in an Armenian girl. This caused tension, of course. Most Iranian Jewish families forbid their children from showing interest in, dating, or—God forbid—marrying goy, a blanket term meaning all non-Jews. In fact, back then the goal of every self-respecting Jew was to perpetuate God's chosen people by having a gaggle of cute Jewish babies. There was a fundamental belief behind this. Repeat that process often enough and eventually what will you have? The Great Big Jewish World, which God, in the Book of Genesis, promised to Abraham.

My poor father simply wanted to get to know this Armenian girl. It was a young crush, probably not even a full-fledged love. Marriage was certainly not on the table at that point. Yet even this early interest was not tolerated by Yeshayahu's family, nor that of the Armenian girl.

Young love, as the elders liked to say, is one of the most uncontrollable forces in the universe. My father's family believed that he would be putting himself and this Armenian girl in peril if he showed interest and she began to reciprocate. According to family lore, she was beautiful with white skin, light brown hair, and deep blue eyes. This same family lore said that she wanted to date my father as desperately as he wanted to date her. They would meet in secret to express their forbidden interest in each other. I imagine them telling each other that, yes, they knew the odds were against them. How could they not? The entire cultures of Jewry and the Armenian Apostolic Church, a Christian faith, stood in blatant defiance of their relationship.

Both families began to sabotage the relationship. Marrying a Jew, the woman's relatives told her, would mar an Armenian family for life. My father's family basically told him the same thing. Marrying a goy wife would spell the end of the bloodline in a Jewish family.

"You will tarnish the family name!" my father's brothers thundered at him.

In the end, both my father and this Armenian girl sided with their respective communities and stopped seeing one another. To the best of my knowledge, they never spoke to each other again. While, in retrospect, this friendship threatened my very existence, the demise of it nonetheless strikes me as sad.

Nowadays, my father never talks about his Armenian love. I don't even know her name. I just know that there was once a girl he was smitten with and nothing came of it. I can only surmise he adored her and that she adored him back.

"She was beautiful," he told me once, when I asked about her. That's all he said, those three simple words, which he offered wistfully before turning away.

Many times, I tried to get more details out of him, but I always failed. The reason is simple. Three words could be used to describe why my father abandoned this love: *Family comes first.* A relationship between a man and woman would have to be forged out of obligation, not out of love. As dour as it may sound to some ears, this is probably not so unusual for religious families of other faiths.

Despite my father's choice, I imagine his family must have wrung their hands over his behavior. "Abraham preserve us!" they said. "What will Yeshayahu do next?"

They were right to be concerned. Because, as it turns out, Yeshayahu wasn't through with keeping his family on pins and needles. Once he finished his medical training, he announced he was joining the army.

It's hard to imagine how this was received! The first man in the family to finish high school and medical school—the first doctor in the family—was about to sign up for the army!

"Are you out of your mind?" my grandfather roared.

"Dada, think this through," said Yeshayahu. "I have a medical degree. In the army, that makes me an officer right off the bat. As a doctor, I'll gain experience. I'll rise higher and faster in the army than I ever would in private practice. I figure in two or three years, I'll be running the place."

My grandfather liked this explanation. He recognized it as good business sense. After that, their relationship seemed to improve. They were easier around one another, more content with each other's decisions. But it didn't last long.

A couple days later, my father stopped by the Ben-Israel family home. He had another announcement to make. "Well, I got in the army," he said.

"Excellent," my grandfather said. "Congratulations!"

"Thank you," my father said. "Yes, so as far as the army's concerned, I am now Captain Nasser Tabibiazar."

My grandfather spit out his cardamom-spiced tea. "What?" he shouted. "What?!?"

Yeshayahu began to explain.

My father was no fool. He understood that a Jewish doctor in the Iranian Army would face persecution. Yes, the shah wanted equal opportunity for Jews. But after all, the Iranian Army was. . . well, Iranian. This basically meant almost everyone in it was Muslim.

Would soldiers in the Iranian Army follow orders from a Jewish officer named Ben-Israel? Probably not. In fact, it's hard for me to ponder what would have happened had my father entered the army as Yeshayahu Ben-Israel, a nice Jewish doctor sporting a pencil-thin mustache, who drove a pale green Volkswagen Beetle and had once dated an Armenian girl. He might as well have painted a target on his back, along with an arrow pointing to the bull's-eye and great big letters that said, SHOOT ME HERE! My father knew that changing his name would do nothing to protect him from a serious background check. He was simply hoping it would keep the larger world from taking him for a Jew.

After careful consideration, he chose the name Nasser Tabibiazar. The name Nasser was a clear reference to Gamal Abdel Nasser, then a powerful figure in Middle East politics. After playing a pivotal role in overthrowing the Egyptian monarchy, Gamal Abdel Nasser became Egypt's second president in 1954. Over the next sixteen years, he began to institute widespread public reforms through a basically socialist agenda. He nationalized the Suez Canal, clawed land grants back from aristocrats, and took pride in quashing imperial rhetoric. By taking the first name Nasser, my father was showing support for someone who, at that point, the shah and his minions regarded as a politician worth emulating.

The surname Tabibiazar was partly derived from one of my father's mentors in medical school. Professor Tabibzadeh was a wonderful man who made a profound impact on my father's life and career. When he found out my father was the first man in his family to graduate high school, let alone medical school, Professor Tabibzadeh roared, "O-ho! We've got to look after you then! I know how it is with you Jews! We have to make sure you do well or your mother will hunt me down and give me an earful! Who wants that? O-ho!"

The name Tabibiazar was likewise inspired by combining two words into one. *Tabibi* means "doctor" in both Farsi and Arabic; "-azar" is a common suffix that means "from Azerbaijan." This of course was true of the Ben-Israels who had lived in northwestern Iran since the days when my great-great-grandfather Avram traversed the Caucasus. By this reckoning, they were all "-azars." As it happens, the word "azar" means "fire" in Farsi. It was also a common enough name for both boys and girls. This also turned out to be fitting since my father would often use fire to sterilize his surgical tools.

Why did my father sterilize his surgical tools with fire? Back then, there was no such thing as autoclave machines, no single-use scalpels, or things of that sort. But of course, any tool used in surgery had to be sterile lest it possibly spread disease. So my father's practice back then was to drop his surgical tools into a metal tray to which he added ethanol or rubbing alcohol before touching it off with a match. As a kid, I watched him do this dozens of times. The tools were so hot that, after being burned on occasion, my father learned to wait a few minutes before attempting to handle them.

Thus Yeshayahu Ben-Israel was transformed into Dr. Nasser Tabibiazar.

Eventually, my grandfather condoned my father changing his name. He saw that my father would have to be somebody else in order to be himself. He would have to pretend to be Muslim to live as a Jew. This sort of protocol has been followed many times in the course of Jewish history. In fact, in the time of the Inquisition, it became rabbinical doctrine that Jews could denounce their faith in public if it meant protecting their lives and the lives of their families.

Even today, a special prayer is spoken on Yom Kippur to forgive future sins as they relate to such acts as renouncing your religion to preserve life.

Taking my father's cue, a few of my uncles also changed their names. My first uncle cut his surname short to Bani while the other changed his last name to Radfar. My only uncle who kept the Ben-Israel name was Elyahu, who'd moved to Israel. The brothers who changed their names all said later it helped them avoid discrimination and opened up new possibilities for them in business. They didn't necessarily hide that they were Jewish, but they didn't flaunt the fact, either.

My father's military service ended during the mid-1960s. At which point, Dr. Nasser Tabibiazar decided to move to the heart of the country, the place where everything was happening at that time. He decided to join his brothers who'd moved to Tehran at the start of the White Revolution in 1963.

CHAPTER FOUR

SABZEH

Tehran in the Mid-1960s

MY FATHER'S FAMILY MOVED from Tabriz to Tehran in the mid-1960s. Their choice was influenced by a few factors. Tabriz was a provincial backwater while Tehran was the country's capital city, and therefore bursting with cultural life and economic opportunities. One was slow to adapt to the shah's modernizations while the other sat at the pinnacle of international culture. Jewish life was more prosperous in Tehran. The Iranian clergy tended to bundle Jews together with other non-Muslim religions, such as the Christians, Bahá'í, Zoroastrians, and others.

The icing on the cake was that my father was still single. He was aware that, as a Jewish son, his ultimate obligation was to get married, build a family, and provide his parents with grandchildren. As opposed to Tabriz, Tehran was a city brimming with available Jewish women for my dad to meet and eventually marry.

By this point, the young king, Shah Muhammed Reza Pahlavi, had become a man. Like most men, he was keen to establish his own dynasty. Muhammed Shah had big plans for Iran. With Mosaddegh out of the way and Western countries supporting him, he created sweeping modernizations that nudged his country toward becoming the next bright shining jewel in the crown of Western civilization.

The shah called this his White Revolution, a series of social and economic reforms designed to bring Iran into the fold of modern—that is to say Westernized—nations. The full slate consisted of land reforms, literacy campaigns, profit-sharing plans for workers, and, of course, the social and economic en-franchisement of women and other minority groups, including Jews.

The White Revolution got its name because it was supposed to supplant a "Red Revolution"—an altercation steeped in blood as opposing parties came to blows. Sadly, this happened regardless of the shah's best intentions. The Muslim clergy, in particular, took offense to the shah's plans. The country's majority demographic was devoutly Islamic. It was also the country's least skilled, least educated faction. They saw the lack of prosperity as a direct affront to their way of life and everything it stood for. Their deep dissatisfaction enabled the rise to power of a Shi'a cleric, the Ayatollah Ruhollah Khomeini, who emerged on the political scene in 1963.

Khomeini quickly displayed a knack for galvanizing zealous Muslim fac-tions to riot. His supporters saw him as a fatherly figure who would eventually free Iran from the shah's rule and empower its people to rule themselves. As a Muslim religious leader, Khomeini directed his outrage toward the shah. He was deeply critical of the shah's land reforms, which allowed non-Muslims, including Jews, to own land in what he saw as a Muslim country. He had many harsh words for Iran's relationship with Israel and the West. These relation-ships were proof, he said, that the shah possessed a secular vision for Iran, one altogether different from its Muslim majority. In particular, he preached that revolt against the shah—and martyrdom in the midst of revolt—was sanctioned by Allah.

In 1964, Khomeini was sent into exile. The shah was thus free to continue pursuing his reforms, but there was trouble right from the start. Most people thought the shah had only won consensus for his modernizations by gaining support from Iran's old power brokers, industrialists and media moguls. These individuals promised to cede power, money, and resources to the general population in what was essentially a "trickle down" plan. But this never hap-pened, particularly in the oil industry, where colossal revenue streams never quite reached the middle and lower classes. Rather, they ended up lining the coffers of elite individuals.

The final eruption of these tensions was still years away, but no matter how anyone sliced it, Shah Mohammad Reza Pahlavi inaugurated one of the most prosperous eras for Jews in Iran. Thanks to all the reforms he promoted, by the early 1970s, only 1 percent of Iranian Jews were in the lowest economic class. Fully 80 percent were considered middle class while 10 percent were considered wealthy. Compare this to the ghettos of Kiev, which my great-great-grandfather Avram left nearly a hundred years earlier.

But the shah was not always benevolent. Always worried about the survival of his monarchy, he had his all-powerful SAVAK mitigate any risks to his rule. The actual extent of SAVAK's power remains unknown. However, the common perception back then was that agents of SAVAK were always present, lurking in corners, spying on anyone controversial. If they thought you were too outspoken, they would abduct you, throw you in jail, and torture you. This happened especially to members of the Mosaddegh's Tudeh Party, known as the Party of the Masses of Iran, or Persia's version of the Communist Party. It also happened to my mother's two brothers.

My mother's family was also Jewish. Their surname is Ben-Rouhi. Unlike my father's clan, they had not wandered in from the Caucasus. Their roots run deep through the sunbaked bricks of Tehran, and before that in Yazd, which is in central Iran, where their family had lived for generations uncounted.

In 1944, a little girl was born to this family. Her name was Yafa, which means "beautiful" in Hebrew. She was the eighth and, at that point, the youngest child. Her father, Mirza Agha, had given up teaching French to sell fabric in a little shop he owned while Yafa's mother, Sara, was an illiterate homemaker who diligently tended to her children's needs. At the time of her birth, Yafa's oldest sibling, her brother, Mouis—which means "Moses" in Farsi—was already twenty years old. There were a number of years between Yafa and her siblings.

Yafa would later become my mother.

Her place as the baby in the family was temporary. Eight years after she was born, her parents had another child, number nine, a girl they named Sorayah. Some children don't take kindly to another sibling being born in the family. Not my mother. She was overjoyed to meet little Sorayah. Suddenly, she wasn't the last in line anymore. Now she had a little sister whom she could play with, take care of, attend to, instruct.

From an early age, my mother showed aptitude in science. No coincidence there. Her older brothers, Mouis, Jahangir, and Elyas, were all educated. They wanted to become doctors. Yafa looked up to them. She wanted to impress them. But the one she wanted to impress most was her second-oldest brother, the fourth-born child in her family, Jahangir.

My mother loved Jahangir. He was her hero and role model. He was more playful and lighthearted than her eldest brother and the first child in their family, Mouis. Jahangir spent time with his younger siblings. He played with them, read books to them, and took them for ice cream or to the movies. Jahangir would play jokes on his younger brothers and sisters, but they never minded. He also played jokes on his older siblings and parents. No one was safe around Jahangir!

Though my mother adored Jahangir, everyone else in the family was worried about him. They saw Jahangir as rebellious, untamed. Judging from all that I've heard, he probably was. In the first place, Jahangir was intelligent. He really liked to read books. Secondly, he was a principled man. Once Jahangir got a notion into his head about what was right and wrong, he stuck with the right, no matter the cost. Throughout history, people of this particular bent have also been alienated. Societies consider them dangerous. What can you do with a person like that?

Jahangir's internal sense of fairness influenced his politics. While still in high school, he supported the Tudeh Party, whose socialist agenda of justice, equity, and equality he admired. The party at that point attracted many young, educated students who wanted a brighter future. Oblivious to the broader geopolitical forces around them, they glorified the party as a wellspring of social fairness. Even back then, Jahangir was not shy about voicing such views, much to his parents' dismay.

His grades were good enough that he got accepted at the University of Tehran. While studying there, his political views became, if anything, more pronounced. His outspokenness brought him to the attention of SAVAK, whose officers began keeping Jahangir under constant surveillance. Eventually, they concluded that Jahangir Ben-Rouhi was more than just another Tudeh Party sympathizer. He was a *dangerous* Jewish member of the Tudeh Party, dangerous to the regime of Muhammad Reza Pahlavi. He had to be dealt with.

Nobody seems to remember how Jahangir ended up in one of SAVAK's jails or how my grandparents got notice of his detention. Back then it was always kept secret who worked for SAVAK and how SAVAK operated. For all we know, a neighbor might have informed on Jahangir, or his best friend. SAVAK officers didn't exactly walk around in uniforms, identifying themselves to the public.

But they'd earned a frightening reputation for knowing everything that went on in the country and acting ruthlessly to protect the shah's interests.

One day, members of SAVAK drove an old flatbed truck past Jahangir while he was out walking. Another SAVAK officer was out on the street, posing as a passerby. When he saw Jahangir coming, he waved a cigarette, asking if Jahangir could spare a match. When Jahangir reached in his pocket, men jumped out of the flatbed truck. Throwing a pillowcase over his head, they punched Jahangir in the stomach to knock the wind out of him so he couldn't scream. Then they picked him up, threw him in back of the truck, and drove him to jail, where they tortured him for days.

Years later, in 1984, I met Jahangir in person for the first time. I was thirteen years old, and I remember feeling awed in his presence. Though his eyes could be piercing and stern, when he aimed them at me I always felt love radiating out of them. He struck me as a living reminder of the love he had for his younger sister, my mother. Whereas, with his own kids, he was demanding. I was so proud to be visiting him, proud that he was my uncle. My mother had told me stories about him that, in my imagination, made him seem larger than life. In person, my uncle Jahangir fulfilled these expectations. In some ways, he even surpassed them.

I was shocked by his appearance though. He had no hair on his body. And one day, when I walked past his bedroom, the door was open and Uncle Jahangir was changing his shirt. His whole bare back was one giant, puckered scar.

I screwed up my courage and asked, "What happened to your back?"

He grunted. "A gift from SAVAK. You know, they arrested not only me, but my brother, your uncle Elyas as well."

Jahangir and Elyas were in prison concurrently though neither of them knew this at the time. SAVAK had snatched my uncle Elyas the same way they'd taken Jahangir. They tortured Elyas the same way, too.

Eventually, rumors got out that both my uncles were on SAVAK's execution list. The Ben-Rouhi family was beside itself. Something had to be done. My grandmother Sara went to her husband, Mirza Agha, and begged him to intercede.

Poor Mirza Agha! What could he do? He had very little money. He was a former French teacher with nine kids who owned a fabric shop. By borrowing from family members and liquidating nearly everything he had, Mirza Agha raised enough cash to bribe the proper officials, which is an ancient Iranian custom.

Satisfied that their eminence had been shown the proper fealty, these administrators freed my two uncles on one condition: that they leave the country at once or be recaptured and killed.

"The choice is yours," they said.

This was an offer my uncles could not refuse. They knew that, on one hand, they faced the prospect of vanishing without a trace. SAVAK was famous for making people disappear. On the other hand, they could start a brand-new life in a more enlightened country where the Tudeh's social agenda—and those of Iranian Jews, for that matter—were already signed into law.

According to family lore, my uncles briefly considered moving to America. In the long run, they opted against this, however. For one thing, it was just far easier and more expedient to get to Germany. And moving to America would have sent them half a world away from their beloved family. For another, both my uncles were mystified by American capitalism and imperialism, which, in their minds, was the source of a lot of the evil in the world.

It is said that my grandfather Mirza Agha gave them the last of the money he raised for their bribes to start a new life in Deutschland. It is also said that, when they left Iran, my uncles Jahangir and Elyas had just enough pocket change to buy one kosher sandwich each from a street vendor in Berlin if they could find it.

This may make Jahangir and Elyas sound as if they were observant Jews. In reality, keeping kosher was the last thing on my uncles' minds. Neither was religious. They both went to medical school in Germany, adopted Western culture, and assimilated. When I met Jahangir, he already had two surgical specialties, plastics and orthopedics as they related to sports medicine. He was fluent in multiple languages, including German and English. And both he and Elyas ended up marrying goyim. Which is ironic when you consider that Mirza Agha and Sara were afraid their sons would marry outside their religion if they stayed in Iran. But what could they say in the end? Both their sons became doctors, and both lived to tell their tales rather than vanishing and becoming another statistic of SAVAK's ruthlessness toward the shah's opposition.

My mother had also grown close to her sister Farideh, who was six years older. Farideh and Yafa had a sister between them but she and my mother didn't get along so well. As is common with two siblings close in age, they developed a rivalry and fought often with each other.

They were probably jealous of one another, desperate to garner what little attention their busy parents and siblings could pay them. This can happen with sisters or brothers. But another reason Yafa and her slightly older sister fought is because they had to. Who else paid any attention to them? Everyone else in the Ben-Rouhi family was so much older. They were always off doing their own thing, leaving the younger sisters to their own devices. But instead of two peas in a pod, they ended up being more like an ear of corn and a head of broccoli left on the table in two different kitchens. Discord ensued.

Farideh would turn her back whenever the younger sisters started bickering—which was often. If she had to choose whom she liked more, I suspect that she would have selected my mother. Back then, Yafa was still the baby of the family. Everyone loved her, which is one of the perks of being the baby in any family. My mother admired Farideh because, in many ways, she was like Jahangir, a free spirit. Also, like Jahangir, Farideh enjoyed reading books. She was vocal about her ideas and she entertained dreams about what kind of life she would lead when she grew up.

Farideh was also critical of the many constraints of Iranian society. She particularly did not appreciate restrictions placed upon women and Jews.

"You see how it is?" my mother once heard Farideh grouse. "I call it the double whammy!"

My mother was still very young and naïve. "What are you talking about?" she said.

"If you're a Jew in this society? Whammy! You're discriminated against. But if you're a *woman* and a Jew in this society? *Double* whammy! It's not just Iranian Muslims who treat women with such disrespect," Farideh said. "Iranian Jews—*male* Jews—are right there beside them, waiting to do their worst."

After saying this, Farideh would often pass my mother a book of poetry or politics whose text or subtext called for such higher ideals as freedom of choice, independence, female power, and the merits of individuality over conformity. Either that or the book was a story whose boy hero lived in such a fashion. By implication, Farideh was asking: Why can't we?

My mother nodded to all this. But inwardly, she wondered, *What can anyone honestly do about such things?*

Nothing, she quickly concluded. Nothing at all.

Opening her poetry books, she went back to reading her favorite verses from Hafez, Rumi, and Ferdowsi.

Farideh had a point, no question about it. It was now around the mid- to late 1960s. Anti-Semitism was getting slightly better in Tehran, but the life of a young Jewish woman living in the heart of Iranian society was quite complex.

The role women play in Jewish culture is often strong. Despite all appearances to the contrary—Father Abraham, the line of David, and so on—Jews have a deep respect for matriarchs. One could argue that Judaism is at least subversively matrilineal. Many Jewish biblical heroes are women, like Esther from the story of Purim. And following World War II, the role Jewish women played in politics changed dramatically. It could take center stage even in the Middle East.

Golda Meir spent years inspiring women and men to fight side by side for Israeli independence. She served as the foreign minister under David Ben-Gurion when he was the first prime minister of Israel. Back in the 50s and early 60s, if one believed the rumors, Golda Meir was headed toward becoming the first female prime minister of the new nation. She was a hero who proved that women could also be leaders.

But you couldn't tell that to an Iranian Jewish man at that time. Like their devout Muslim neighbors, they mostly considered women inferior. Women did not lead, they were the lieutenants in a family, soldiers who took orders from either the family's father or eldest son. More than a few Iranian Jewish men disciplined their wives and kids using corporal punishment. In fact, to hear my mother tell it, throughout Tehran's Jewish quarters, one often heard arguments filtering out of windows, lying like mist in the streets. Then screaming, followed by the crack of a man's belt as it raised livid welts on his wife's exposed flesh. More screaming. More cracks. Then the tears.

"Domestic violence?" my mother once told me. "I only heard that term when we arrived in America. I remember thinking, 'What does this mean, domestic violence?'" She shrugged.

If the westernization of Iran was happening too fast for the Muslim clergy, it wasn't happening fast enough for the country's women. In those days, a woman's education was still considered far less important than a man's in Tehran. Women were expected to do what their husbands told them, to remain silent, to have lots of children, and to raise those children to be fine upstanding Jews. Punishment for deviating from this script in any way could be awful.

Farideh had a hard time living under such conditions. She had all the positive characteristics of her older brother, Jahangir—the intelligence, the joie de vivre, the innate understanding of right versus wrong. But alas, she was not a man, and this made her life a living hell in a male-dominated culture. While the rest of her family would laugh and encourage Jahangir's free-spirited antics, they cracked down hard on Farideh.

"Why do you behave like this?" asked the husband of one of her sisters. "No! Do not look me in the eye. How dare you? Cast your eyes downward when you speak to a man! Yes. Like that. Now leave us alone. We are doing very important things here, manly things, and you are not wanted."

My mother's brothers-in-law were businessmen in the mode of Jewish Iranian *bazari*, a word that, in Farsi, means "from the market." To her, they came across as loud, proud, arrogant, and chauvinistic. When she was younger, she could not stand them. But her father was getting older and her brothers, Jahangir and Elyas, were away in Germany. Mouis, by this point, had emigrated to America. The brothers-in-law were the only remaining men in the family. They ruled the Ben-Rouhi household.

Both men were good-looking and, to hear my mother tell it, unafraid to flaunt it. They always wore suits, even in the most absurdly hot Iranian weather, and they always kept their shirts slightly open to show off their chest hair. Nestled among that thicket, each man wore a gold chain and, occasionally, their Magen David—what Westerners call the Star of David. Picture a cigarette dangling perpetually out of a corner of each of their mouths. The way it bobbed up and down when they talked—which meant that it constantly dipped.

Both men had grown up in challenging circumstances. In many ways, they were victims of their environment, raised to survive in a world that was hard and unkind. Corporal punishment had been one of the primary tools their own parents levied to keep them in line. Small wonder they applied it to their own kids. They were following what they'd been taught by their own role models, same as anyone does.

Persian mothers have doted on their sons for millennia. The sons in a family can do no wrong. Since time immemorial, sons have been considered assets to a family. Daughters, by contrast, are viewed as liabilities.

Where did this bias come from? In ancient times, since girls were not as physically strong as boys, they were forbidden from going into business or earning their own living by some other means. In a male-dominated society, the primary benefit females conveyed to their clan was through marriage to a husband from another politically or economically advantageous family. Thus, women were forced to accept the support of their family until they were married. Any girl who left her parents' home before marriage was called a *jendeh*, a word that, in Farsi, means "whore." Sometimes they were stoned to death by mobs or murdered by their own kin in what, ironically, was termed an "honor killing."

As centuries passed, such practices reaped many casualties. The history of Iran—one might say the entire Middle East—is dipped in the blood of its suffering women. And yet, such customs persisted. As generations ground by, oppressive men were always in charge while the females were cast in subservient roles. To look at things differently, the two brothers-in-law were simply doing the same thing their Muslim neighbors were doing. In Iran, a man who did not discipline his wife and children was thought of as weak. Other men would not trust them. They thought, *How can a man not be the boss of his home yet run a good business?* This was the standard against which Iranian men applied their business and family lives. I mention all this to say that my mother's brothers-in-law were not bad men. They had enormous hearts insofar as their families were concerned. They just had a funny way of showing their love according to Western standards.

"In fact," my mother once told me, "I saw a much different side of my brothers-in-law as they grew older. They began to calm down a bit once time had weakened their muscles and melted their bones. It was fun watching them become more docile. One time, I even watched one of them burst into tears when his favorite song—an old Jewish classic—played over the radio." My mother shrugged. "They weren't so bad, really. Their kids missed them after they died."

"What about their wives?" I asked.

My mother pursed her lips and gave this some thought. "That was a bit trickier. No," she finally said. "Both sisters had a hard time forgiving their husbands after the decades of physical and emotional abuse."

"And what about you?" I asked. "Did you forgive them?"

"For what?" my mother asked.

"Are you kidding?" I said. "For treating you so poorly! For convincing your father that you shouldn't go to medical school!"

"Oh, that." My mother turned away.

Again, I mention all this to illustrate how Farideh and Jahangir got treated differently merely by virtue of their gender. For instance, Jahangir seemed to have a different girlfriend every week, and this was applauded.

"My, what strength he has!" they would cheer. "Such virility! Such machismo! This is our very own son, Jahangir!"

One time, Farideh mentioned a boy whom she thought was nice. Her brothers-in-law called her *jendeh*.

Little by little, these disparagements began to add up. Farideh grew more self-absorbed. She stopped reading as much as she had and turned to writing more and more.

"Writing," she once told my mother, "is like an escape hatch from reality."

My mother was still very young then. She did not understand, and she said so.

Farideh held up the black rectangle of her journal. "You see this? Whenever I don't like something out here. . ." She waved a hand as if to indicate not just the room they were in but the whole wide world. "I open this magic door. . ." Here she opened her journal. "Using this key." She held up her fountain pen. "And just like that, I escape."

My mother was very impressed by this explanation. She had never heard anything like it.

I think it's fair to say that my mother worshipped Farideh. They bore a striking resemblance to each other and were both considered the family's ugly ducklings, girls who were *sabzeh*—a Farsi word meaning "olive-skinned"—rather than white-skinned, which at that time was considered a prettier quality. Both girls were deeply intelligent but also deeply shy. They kept their aggressions, and therefore a certain quantity of their feelings and thoughts, locked tightly within them.

And both girls got picked on in school. Farideh's challenges are particularly worth noting.

Mirza Agha reached deep in his pockets and shelled out the money to send Farideh to one of the best private schools in Tehran, the same school the shah's wife, Queen Sorayah, attended. What convinced him to think that such a grand expense was necessary? Part of it was his own vanity, I think. French wasn't taught in the regular school system. As a former French teacher, Mirza Agha longed to have at least one of his children speak what he called "the language of aristocrats."

When she was still a girl, Mirza Agha approached my mother's eldest sister to learn French but she flat out refused. She called such training outmoded and ineffective. English was the only true international language, she said, not French. That left Mirza Agha to send Farideh to private school in place of the older sisters. My mother was still too young to be caught in the fray.

I feel certain that Mirza Agha thought Farideh's problems would simply vanish once he sent her to the ritziest school in Tehran. If anything, the opposite happened. Farideh's life became a living hell.

The chief problem was that Farideh was poor, dark-skinned, wore glasses, and was no raving beauty. The other girls at her school were wealthy, lighter-skinned, and aspired to be seen as European. Socio-economically, Farideh was out of her depth. This made her an easy target for bullies. They started calling Farideh *kaka sia*, a Farsi term that literally means "black shit."

Also, what Mirza Agha hadn't counted on was that private school students need a lot more money than tuition. Farideh's classmates had fancy new clothes and cars and plenty of cash to spend on restaurants, cafes, and trips. But Farideh's pockets were empty. This additional pressure proved very destructive. The wealthier kids added Farideh's poverty to their list of reasons to pick on her. Now, to them, she wasn't just ugly, shy, and nearsighted. She was broke! Farideh had gone from being a poor Jewish girl to being a second-class citizen in one school to something worse than that in another.

To make matters worse, her situation at home was becoming more challenging than ever. As one of the younger children, a girl, and an ugly duckling to boot, she became the butt of everyone's jokes.

There was one episode my mother remembers well involving a suitor who called on her oldest sister, Helen. This man was not very attractive. He had very little going on in his business and was widely deemed a poor marriage prospect. He became the laughingstock at the Ben-Rouhi dinner table. Helen refused to marry him and everyone else agreed.

"His suit is absurd," said one of the men at the table. "But don't dismiss him outright. We should keep him in mind for Farideh!"

CHAPTER FIVE

A WOMAN, A
STRUGGLE, A TRAGEDY

Tehran in the Mid to Late 1960s

THE SOUND OF THE front door opening at our house in Chattanooga breaks the spell. Liam and I blink ourselves out of conversation and back to the present as my wife, Kelly, files into the kitchen with our daughters, Eliana, fifteen, and Addison, thirteen.

The women look surprised to find Liam and me sitting alone at the kitchen table. "What are you two up to?" Kelly asks.

"We got a phone call," I say. "From Mom." Kelly's look grows concerned and I nod. "Dad's not doing so well so I'll move things around and fly out to see him tomorrow."

"Pappy was telling me family history," Liam says. "Like, I didn't know that Fafa had a sister named Farideh." He shakes his head. "I didn't know half the stuff that he's telling me."

Addie quickly pulls up a chair. "Who's Farideh? I've never heard of her."

Kelly and I exchange glances. She knows this tale. I told it to her long before we were married. She knows what happens next and she knows it's not a subject for children. Or is it?

Our daughters are teenagers now. They grew up in a world where certain facts of life are assumed, particularly where gender differences and the roles women play in society are concerned. I've always felt uneasy with this. Not that my daughters enjoy such a relatively comfortable existence that they might not understand how different life would have been for them had they not been born in America. Had they not been a part of this modern age whose awkward but earnest attempts to reconcile rights could be taken for granted.

Eliana opens the fridge and pulls out some bottles of water for everyone. "We have a great-aunt named Farideh?"

Kelly nods at me, barely perceptible. *It's okay*, she's telling me. *This is the time.*

"Wait," Addie says. "Before we talk about Fafa's sister. . . I don't know anything about Fafa's childhood. Can you tell us that first?"

I nod. "Yes, I can."

My mother did not have an easy childhood. She was a little Jewish girl growing up in the Muslim-choked streets of Tehran. Her family was so poor, she owned only one pair of little white shoes, which had long ago started falling apart. Despite their awful condition, she wore those shoes everywhere. To school. To play in the yard. To work in the fabric shop with her father.

This was the life little Yafa led, a life that, in so many ways, was defined by her one set of shoes to fit every occasion. Which, of course, it did. What choice did she have? To wear her awful shoes or go barefoot. Some would say this is no choice at all. But my mother said, "Necessity is the mother of invention," and then set about making something positive out of something negative.

Along with poverty, the word "no" hounded Yafa at every step. The adults she interacted with tended to use that word a lot. As in: "No, you cannot do that." Or: "No, that is impossible. Poor little Jewish girls cannot do that." And: "No. That is my final answer. Just no—and no, you do not get an explanation for why I'm saying no. No means no, and that's final. No."

To hear my mother tell it, the only two people who took her seriously were her older brother Jahangir and her older sister Farideh. But for much of Mom's early years, Farideh had troubles of her own and Jahangir was being spied on by SAVAK while he studied at the University of Tehran. So any help they may have given her was limited at best.

My mother was one of the only Jewish girls at a predominately Muslim school. She once told me how hard she tried to fit in with the other girls, how she yearned for their attention, camaraderie, and validation. Even simple acknowledgment would have been a blessing. But this was never to be. Walking the hallways, she felt invisible. She was the last one chosen for teams in a sport, the last student the teacher called upon in class though Yafa constantly raised her hand first.

"That hurt me so much," my mother once told me. Then she shrugged. "I was a teenager. Was there ever a teenager who didn't care if people liked her or not?"

She became conflicted. At a very young age, a profound sense of isolation burrowed deep in her psyche and set up house there where it started to clash with her intense desire to fit in, to be seen, to be valued.

Complicating matters, Yafa had entered this world equipped with a near-adamantine sense of self-identity. "I only fought so hard to be liked," she once told me, "because I knew how much I was worth helping."

In my opinion, it was these two forces—a strong sense of self-identity plus an equally strong desire to fit in—that created the deep internal struggle that followed my mother the rest of her life.

With no friends to play with, Yafa often went directly to her father's fabric shop after school. Sometimes, she sat on a stool in the back, reading books and doing her homework. At other times, she would march about, helping the customers make decisions. Being good in math, even at young age, she would help her father, Mirza Agha, with accounting.

I can imagine my mother engaging customers. "What are you thinking of making?" she would ask them. "Some drapes? I see. For what room in your home? Aha. Look at this, then. It's a hundred percent linen, from Italy. A bit more expensive, that's true, but it is what we call an all-seasons fabric—not too heavy, not too thick. And look here. Strong fibers with a hollow core block out the light while allowing air and moisture to circulate. See?"

In this way, Yafa developed a sense of pride. Yes, she was helping her father, which meant she was also helping her family. But she was also gaining confidence being a woman asserting herself in what she had already come to think of as a world planned, built, and managed by men.

One day, Mirza Agha placed Yafa in charge of the fabric shop while he left to perform some errand. A couple hours later, he came back and opened his book of accounts. Flabbergasted, he stared at the lines of new ink carefully scrawled in the margins. Aghast, he noticed his sums had been changed.

"What happened here?" he demanded of Yafa. "What did you do?"

My mother led him through the figures, showing him all the mistakes he had made. "I see," said Mirza Agha. "I see." After which point, rather proudly, he turned the store accounts over to her. From that point forward, she did all the bookkeeping.

Eager to show respect, my mother would take her accounts for the fabric shop to be checked by her sister, Farideh. Farideh reviewed Yafa's math and she shrugged. "Again, you're right and he's wrong," Farideh said. "That's the beauty of math. It is not an interpretive art." She made a few strokes with her pen in her journal. "Not like literature, anyway. Here." She held out the journal to Yafa.

"What's this?" my mother said.

"A new story I wrote. Read it."

So my mother did.

She knew that Farideh understood math and science quite well since sometimes she helped Yafa study. Farideh had also made it clear that Yafa had sufficient aptitude to pursue academic studies if that's what she wanted to do. Farideh could talk politics with the best of them, guided as Jahangir was, by a strong sense of right and wrong.

And Farideh, of course, was a writer. Writing, my mother thought, is where Farideh truly excelled. Because, Yafa thought, no matter what Farideh wrote, no matter what fictions she conjured, she always told the truth.

Inspired by Farideh, my mother once tried writing as well. Later, she told her sister what she thought of the process. "It's so difficult!" my mother exclaimed. "This business of telling a story and telling it straight, so other people will understand it. Of finding the right word and setting it down so it matches precisely your feelings and thoughts! My goodness! I've been writing here at my desk these past few hours. I struggle to write a few words that I like. But you!" She pointed at Farideh. "You tear through page after page, hour by hour and day after day! I don't know how you do it!"

To this, Farideh just nodded. Silent, she watched my mother with dark hooded eyes while her pen, as if animated by its own spirit, scratched its nib across a fresh page in her journal. "Be honest," she told my mother. "What, in the end, is more tragic? Living somebody else's life or dying the way you would like to?"

"If only I'd listened," my mother once told me. "If only I'd understood what she was trying to tell me. . ." At which point she burst into tears.

Today, more than sixty years later, the wound is still fresh. My mother still cries whenever anyone mentions Farideh's name.

In 1966, Farideh was nearly eighteen and just about to finish her last year of high school—which, given her circumstances, she was barely surviving. Her parents fought often and loudly about money. The kids, who were mostly afraid of their father, would approach Sara whenever they wanted to gain a toehold on what they were lobbying for. Their mother, in their eyes, listened to their troubles with a keener ear and dispensed her advice more fairly.

One day, there was a terrible argument. I would love to divulge what all the shouting was about but, to this day, my mother insists that she cannot recall. All she knows is that the fighting ripped through the entire household. No one was spared from it. Everyone had to take sides.

Things got so bad that for several days, nobody spoke to each other. Suddenly, Sara's sister arrived on the pretense of paying a visit, when everyone knew she had come to broker a peace.

She was mostly successful in this. The children and their parents let bygones be bygones. "Come kiss your mother's head," Sara's sister told my mother and her siblings. Everyone complied except for Farideh.

The aunt took Farideh's obstinacy quite personally. When it became clear Farideh would not relent, the aunt started cursing her, calling her ugly, an ingrate, and other unflattering things. Farideh fled to the basement, where she locked herself in a room. Yafa and my mother's sister Victoria tried getting her to come out but to no avail.

"We thought it would be a good idea to let her cool off," my mother told me, many years later.

My grandmother and her sister left the house and went for a walk to calm down. At this point, everyone thought that was that. There had been an explosion. Hard words had been spoken but things would be fine in just a little while.

"I felt the same way," my mother recalled. "I was upset. I mean, everyone was. But I never thought. . . I mean, I just never. . ."

This is the part where she normally bursts into tears.

Sara and her sister had only been out of the house thirty minutes when Sara was struck by a dark premonition. Something was terribly wrong. She just knew it. She told her sister they had to get home, and not just quickly. "This instant!" she said. By the time they arrived, Farideh's body was already cold.

This is what they pieced together later. Once the house was essentially empty, Farideh let herself out of the basement and went upstairs to one of the bedrooms. The house they were then living in was similar in design to Spanish haciendas. It had a central interior courtyard, which the house surrounded. Farideh found a rope somewhere and used it to hang herself out one of the bedroom windows.

Rushing back home, Sara was the first to discover her daughter dangling over the courtyard, blue and cold. She let loose a loud and ominous screech that told everyone in the house something tragic had happened. But in their wildest nightmares they couldn't have imagined this.

"She was already gone," my mother sobbed. "There was nothing anyone could do."

Mirza Agha covered his face with his hands and wept. His tears, my mother told me, were like diamonds of sadness, anger, and regret. But mostly despair. How could Farideh have done this? Why would she have done it?

The local newspapers ran articles about Farideh. Suicides were rare among Jews back then. Doubly so when it came to women. Some of the papers speculated openly that Farideh must have gotten embroiled in some love affair that went horribly wrong. This cast an unfavorable light on the Ben-Rouhi family. Mirza Agha approached a private medical examiner to autopsy his daughter's body and confirm that she had died *dokhtar*, meaning a "girl"—a virgin. He made certain the medical examiner's findings were duly noted by the papers. This went a long way toward preserving the family integrity. But the fact remained that Farideh Ben-Rouhi had taken her own life. Why?

When people asked "What happened?" they got a variety of pabulum in response. "Farideh was always so nervous." Or: "Farideh was just too good for this world." Whatever that means. Or: "She was always under such strain. The pressures of being a poor young Jewish woman in Tehran? You know how it is."

Less openly talked about, of course, were the pressures she faced at home, where she was constantly told what to say, how to act, how to think, what to read, who to talk to, who *not* to talk to, who she was, and, most importantly, who she could be. What the Ben-Rouhis never dared admit was that, in the end, it was their culture that killed Farideh. Farideh had always understood that she was not free, that everyone else made all her decisions for her. For a young woman with such a strong sense of self, this was untenable. In her own understanding, taking her own life was undoubtedly viewed as an assertion of her control. It was the best way to preserve her identity, which she'd worked so hard to construct. In this regard, Farideh taking her own life wasn't tragic. It was an act of courage and independence. It was the ultimate act of defiance.

A death like Farideh's can devastate everyone touched by it. "When Farideh died, everyone had their own reasoning," my mother once told me. "They simply refused to see the truth. Her life was a constant source of stress. She was always ordered around. 'Go to school here. Behave like this. Do not talk to this person, talk to this man instead. If we tell you you'll marry him, that's what you'll do.'" She shrugged. "In the end, she took control of her fate the only way she knew how."

I have always been torn on the matter of Farideh's death. To be clear, I cannot condone anyone so young taking their own life. Suicide is a permanent, tragic solution to problems that time and understanding often prove temporary waves required for growth. Still, I credit her as a hero because hers was the ultimate act of defiance. She felt helpless and out of control in her life. She was not free with everyone else making decisions for her. Her attempt to take back the reins of her existence evidently demanded she pay the ultimate price.

In the end, however unwittingly, Farideh highlighted the need for more compassionate communication in our family. Moving forward, everyone was more sensitive to each other's needs.

A quality common to all heroes is their willingness to sacrifice their own desires—indeed, to sacrifice themselves if that is required—for some greater good. This is precisely what Farideh did, I think. She chose to end her own life in service to the greater good that was her identity as a strong, young Jewish woman who knew her own worth and refused to play various roles her society demanded she play. How many of us would make the same choice when challenged? How many of us would remain so true to the values we hold dear?

The Ben-Rouhi family was so devastated by Farideh's passing that no one mentioned it to Jahangir or Elyas, who were then living in Germany. They only learned that their sister had died a year later when Jahangir came home to visit. Hearing what happened, he lost control of himself for a time. He was upset and angry, shattered and hurt. But he didn't know who should be blamed.

"What do you *mean* you didn't tell me?!" he cried.

"We didn't want to upset you," Sara said.

"Of course, I'm upset!" Jahangir screamed at her. "Of course, I'm upset. Do you see?"

After Farideh's death, life changed dramatically. It would be an understatement to say that my mother was decimated. She was twelve years old and the loss of Farideh was incalculable. Farideh had been everything to Yafa—her advocate, role model, teacher, mother, sister, and friend. They had even slept in the same bed together.

How was Yafa supposed to keep living without Farideh there to guide her? It was like losing a part of her brain, like waking up one day to find that everything you thought you were—your memories, talents, feelings, impressions, your very sense of yourself—had all been a great big lie, and now you had to start over. But how?

My mother remained bedridden for months after Farideh's death. She only got moving again once she concluded that her wound would never truly heal. To this day, no one can mention Farideh's name within earshot of her without her eyes tearing up, after which she quickly slips out of the room.

Later, to honor her sister's memory, Yafa changed her name to Flora. Doing so followed one of several strong naming conventions laid out by both Ashkenazi and Sephardic Jews. By this custom, new children are named after family members who've died. In this case, the child being born was my mother—metaphorically. She honored the memory of her sister by taking a name with the same first letter as Farideh's. That way, from that point forward, whenever someone called her Flora, it would recall her dear Farideh. Changing her name was a very deep, personal commitment for Yafa. She was altering her very identity to accommodate all that her sister had been. In this way, Farideh's memory would not simply pass from the world. She would live on in her sister Flora and in the rest of their family, as well.

Yes, you read that right. I said, "the rest of the family." My mother's siblings made similar commitments. All seven of them gave at least one of their children a name that begins with an F.

My mother, now called Flora, tried going back to the life she had led but she found this next to impossible. No matter what had happened, no matter by what name she went, she was still a poor Jewish girl living in Tehran. Which meant she was assailed by the same constrictive society that had driven her sister to take her own life. The only difference now was the measure of grief my mother was forced to endure. Now, on top of all her other adversities, she carried the burden of losing Farideh.

"I sometimes wondered why I even went home," she once told me. "That house didn't feel like a home without Farideh. She was like my beacon of light in a very dark place. Sure, I had other siblings. I had my parents. I had people to talk to. But without Farideh, I felt lost and cold."

The next few years marched past. Flora's brothers all went on to pursue careers in medicine of one sort or another. Jahangir and Elyas became doctors while her older brother, Mouis, became a pharmacist. Uncle Mouis was one of those characters every family tells stories about but the most memorable thing about him was the reason he eventually left Iran.

He had fallen in love with an Armenian woman, a goy. Everyone in his family pleaded with him to leave her. "What are you doing?!" they would shout at him. "Are you crazy? She is not Jewish! Only pain and destruction will follow this!" But Mouis would not relent. And so, where his younger brothers had fled the country because they were persecuted by SAVAK, Uncle Mouis fled the country because he was persecuted by his own family. He and his wife went to America, where they eventually had children. But their lives were difficult.

In America, Mouis found he was no longer licensed to practice as a pharmacist. And so, like a lot of Jewish men in those days, he became an entrepreneur. That might be stretching the word just a bit. By "entrepreneur," I mean that Uncle Mouis cooked up schemes and ideas whose ultimate ends were to make money. Sometimes he bought, renovated, and sold cars. Sometimes he did the same thing with real estate. Sometimes he bought a medical office or rental building. Sometimes he succeeded in business. Sometimes he didn't.

Ultimately, he failed in love. His Armenian bride, the woman his family had warned him about, announced one day she was leaving him. She took the kids with her. Uncle Mouis was a kind person with a hard shell. He was a survivor. I remember him having garlic in his pocket and eating it like candy to protect his cardiovascular health and ward off heart disease. In the end, he died of a stroke from a brain stem hemorrhage, small enough to barely see on an MRI but consequential enough to plunge him into an irreversible coma. This happened when he was in his late sixties.

For years before his death, Mouis's story had become something of a cautionary tale in our family. He became a living example of what happens to good Jewish men who marry outside our religion. His story was doubly sad because I liked Uncle Mouis. He was always kind and generous to me and my siblings. Also, as I got older, I began to recognize the tremendous strength of character he must have had to leave his family behind and pursue the life he envisioned for himself and his family.

With Jahangir and Elyas shipped off to Germany to escape the clutches of SAVAK, my mother and her four surviving sisters—Helen, Victoria, Lilly, and Sorayah—found themselves in a house run by Mirza Agha, but that was a problem. Mirza Agha was getting older. His powers were waning even as my mother's *bazari* brothers-in-law rose in prominence.

Neither man had a history of keeping an open mind where women were concerned. If anything, their views began to get stricter. Both men continued to act as the self-appointed gendarmes of our family's reputation. They focused particularly on keeping our family's women in line. Like all Jewish men of that era and time, they disciplined the women over even the tiniest infractions, lest they wound up shaming everyone. It went without saying that women could not entertain dreams of academia, nor could they hold a job. Having women become educated and self-sufficient would turn the men's carefully structured society into chaos. The daughters of a family were expected to marry, rear as many children as possible, and support their husbands unerringly. Unfortunately, my mother had no plans of doing any of these things.

Farideh's death was still like an anvil dangling constantly over Flora's head. She refused to succumb to the forces that had crushed Farideh's spirit, nor would she compromise on the matter of men controlling women's lives. Flora decided her only logical course was to bury herself in her studies. Any subject her school did not teach her, she vowed to learn on her own. And so, day after day, once school was finished, Flora hiked the short distance to her father's fabric shop. There, after working through piles of receipts and correcting his math in the store's accounts for the umpteenth time, she sequestered herself behind a literal wall of books.

The bubbly girl named Yafa who once greeted customers amiably disappeared. In her place was this new young woman, Flora, who was darker, quieter, shyer, and yet more driven—a doppelgänger of Yafa. Increasingly, this Flora became more isolated, withdrawn.

"I sort of knew what was happening to me, even then," my mother told me once. "Today we might call it an existential crisis, but I didn't care. I was young and I had ambitions. At that point, my chief aim in life was to prove that the rest of the world was wrong. Wrong about women and girls, wrong about Jews, and most of all, wrong about me."

Flora dreamed of becoming a doctor, like her brothers. She had the aptitude for it. *People will respect me once I'm a doctor*, my mother thought. *As a doctor, I can help people. Therefore, I will be appreciated.*

Back then, in order to qualify for study at an Iranian university, all candidates had to pass the standardized test we called Konkour. The word is Persian, derived from the French *concours*, meaning "competition." It's an apt derivation. Konkour is a rigorous academic ordeal. Student candidates nationwide vie with each other for the limited number of spots available at institutions of higher learning.

In some ways, Jews had an edge at Konkour. Since the start of the twentieth century, the literacy rate among Iran's Jewish minority was significantly higher than that of Iranian Muslims. Studies show that in 1945 about 80 percent of the Jewish population was literate, whereas most Muslims—the country's vast and insolent majority—could not read and write. This condition didn't change much as time went on. By 1968, only 30 percent of Muslims were literate while Jewish literacy stayed high at 80 percent. It could be that since Iranian Jews, like their eastern European counterparts, were legally barred from owning and farming land, they turned their energies toward trade and education.

Konkour is still in effect, by the way, though it's changed a bit. Over the last few decades, the Iranian government expanded the number of universities throughout the country. They likewise modernized the parameters under which candidates can sign up to take the exam. But even with such alterations as these, only 10 percent of Iranian students who go through Konkour earn a chance to study at university. This percentage was even less in my mother's era.

Flora understood how badly the odds were stacked against her, and yet she refused to be deterred. Come hell or high water, she was going to battle. The foe she would face was Konkour. She studied hard for months with an aim of attaining a spot at the best school her country had to offer: the University of Tehran. Only the cream of the crop went there.

Through all this, her parents had no idea what she was doing. None whatsoever.

Flora was very excited when her scores came back. She had practically aced the exam! Her performance placed her in the uppermost percentile. She could study wherever she wished. Every university in the country would welcome her with open arms.

A bit stunned, Flora shared the good news with her family at dinner that evening. When she finished her announcement, everyone seated around the table stared at her. Nobody said a word. Finally, Flora said, "Don't you get it? I can become a doctor now. This is what I've always wanted!"

"Why?" snickered one of the brothers-in-law. "So you can look at naked bodies? That's what doctors do, you know."

"That's what you really want, huh?" the other brother-in-law chimed in. "To spend all day looking at the naked bodies of men who are not your husband? Like a *jendeh*? How can you say such things at this table? And here with your parents sitting beside me! Pass me the salt."

Flora turned to her father. "But Baba—"

Her father stared down at the meat he was cutting. "They make a good point," he said.

"What point? Why is it okay for boys to be doctors but not girls?"

"Because boys and girls are different," her mother said gently.

Flora's father nodded. "*Very* different. Where have you been all your life that you have not noticed this?"

"I have been here," said Flora quietly, keeping her father locked in her sights. "I have been right here all this time."

Her father kept his eyes down on his plate. If he caught her tone, he opted not to comment on it. "Medical school is no place for a nice Jewish girl. A woman's place is at home, rearing children and obeying her husband," he said. "Women doctors are not part of our culture. Will there be boys in this medical school who are not Jewish? Yes?"

Flora stared at him, flabbergasted. "I will not be there to meet boys. I will be there to study to be a doctor!"

"If you want to be a doctor, marry one," said Mirza Agha. "People will still call you Mrs. Doctor and all will be well."

"I earned this!" Flora shouted. "Do you have any idea how hard I worked? How much I've always wanted to do this?"

"You have not listened to me. No! You will not go to medical school to see naked boys!" With that, Mirza Agha set his knife and fork down—*clank!*—on the edges of his plate. The sound they made—so sharp, so abrupt—made it clear that, in his mind, the matter was closed.

Incidentally, my father also took Konkour. It was the only way for him to get into medical school. My father didn't score as well as my mother did. This has always led me to believe that, had my mother gone to medical school, she might have become a better doctor than my father. And he was a very good doctor.

Sometimes I think about all the talented people whose gifts were never allowed to contribute to the greater good. And why? Because they were women? This seems like a very poor reason, indeed.

Flora cried and cried but her tears did nothing to help her case. She stopped eating and went on a hunger strike but this did not help either. Her father and brothers-in-law remained unmoved, and it wasn't just the men in her family who said she should not attend medical school. The women were dead set against it, as well.

"Why are you being so hardheaded about this?" asked one of Flora's sisters.

"Oh, *I'm* the one being hardheaded?" Flora said.

"Of course!" her sister replied. "What do you think, that the rest of us like being pushed around by men?"

Flora just stared at her. "So what are you saying? I should join the rest of you in being persecuted because the more women there are being persecuted, the better off women will be?"

Her sister glared at her. "Of course not. That doesn't make any sense."

"Exactly!" Groaning, Flora threw up her hands and began to walk away.

Her sister called after her. "Why not try a vocational school?"

In those days, the option to attend vocational school was one which Jewish men of Tehran condoned for women who absolutely insisted they receive some education.

"Really, Flora," said the men in her family. "If you like medicine so much, why not go to vocational school. You could be a phlebotomist. Or maybe work in a lab where they process tissue samples."

By this point, Flora's voice had gone flat. Her shoulders seemed to have fallen into a permanent slump. She had the dead eyes of a veteran soldier or someone who's barely survived some trauma. "I don't want to do any of those things," she said quietly.

"It wouldn't be so bad," her sister continued. "It would only be temporary, right?"

Flora looked at her. "Temporary?"

"I mean until you marry a good Jewish man and start a family. After that, you won't have time to work. You must stay home raising the kids."

Outraged or not, despondent or not, Flora saw the writing on the wall. When she boiled everything down, she had only two options: attend vocational school or work in her father's fabric shop full-time. But how could she work with her father after he'd played such a big role in crushing her dreams? Being back at the store would have reminded her of all the days, weeks, and months she had already spent there, hunched behind piles of books while learning the science she loved more than anything else. She chose to attend vocational school. In my mother's mind, it was a way to delay, if not precisely escape, her fate. *And who knows?* she thought. *Maybe one day I can try again to become a doctor.*

The irony of all this is that, as bad as things were for my mother, her sister, and all Jewish women who lived in that region, conditions in Iran were actually improving for them through the mid- to late 1960s. In addition to the shah's slate of westernizations, more and more families were leaving the country and moving to Israel or America. This meant that more and more women were seeing what it meant to be free, to have options that allowed them to carve their own path out of life.

The men of Iran—Jews and Muslims alike—began hearing these tales leaking out of the West. Tales of justice for women. Of women's liberation. Of the sexual revolution. American politicians talked openly of something called an Equal Rights Amendment being added to the U.S. Constitution. Jewish women learned that the Western legal system had a name for the act of a man abusing his wife: "domestic battery." That police who responded to such situations could take a husband away from his family in handcuffs and put him in jail. That the judicial system could not be bribed to look the other way when a husband battered his wife, as occurred often in Iran. Western judges punished men who beat women. What a concept!

At the vocational school she attended, my mother trained to work as a microbiologist and lab technician. While there, and strictly for work purposes, she changed her name to Ghodsieh, an Arabic name, meaning "Holy." As my father had done before her, she found it easier to go by an Arabic name and thus avoid the bulk, if not all, of the various discriminations leveled at Jews.

Working in the labs kept Flora in the vicinity of her first love, medicine. The attraction proved irresistible. My mother craved learning medicine the way flowers crave sunlight and water. Once again, she was borrowing books and barricading herself behind them, gorging herself on their rarified knowledge. Once again, she was pushing herself to the limits, her father and brothers-in-law be damned. Only, this time, she wasn't alone.

While attending vocational school, my mother met other Jewish women who, like her, had been denied opportunities based purely upon their gender. This was a watershed moment for her. She bonded with her fellow students and found solace in the friendships she made. The bonds my mother made with those girls in the mid- to late 1960s turned out to be stronger than some of her family bonds. As I write this, some of those relationships have lasted more than five decades.

Once she'd finished vocational school, my mother took a job processing tissue samples in a hospital laboratory. She liked the work. It kept her engaged, made her think. However, within a few months, her parents and sisters began pressuring her to marry. And they weren't the only ones.

Her sisters' husbands were the loudest voices, as well as the bluntest, urging her to wed. "God, Flora! What are you doing with your life?" one of them asked her.

They were in the kitchen. My mother was drying a dish at the sink. She kept her eyes glued on the towel she was working across the plate, her voice level. "Could you be more specific?"

"You're twenty-four years old!"

"That is correct. What is your point?"

"You're getting really, really old!" he said, as if this was the most obvious thing in the world.

My mother looked up at him, startled. Embarrassed.

This is the point, she later told me, where she started to think about finding a husband. If nothing else it would keep the men in her family from pestering her to get married.

CHAPTER SIX

A MARRIAGE
OF EQUALS

The Late 1960s, Leading Up to the Revolution

ELIANA AND ADDIE SIT across from me, wearing stunned faces.

Addie speaks first. "How could anyone treat people like that?"

Again, I meet Kelly's gaze before I respond. "It was a different time and culture, Addie, where people held much different values."

"Well, that could never happen here."

She's probably right. Though, these days particularly, I'm often not so sure.

"What happened next?" Eliana says.

So I tell them.

By the time she was twenty-four, now working as a young lab technician in a local medical clinic, Flora suffered daily harassments over why she had not yet married. The taunts and sometimes outright threats from her family and her brothers-in-law began to increase in both their frequency and aggressiveness.

"What is *wrong* with you?" one of her brothers-in-law would say. "Only a *jendeh* refuses to marry! And do you know *why* a *jendeh* refuses to marry? She wants to keep her options open. Options!" He spat the word out. "God, Flora! Do you think we are stupid? We see what you are doing. We know how the world works! We are *men*!"

The situation grew increasingly uncomfortable. Throughout it, my mother had one saving grace. Unlike her sisters, she had a job. She made her own money, which meant she was less dependent on either her family or the financial largess of potential husbands. Flora needed no man to provide for her. She handled her own expenses while donating generous sums toward the household bills whenever she cashed her paycheck. And while her income wasn't as great as those of her brothers, it was more steady and honestly earned than any among the *bazari* could claim.

Contrast her predicament with that of one of her sisters, whose husband forbid her from working. My mother's sister saw all the freedoms her younger sister possessed. She noted the way Flora carried herself—with dignity, pride, and a deep self-assurance. She quickly grew resentful of Flora. This presented a new sort of crisis.

The husbands had taken note of how many of the women in their family yearned to emulate their younger sister. This made them angry. What would happen if each sister began to insist that she take a job, as Flora had? What would happen to the husbands when their good, obedient, servile wives were exposed to the world Flora knew—a world outside the Ben-Rouhi household where women all throughout Tehran were developing strange new ideas about their place in society? What would the rest of their community think of their family? That the wives needed to work to support the family? That the husbands couldn't make enough money so their wives had to work? No, no. If that ever happened, the value of men would diminish in the eyes of the community. That sort of nonsense had to be stopped and stopped quickly.

"Flora!" the brothers-in-law would say. "This independent life you lead is a terrible thing! Those books you read are ruining your mind! Before you know it, no one will marry you. What do those books talk about, anyway?"

"Politics, mostly," Flora replied.

The brothers-in-law nearly went apoplectic. "Politics? *Politics*, did you say?! An *unmarried woman* reading *politics*?! Who told you that you could do that?!"

"Jahangir recommended this particular title," Flora said.

Though living in Germany then, Jahangir was, in many ways, closer to Flora than ever. They often spoke by phone. In her heart, I think, my mother still compared every man she ever met to Jahangir—and all of them fell short of that ideal. No matter how rich they were or how poor, how old or how young, how handsome or ugly. . . if they were not Jahangir—which of course they were not—my mother wanted nothing to do with them.

It's not that my mother didn't have suitors. Quite the opposite. There was a certain breed of young man who found Flora scintillating, mesmerizing—"a catch," as people used to say. But most of these suitors were *bazari* or *mahale-yee* (in Farsi: "from the streets"). They were often brazen middle-class merchants and traders who conflated life with the status of the national economy. They had little formal education, and sometimes no education at all.

In those days, the *bazari* were an especially powerful force in Iranian culture. Devoutly Persian in their traditions, they maintained close ties to the Muslim clergy and thus were major proponents of social conservatism throughout Iran. By and large, they despised the government of Shah Muhammad Reza Pahlavi. They viewed his efforts to make Iran more progressive as a threat to their class, their beliefs, their very way of life. What would happen if the shah continued industrializing the country? What would happen if Iran became a player on the international stage? Why, the *bazari* would be trampled into the dust and left behind, they thought. And so they began to rattle their sabers.

The Grand Bazaar of Tehran became like a cauldron bubbling with pro-revolutionary sentiments. Throughout the late 1960s, traders spoke openly and with hostility toward the shah, his policies, and his government. Their fervor hit many of their customers like a virus. The internet had not yet been born and media was not yet digitized. Still, they transmitted this deadly disease throughout the nation using the means of the day. Phone lines jangled with outrage. Newspaper editorials grew increasingly caustic. Conversations with family and friends over dinner or tea could explode at any moment.

Looking back, it seems clear the *bazari* were one of the primary instigators of the revolution that finally broke out in 1979. Their passions, already so hot, went practically nuclear during the Iranian oil boom between 1974 and 1978. A lot of money got made in those years but very little of it trickled down to the *bazari*, who took this as confirmation of their beliefs.

"You see?" the *bazari* would trumpet. "The shah is not for the working class! He has set himself against the common businesspeople who make Iran work. Against Persian culture itself!"

In this manner, certain members of the middle class began to align themselves with the country's most conservative political forces. This included the Muslim religious establishment, which eventually gave rise to the Ayatollah

Khomeini. And Khomeini, of course, was responsible for toppling the shah. In the power vacuum that followed, he founded the Islamic Republic of Iran and became the new nation's first supreme leader.

Word to the wise: whenever a nation is led by someone who calls themselves "the supreme leader," trouble is bound to follow.

Flora was growing increasingly hopeless. Most nights, she cried herself to sleep while reviewing the options before her, none of which looked good. Should she knuckle down even more to endure the increasingly hostile bombardments cast at her by her family? Should she marry some bombast from the *bazari* just to shut them up?

Flora was keenly aware that some of her suitors were rather well off. In theory, they could make a good life for her. But at this point, she cared far less for money and comfort and more for the vibrancy of her mind and the freedom to carve her own path in life. No *bazari* would ever allow her to follow her dreams. Like her brothers-in-law, they would insist that she correspond to the bit part women traditionally played in Iranian culture. To this, my mother would never consent. And so, to escape her home life, she worked longer and longer hours. She could not go out after work with her friends—in Tehran, in those days, only *jendeh* did that. Each time she got home, she fled directly to her room, where she buried herself in her books. And she thought about Farideh.

Increasingly, my mother understood why her sister had chosen the path that she had. She realized she did not want this path for herself. Some other way must exist, she thought. But what?

One day, one of my mother's brothers-in-law came home from work. Proudly, he announced that he had found a suitor for Flora. This brother-in-law said he knew a guy, a shrewd businessman from Tabriz whose younger brother was single and a doctor. His name was Nasser Tabibiazar. He'd just moved to Tehran and—unbeknownst to this brother-in-law or anyone—had just come off an ill-fated love affair with an Armenian woman.

Nasser's family was interested in bringing Nasser back into the fold of ancient Jewish custom. The proverbial light bulb went off inside the brother-in-law's head. This Dr. Nasser Tabibiazar would make the perfect husband for his rather infuriating sister-in-law! So Nasser's brother and Flora's brother-in-law decided to play matchmakers. They conspired that Nasser and Flora would meet. Soon after that, they would marry, at which point, Flora would leave this ridiculous job she kept slaving away at, the happy couple would have many children, and all would be right with the world. But there was a problem.

Unbeknownst to this brother-in-law, there was another man in the family (another brother-in-law, in fact!) who was keen to play matchmaker for Flora. This man also had a suitor in mind from among his *bazari* contacts, a man I'll call Fazel. Fazel was an older, good-looking gentleman whose excellent business had made him quite wealthy. This made the brother-in-law very eager to recommend Flora for marriage; he wanted to forge a business connection with Fazel and finding him a young wife seemed like an excellent way of accomplishing that. This brother-in-law began pushing Flora and Fazel to meet, which they eventually did, in the ancient ritual of *khastegāri*.

The Iranian process of courtship is a highly structured affair whose roots predate Islam. Even today, practically everyone in the country observes the steps of *khastegāri*, regardless of their ethnicity or religion. It goes like this. When a young man is ready to marry, his relatives seek out eligible young women among the families they have relationships with. Once a possible bride is found, a meeting is set where the families can mingle. The bride's family is expected to entertain and furnish refreshments. The young man and young woman are introduced to each other. The prospective husband presents the prospective bride with a bouquet of flowers. If things go well, the couple can meet again under customary circumstances. But either party may decline a second visit.

Fazel and Flora first met during a formal *khastegāri* arranged by my mother's brother-in-law. They barely spoke a word to each other. Despite this, Fazel took a liking to Flora. He later said he liked her looks. My mother was far less impressed.

"I thought he was. . . okay," my mother divulged to me many years later. "I mean, he was nice enough looking. He was a gentleman and he had money, which I knew could be useful in life. He also liked to read books so I thought I could at least hold a conversation with him. But he had two big strikes against him."

"Oh?" I asked. "What were those?"

"First, he was a *bazari*. Second, he was a friend of my brother-in-law."

Flora began to ponder whether she wanted to meet Fazel a second time.

Noting her hesitation, her other brother-in-law saw opportunity. Plotting with my father's brother, he pushed to initiate a *khastegāri* of his own. Not long after that, Dr. Nasser Tabibiazar was invited to call on Flora Ben-Rouhi.

Family lore tells the story of how, when my parents first met, my father gave my mother a bouquet of plastic flowers. He thought the fake flowers looked nicer than fresh flowers. Also, he reasoned, they would last longer, never die. For this and many other reasons, we could hardly say there was love at first sight.

"We had zero chemistry," my mother recalled later on. "I mean, zero. Your father was so quiet and withdrawn, the matchmakers did most of the talking that evening. Your father just sat there, staring holes in the tablecloth. He was short with a big nose. His movements were clunky and he had already started going bald. That plus the thing with the fake flowers?" Exasperated, she threw up her hands. "I mean, what sort of suitor would do that? Nobody did that. It was just weird."

In fairness, my mother wasn't the friendliest person back then. She was still sad over Farideh's death and more than a little bit angry over the predicament she found herself in. All of which is to say, she put little energy into making suitors feel comfortable in her presence. "I guess I barely spoke, too, when I first met your father," she later admitted. "I saw myself as an independent woman. Basically, I attended the *khastegāri* because I was told to. I'd calculated the risks and I knew that my brother-in-law would give me a terrible time if I refused him."

Flora knew that Nasser wasn't rich. Still, he was a doctor, which meant he was smart. Intelligence intrigued her, as did my father's quiet demeanor, which suggested that, unlike the *bazari*, he'd never physically abuse her. After watching the ordeals her sisters had weathered, such notions were foremost among my mother's considerations when choosing a husband.

Nasser saw Flora along similar lines. She was a nice Jewish girl whom his older brothers approved of. If he married her, he could be done with their ribbing, their shouting, and all the exhortations that came from his still being single. In one fell swoop, he could get his family off his back. To my father, this was a priceless gift. He knew he and Flora would not be in love with each other like he'd seen in all the American movies. Who cared? At least both he and Flora would never *pretend* they loved each other. They were both up-front and honest about how tepid they were about marriage.

The couple's lack of chemistry wasn't lost on their families. Everyone tried filling the silence with stories and jokes to the point where the atmosphere in the room became uncomfortable. They all knew the truth of the situation. Flora was the last daughter in the family to wed—Sorayah was still too young to be eligible. Nasser had reached a similar juncture. His brothers had kids who were nearly as old as he was. Both families increased the friction, hoping that sparks would start flying, but no. Nasser and Flora stayed cold toward each other.

But then something unusual happened.

Once the party was over, Mirza Agha approached his recalcitrant daughter and asked what she thought about Dr. Nasser Tabibiazar. Flora shrugged and said, "I will marry him."

This was the right answer since Mirza Agha had made it quite clear to her she had no other choice.

In a different household in another part of the city, Nasser's brother "strongly recommended" to his younger brother that he marry Flora Ben-Rouhi.

Nasser just shrugged. "Fine," he said. "I will take her to wife."

My parents were married a few months later in the early spring of 1969. The wedding pictures show an unsmiling couple. They look neither happy nor sad. The whole affair felt more like a job that had to be done, so they did it. Already the die had been cast. Their marriage would not be a labor of love, more like a workshop where sacrifices would be made in order to build a family, the most important job any young Iranian Jewish couple could perform. Period, full stop.

The first night of their married life was a testament to this. Since my mother and father both lived with their parents, once the wedding was over, each returned to their respective homes. My mother once told me she cried herself to sleep. The next morning, she got up, packed her books and clothes into boxes and bags, and moved into the Ben-Israel home. She and Nasser planned to reside there among his parents, siblings, and cousins until they could figure out what to do next. But the troubles started immediately.

My mother and father had seen each other as a way to escape their terrible home lives. They hadn't looked hard at the details, however. The chief complication was that Nasser and his family were not Persian. They came from Tabriz; they were Turks, and thus spoke Turkish, a language that Flora had no facility with. Whenever she tried speaking Farsi, Nasser's family made an attempt to reply but just as quickly gave up. They couldn't be bothered to learn the language. *Besides*, they must have thought, *this is our house. We speak Turkish here. If you live here, you must also speak Turkish.* Nasser's family went about their business without any effort to include Flora. She was just a woman, there to serve Nasser, more like a maid in the final assessment of things.

On top of this, Nasser was not liked in his own home. He had to be brash and hard on his young nieces and nephews to keep them on track with their studies while he worked hard at his own pursuits. This meant that he wasn't around very much. Then there was his demeanor, which everyone said was too serious. My father didn't know any jokes. He wasn't interested in entertaining people. He did not suffer fools nor did he stand up to his family when they castigated his new wife. By all reports I have heard, Dad didn't seem to care that my mother was there. At the dinner table, though he knew his wife only spoke Farsi, he continued to speak Turkish with his family while Flora just sat there, still as a totem, staring at the empty plate before her. He never offered to translate what was being said to her. Like his brothers, he preferred to adopt a macho attitude where he barked orders at her. The only real difference was that, while Nasser's brothers had married illiterate Turkish women, Nasser had married a woman whose marks on *Konkour* should have let her study at the University of Tehran.

By the time Flora realized the mistake she had made, it was too late to do anything about it. Often, she ended up fleeing to the house of her sister Victoria, where she cried a lot but also soaked up every word spoken to her in a language she could at least understand. To say she felt isolated during this period would be a drastic understatement. It was as if she was back in middle school again. Once more, despite all her triumphs, she was that young child the other girls denigrated because she was Jewish and poor. All the pain she'd suffered through high school in the wake of Farideh's death came rocketing back at her. All the confidence she'd built up in her work got erased. And the worst was yet to come.

After their wedding, Nasser told Flora she had to quit her job. Flora vehemently disagreed. The fights that erupted over this subject were epic but my father held firm. He told my mother that none of the wives of other doctors worked. It would set a bad precedent if she had her own job. No, the safest, most acceptable thing for her to do was to stay home like all the other wives and raise children.

"Why would I do that?" Flora shouted at him. "Stay home and raise kids with a bunch of other women who don't like me and don't even speak the same language?!"

She acquiesced eventually, but also temporarily. From that point forward, she began looking for ways to assert her independence. It helped that she quickly discovered she knew more about medicine than my father did. Moreover, she noticed that Nasser was not a good businessman. Practically every other doctor in Tehran was making great big piles of money but Nasser was content making the bare minimum at his little practice. He understood how a Jewish doctor of Turkish descent who spoke heavily accented Farsi was viewed among Persians. To the more cosmopolitan set in Tehran, the word *Turki* was synonymous with *donkey*. To call someone *Turki* meant they were stupid. Who, my father wondered, among the elite in Tehran would want to be treated by a *Turki* doctor?

Up until that point, Flora hadn't cared much for money either. Now, however, she saw a new use for it: getting out from under her in-laws' thumb. Suddenly, everything Jahangir had taught her—all the idealism of her Tudeh, socialist/communist political upbringing—got tossed out the window. If money was what she needed to buy her freedom then money is what she would have. She didn't know how to get it just yet but once she set her sights on that, the whole Earth moved to accommodate her.

A few months into their marriage, my father brought up the notion of moving. His younger sister, Simah, had recently married a Kurdish doctor named Saeed who came from the city of Kermanshah about five hundred kilometers southwest of Tehran. Saeed had told Nasser there were plenty of job opportunities for doctors throughout southern Iran, in Khuzestan. The region was ripe with oil fields, which the shah's government was developing to boost the national economy. One city looked particularly promising, Saeed said. A city named Abadan on the river named Shatt Al Arab, which marked the border between Iran and Iraq.

My father's interest was piqued for four reasons. First, he wasn't in love with Tehran, which he'd found to be far too big and bustling a city to take any comfort in; it was also a very competitive place for doctors to start a practice. Second, the new city presented an opportunity for my father to establish himself and work with underserved communities, something he'd always wanted to do. Third, Saeed and my father had known each other since medical school. They were fast friends, more like brothers, whose bond, as it turned out, lasted the arc of their lives. My father knew that Saeed was a much better businessman than he was. If Nasser pushed him a little, perhaps his new brother-in-law would teach him techniques to increase his finances.

Fourth, and perhaps most important, Saeed floated the idea that my father could make lots of money if he took certain positions within the government's nationalized hospital structure. This notion intrigued my father. He'd been in the military. He knew what government work was like. He brought up the matter to Flora and asked what she thought of it. Flora said yes right away.

She, too, had harbored dreams of helping the underserved. Jahangir and his talk of Tudeh politics had inspired her socialist—one might even say communist—leanings. But moving to Abadan would be much more than that, she thought. It was the chance she'd been waiting for to get away from Nasser's family. Once they had done that, she imagined herself asserting more control in her marriage.

And so the decision was made. In 1969, my parents moved to Abadan and set up house in a two-story home across from a pharmacy owned by a friend of Saeed. My father arranged his clinic on the first floor while he and Flora took up residency on the second floor. Flora did not work when they first arrived. Still, she was happy to make a new home there, happy that everything seemed to be turning out right. Until it didn't.

Within a few months of their moving to Abadan, Saeed, who was really their lifeline, announced he was picking up his family and taking them back to Kermanshah. Nasser and Flora were stunned by the sudden announcement. They debated the matter and ultimately decided they would stay. But that was just one of many problems they faced.

"Our marriage did not have much love," my mother once shared with me. "I had read dozens of books where the husband and wife just adored one another. But I had your father." She rolled her eyes. "I wanted us to be closer and I assumed that having a child would turn that around. So I got pregnant." But this only made matters worse.

Convinced that Nasser and she would never make a good match, my mother packed her bags and took a train, alone, to Tehran. She told Nasser she was going there to have the baby. At this point, our family's entire future was deeply uncertain.

That baby, of course, was me. I was born in August 1970 in Tehran while my dad was still in Abadan. It was a particularly hot summer, which is saying something when you live in Iran. Flora was on a picnic with her entire family when she felt the contractions. With her younger sister, Sorayah, she headed to the hospital. And soon after that, I arrived in this world.

It was Mirza Agha who named me Raymond. According to family lore, my grandfather took a special liking to me. Everyone said he liked my constant smiles, which, as a physician, I now understand was probably me passing gas.

Naming an Iranian Jewish boy "Raymond" is unusual even by today's standards. But Mirza Agha had his reasons. "Raymond is a French name," he said, revealing again his passion for the French language. "A name borne by kings and aristocrats. It fits him, I think."

My mother was not so convinced. "It is neither a Persian name nor a Jewish name," she said. "When my child goes to school, other kids will make fun of him. So tell me. Exactly how does it fit?"

"Ah, be patient, Flora. You will see," said Mirza Agha. "One day very soon, that beautiful boy in your arms will be a great doctor in America!"

This all happened during a period when Mirza Agha assumed that our family would soon emigrate to America. He had no idea that his premonition would be delayed by approximately twenty years. Nor that, when we eventually did arrive in the States, we would do so under the most curious of circumstances.

Despite her doubts, and with her typical air of resignation, my mother let "Raymond" stand as my official name. Privately, however, she called me Farzin, a name derived from an Urdu word meaning "one who is learned" or "wise." Perhaps most important to her, the F in Farzin commemorated her late sister, Farideh. Soon, everyone on her side of the family started calling me that name. To them I was Farzin, not Raymond.

My father showed up a couple days after I was born. Among our family photos, there is one showing Nasser and Flora together. They are holding me. And they are smiling!

"I thought that my big plan had worked," my mother said later. "That maybe we'd finally found that spark I'd read about so many times. I hoped that we had but I still wasn't sure."

Apparently, neither was Nasser. After only a couple of days, he took the overnight train back to Abadan. Flora promised to follow him later.

The family Tabibiazar had now grown to three.

CHAPTER SEVEN

LUSH CITY

Tehran, Abadan, and Khorramshahr in the Early 1970s

THE EARLY 1970s WERE perhaps the most prosperous time for Iranian Jews in recent history. This isn't to say that long-held social biases against Jews just evaporated overnight. If anything, they were more dangerous now since certain groups in Iranian society kept fighting so hard to suppress what they saw as destructive westernizations. With modernization still on his mind and yearning to possess a military similar to the Israelis', Shah Muhammad Reza Pahlavi praised the small nation often and loudly for its tenacity, fearlessness, and disproportionate strength. He began shifting more and more of his allegiance toward Israel while strengthening his relationship with Israel's key Western backer, the United States.

A lot of this economic and social prosperity had to do with the close relationship the new state of Israel forged with Shah Muhammad Reza Pahlavi. They shared a common enemy—Arabs—and the role they played on the world stage shifted dramatically after the Six-Day War. Iranian Jews were viewed as part of this movement. Many of their countrymen considered them aligned with the shah and his progressive policies rather than conservative Muslim hierarchy—the mullahs. In the final assessment, Iranian Jews continued to enjoy status and opportunities. But beneath the veneer of Iranian society, a backlash was gathering strength.

It was during these golden days that Nasser and Flora's marriage blossomed into something akin to a true partnership. As my mother later confided in me, their marriage had trudged along without romance or passion. But now, more than ever, they relied on each other to stabilize their jobs, create a home life, and care for their new child—me.

"I began to resign myself to it all," my mother told me. "I suppose I began to see that being somebody's wife wasn't going to be like what I'd read in a fairy tale. It was harder. It was painful at times. But it was more worth it than ever."

She returned to Abadan with me a few months after I was born. She was now a fully hands-on parent, a tower of emotion and strength who fed me, clothed me, bathed me, read to me, disciplined me, and set boundaries. My father, by contrast, was fully hands-off. In fact, he was rarely around. My mother and I were always upstairs on the second floor of our house while my father was downstairs, at work in his clinic.

I was still just a toddler when, one day, while walking to Dad's clinic, my tiny foot slipped and I fell backward down the hard metal stairs. My head struck the corner of a large aluminum container filled with heating oil. The lip of the container gouged a massive cut over my right eyebrow. There was a lot of blood. I went unresponsive as a seizure rippled through me and I started foaming at the mouth.

My mother was up in our apartment. She heard me tumble and rushed out to see her baby boy thrashing about, bleeding like a mortally wounded animal. Screaming, she raced down the steps. "Nasser!" she shouted. "Nasser, come quickly, your son has died!"

My father rushed out of his practice and quickly examined me. I was still breathing, he said, and my heart rate was good. The blood was impressive but head wounds always bleed a lot. Calmly, professionally, he told my mother I was fine.

"Fine?!" my mother shrieked. "He is *not* fine, he is *dying*! Give him to me!"

She reached out to take me but Dad wouldn't let her. "There is nothing to do until he wakes up," he said.

"What are you talking about? You are a doctor!" Flora screamed. "Call an ambulance! Call a helicopter! He must go to a hospital! Do something! What kind of father are you? Save him!"

Calmly, my father explained, "If we take him to a hospital, they will put him through trepanation."

"What does that mean?!"

"They will bore a hole in his skull, which will maim him at best, maybe kill him at worst." Gently, my father wiped blood off my face with his handkerchief, shaking his head. "I give him a fifty percent chance if we just let him be and we see how things go. If he goes to a hospital?" He shrugged. "There's a hundred percent chance this will scar him for the rest of his life."

Weeping, my mother shook her head. "No! I do not believe it! That is ridiculous! That is—"

"That is how medicine works," my father said. "Now please, go into my office and bring me my black leather bag. Tell the patient in there he will have to wait. I have to clean up this cut and suture that eyebrow, then get back to work."

My mother started yelling. She cursed my father and his primitive Turkish family. His stupid parents, his idiot brothers and sisters, his mouth-breathing ancestors—everyone and everything she could think of to associate with him got cursed. My father bore all of it. As stoic as ever, he stood there, withstanding my mother's ferocity. He knew what was happening. She was a mama bear protecting her cub and he was wise enough to know that men seldom triumph over such powerful female energies.

Finally, in his best level voice, he said, "Everything you are saying is true. I am callous and insensitive. I am probably unfit to be a human being let alone a parent to this wonderful child. Now please. Bring me the black leather bag in my office. It's right on the floor by my desk."

It was one of those watershed moments in a couple's relationship where they rue the day they married each other. Each, I was later told, saw the other as falling short of their expectations, both as partners and as parents.

I woke up the next day with a headache. I was thirsty. I asked for some water. When I said I was hungry, they gave me fruit to chew on. And that, as they say, was that.

It was not my last childhood injury, nor would it be the last time that my father saved my life.

Despite their relative antagonism toward one another, my parents settled into a more placid routine and soon welcomed their second child. I was not yet three years old when my brother, Ramin, was born in June 1973.

I remember my mother was in the hospital just outside Abadan, preparing to deliver. My father came to pick me up in his car. "You will see, Ray," he said. "When we get to the hospital, you will have a new baby brother waiting for you."

Even now, nearly fifty years later, I remember how excited I was to meet him. I imagined my new brother would want to play with me right away—my very own personal live toy brother!

The drive to the hospital took about thirty minutes. I remember my father let me sit up front with him. In those days, especially where we lived, there were no rules about child seats or anything of the sort. Minute by minute and kilometer after kilometer, I peppered my father with questions. *How is Mom? What will the baby look like? Will he look like me? Like you? Like somebody else?*

My father answered my questions with his customary patience. By that point, he was used to my curiosity, especially when it came to toys, of which I'd become a connoisseur. I had a remarkable number of toys because my mother had gone back to work following her pregnancy. She felt guilty about leaving me in a nanny's care and so, each day, she would buy me a toy to distract and appease me as she left for her job. I ended up breaking most of them by the time she got back. So she bought me another. And another.

My nanny would chastise her right in front of me. "Don't you see you are spoiling this boy? You are also wasting the precious money you keep telling me you do not have!"

"Farzin is curious," my mother said. "He is breaking the toys to see how they work. Someday he will be a great inventor."

I'm not sure if "great" is the proper adjective. But in other respects, this turned out to be true.

At the hospital, I remember entering the room where my mother lay in bed. She was smiling and she held this odd, squirming bundle in her hands. Dumbfounded, I stood there and stared. "Come, Farzin. Move a bit closer. Do not be afraid," my mother said. "He will not bite you. This is your new brother. His name is Ramin."

To this day, I can recall everything about that experience, the same way I recall everything about my childhood with surprising clarity. Early on, when I would recount my memories, friends and relatives would tell me I wasn't actually remembering things but parroting my mother's stories about these events. This might have been true. Except that I could recall—and still re-call—the colors of the walls and doors and even the sheets on the bed in that hospital room. I remember the pictures that hung in their frames on the walls. I remember the thick heavy curtains that hung from the window, the bed's brown plastic headboard, and the smell in the room, which was a mixture of chemical hospital odors and the pungent cinnamon sweetness all new babies seem to give off.

Mostly I remember seeing Ramin for the first time. It was not love at first sight. "What is wrong with him?" I asked.

"Wrong?" my mother said. "What do you mean?"

"Why is his skin so gray and scaly?"

"He was just born," my father explained.

"Why are his eyes closed?"

"Being born is a huge ordeal." My mother sighed wearily. "He is exhausted."

"But why is he so small?" I asked. What I really meant was, how can something so small as this play with me and be my friend?

My parents shot knowing looks at each other. "He will grow," my father said. "You will see. And then he will be a great friend to you. Maybe your best friend. Just be patient."

I remember not being able to recognize the feelings coursing through me right then. It wasn't sadness, nor was it happiness. Rather, the sensation seemed to lie dead center between the two. It was muted but also intense. It was light and heavy at once. Moreover, this feeling was oddly warm and comfortable. It was relaxing. Up until that point, I hadn't had any idea such a feeling was possible.

That feeling has stayed with me always. It is here with me now, as I write these words. Many years later, as I continued to grow, I understood that the feeling was love. A love that, despite its many ups and down, would last a lifetime.

Walking to my mother's bedside, I looked down at the infant asleep in her arms. "Ramin." I said his name out loud. "My name is Raymond but you can call me Farzin. You will be my brother and my best friend. And you will be my toy."

"That's lovely, Farzin Joon," my mother said. In Farsi, *joon* means "dear." "But remember, please, not to break this particular toy. Promise me that?"

After Ramin was born, my mother and father again turned cold to each other. Despite a shared focus on their children's well-being, they seemed to lack the fundamentals for marital harmony. They fought about everything. Constantly. Loudly. A lot of their tensions revolved around money and specifically my father's seeming inability to earn any. Despite seeing more patients than any other doctor and despite having lines of patients waiting to see him—patients who said he was a great doctor and recommended him to other patients— his practice was not generating enough revenue. He was a doctor first and a businessman second, always more concerned with his patients' welfare than whether or not they could pay him.

At the same time, my mother had started to notice that most of her friends had husbands who worked very little. Nonetheless, they bought big houses, rode in nice cars, and took their families on expensive foreign vacations. My father worked from six in the morning to ten each evening and had practically nothing to show for his efforts.

I remember the terrible fights Mom and Dad had over his billing procedures. If a patient didn't have money, Dad never insisted on it. Quite often, he allowed the people he treated to give him presents and food for services rendered. Looking back, I think part of his reason for doing this was that we were Jewish and therefore outsiders in that community. Abadan, at that time, was also an underserved community. My dad simply wanted to help people who needed it most.

While we never went through periods of scarcity, money was certainly not abundant in our household. My mother told my father he was sacrificing his own family for the sake of his patients. "Each time you do not charge a patient, you take money away from your children! Do you not see this?" she shrieked.

But my dad couldn't imagine asking if someone had money before he treated them as a patient. "I cannot squeeze wine from a raisin," he told her.

They both acknowledged that my mother had more fire in her belly, more business savvy than my father possessed. "You need to try something different," she said. "It's a fact that other doctors are making more money than you. Let's not try to reinvent the wheel here. Let's ask ourselves how they're doing it and try to do what they're doing."

A lot of doctors in Abadan were working for the oil company, which paid very well. But my father had no interest in this. He'd already been in the military and worked for the government, which meant he'd grown wary of hierarchical, administratively top-heavy organizations whose resources rarely trickle down to the people such companies claim to serve. Still, he knew plenty of other doctors who profited by aligning themselves with a pharmacy and referring patients to each other.

"Wonderful!" my mother said. "Why not do that?"

Dad nixed the idea. From his point of view, no good doctor colluded with a pharmacy. He found this sort of "you help me, I'll help you" relationship among medical professionals offensive, particularly since they always seemed to prosper at the patients' expense. His ethics would never allow that.

By this point, he was working at the government hospital during the day. The job didn't pay very well so he kept up his personal clinic, hoping to make ends meet by working two jobs. At one point, he floated the idea of going fully into private practice, to which my mother said nothing. I think she didn't want to encourage him. In the back of her mind, if he went into private practice, he could lose more money than ever.

Again and again, they fought over finances. Finally, my mother pointed out that Dad had two business-savvy brothers. "Why not give them some money so they can invest it for us?"

So that's what he did. Dad reached out to his brother, who was happy to help his younger sibling. "You want to make money in business? Why, sure! I can help you with that!" he said. "How much have you got to invest?"

Impressed by this eager response, my father liquidated his life savings and gave them to his brother.

"How much are you giving him?" my mother asked.

"*Khanoom*," my father said, "do not nag me. This was *your* idea. I'm just trying to do what you told me."

"It's true it was my idea to give your brother some money," Mom said. "But I didn't say give him *all* of it!"

Time went by. Periodically, my mother would ask for updates. Each time, my father reported his brother had told him there was nothing to report. This wasn't good enough for my mother, who insisted he fly to Tehran and figure out what was going on.

"While you're there," she said, "ask if you can get part of your inheritance now. We are practically starving here!"

My father flew out to Tehran and came back bearing gifts for me and Ramin. I got a large battery-operated fire truck. Ramin got a massive, cuddly teddy bear. But there was no money, he said.

"What do you mean there is no money?" my mother said. "You gave your brother your life savings. Where is it?"

My father looked away. "You know, Flora, business is full of ups and downs. Every new venture has risks."

"*Where is it?!*" my mother shrieked.

That's when my father told her everything he'd given his brother was gone.

"Gone?!" my mother said. "*GONE?!?*"

Furious, she snatched up my brand-new, bright red fire truck. Even today she maintains her intent was to throw this ridiculous icon of their poverty in the trash. As it happened, she picked up the truck by its ladder and whipped it around at precisely the right arc that it struck my father's prodigious nose. Blood exploded everywhere and that wasn't the worst part. No, the worst part was my father's explanation.

As my mother continued to hound him, he told her what he'd learned. His brother had just bought a nice new apartment building. For his mother-in-law, he said.

"But what about us?!" my mother shouted. "What about the money we gave him to buy something valuable for us?!"

"He said he put that money into a separate venture, and that one didn't work out so well. We were just unlucky," Dad said. "That is how business is. Sometimes you win and sometimes you lose."

"Get it back!" my mother shrieked. "Get it back!"

"Flora, I cannot. The money is gone!" Dad roared.

Mom burst into tears. "What about your inheritance?"

Dad crushed a handkerchief to his nose. "I asked about that, too."

"And?"

"My family said I'm a doctor and doctors can make money easy. But they are businesspeople. They need capital to make money. So. . ."

My mother called my father many names, most of which centered on the fact that he was a Turk, and Turks are donkeys, she said, as stupid as rocks in the desert. The worst day of her life was the day she married him, she said. Just like that, any ambitions they'd had of moving to America were crushed.

Ramin was still very young and asleep in another room. I, however, was present through all of this argument. I remember I started to cry. Not because my parents were fighting again. That was normal. I'd come to expect that. I was crying because my new bright red fire truck had broken when it hit my father's face.

In retrospect, that was a super expensive toy. My father had bought it with all the life's savings he'd given to my uncle, as well as the inheritance he'd hoped to get from my grandfather.

In 1974, I was hit by a motorcycle while playing soccer in the street outside my father's clinic. On that day, as on most other days, the waiting room of Dad's clinic was full. There were so many patients hanging around to see Dr. Tabibiazar that half their number had lined up outside the building. They watched as my friends and I would play in the street. The adults would smile and laugh while giving us pointers on kicking and footwork. It felt like a great way to grow up. It felt safe, like the whole community was my babysitter. Which is why this next incident was so traumatizing.

One day, some kid about seventeen years old came rocketing around the corner on one of those smoky, noisy *put-a-put* bikes. To this day, I remember what he looked like, the long pants he wore, how he wore his shirt open, the fact that he wore no helmet. Then—*whoomp!* He ran me over. I was four years old.

I remember a second of deafening silence, which I broke by leaping back onto my feet. Boldly, I stared down the crowd. It suddenly felt important that I reassure everyone. "Nobody worry!" I said. "I'm Superman and I'm strong!" After which, passing out, I fell over backward.

Vaguely, I recall people screaming and shouting my father's name. The next thing I knew, strong hands were picking me up and I opened my eyes. My father was holding me. "Are you alright?" he said.

"Yes, Baba," I said. And I was. I had scratches, my ears were ringing, and my head hurt a lot. But I was fine.

The motorbike's driver didn't get off so easy. When I blinked my eyes into focus, I saw that the crowd had pulled the young man off his bike and was beating him with fists and feet and handbags. Still clutching me, pushing his way through the crowd, my father shouted at everyone. "Stop!" I remember him saying. "Don't hit him. Stop! My son is fine! It was only an accident!"

It took everyone several minutes to calm down, at which point the police arrived. I was taken into the clinic where my father examined me. He said I had a concussion. I had no idea what that meant. All I knew was that, over the next few days, my headache was ferocious. Then that, too, subsided.

A few days later, I asked my father why he'd gone to such lengths to protect a man who'd nearly killed me. I remember him checking my forehead for swelling. For a long time, he didn't speak. Then he said, "Farzin, in this world, there are very few people who try to do wrong. If there's any trick to living it's knowing when to demand your pound of flesh and when to let bygones be bygones. Do you understand?"

I was only four years old and I'd just been hit by a motorcycle while playing soccer in the street with my friends. Nothing my father had said registered to me but I wanted him to know how much I appreciated him caring for me. So I lied. I nodded. "Yes, Baba," I said. When, in fact, many more years would pass before I had the faintest inkling what he was talking about.

Because of this incident and many others, my mother grew increasingly discontent with our life in the south. She wanted us to be closer to her family so they could watch us kids. She thought this would give us more financial security, more prestige, more social opportunities. "We would have all that if we lived in Tehran!" she insisted.

My father disagreed. He couldn't care less about such things. He'd never craved the limelight. Also, notwithstanding the loss of his life savings, he thought we had enough money. "We have good food on our table and a good roof over our head," he would say. "Should we not be thankful for this? We are much better off than the patients I treat."

"You're saying you want to be as poor as your patients?" my mother shouted.

"I'm asking you, why should we throw away everything we've built here and go to Tehran?" my father said. "So we can grovel and try to impress a bunch of arrogant, uptight, snooty people who live there? I do not want this."

"We are isolated here!" My mother's shriek blasted twin plumes of smoke through her nostrils. By this point, driven by stress, she had become a chain-smoker. She ashed her cigarette into the sink. "Even your sister and her husband—your best friend—have left. Sima and Saeed are not fools. They saw this place for what it is, a trap. That is why they moved back to Kermanshah!"

My father shook his head. "This place is not a trap. Sima and Saeed just didn't give it a chance. Saeed was right. The fields around here are pregnant with oil. There will be plenty of prosperity here soon enough, and to spare. You will see."

My mother was so unconvinced, she decided to leave my father. It's hard to describe to a Western audience how countercultural this would have been in Iran at the time. Divorce was unheard of, of course, so my mother did what a lot of women did back in those days. She took her two sons and went to "visit family."

"This will be so much fun," she said. "You will see. It will be a chance for you to meet your cousins."

I was still very young at this point but I recall being dimly aware of the tension between my parents. Their personal life had begun to emulate the Cold War, which the United States and Russia were deeply embroiled in. The rivalry they engaged in was open but deeply restricted, a conflict whose delicate balance required constant tending lest it destroy the world. And so their tensions raged on, subversive and awful, scarring the landscape wherever they went. Through all this, my brother and I went along for the ride. What choice did we have? We were kids.

It was during this visit to Tehran, in 1974, that Mom became sick and required hospitalization. Doctors discovered great clusters of cysts in her lungs. She had to have surgery.

I remember my mother dropping Ramin and me off with her sister, our *khaleh*, Aunt Vickie. Ramin and I were excited by this. Khaleh Vickie had children our own age. Their names were Amir, Mojgan, Farnaz—whom everyone called "Essi," short for Esther—and Michael. So it turned out Mom had been right. Ramin and I were finally getting a chance to spend quality time with our cousins.

She stayed in the hospital about three months, long enough that, by the time she came out, Ramin, who was then only one year old, no longer recognized her. He'd started calling Khaleh Vickie his mom. When my mother heard this, it crushed her.

I remember Khaleh Vickie attempting to console her. "There, there, Flora," she'd say. "Children bond with adults. This is natural, don't you see? The important thing is that Ramin has felt loved all this time. Once you spend time with him, he will remember that you are his mother and all will be right again."

Khaleh Vickie was correct. Eventually, Mom got better, and she and Ramin became closer again. Soon after that, Mom told us it was time to return to Abadan. Ramin and I got excited by this.

"It will be just like it was before!" I said.

My mom shook her head. "Not exactly like before."

She knew something we didn't. In our absence, my dad had been promoted. He'd joined the staff of a local hospital in Khorramshahr. This hospital was bigger and more prestigious than the one he'd worked at in Abadan and it paid better. He'd also kept his private practice, where he saw patients on evenings and weekends. And in this way, because he committed to that course and worked very hard, we began to have a little more money. My parents had less marital stress.

Little by little, things got better.

Once we got back from Tehran, my mother kept pushing my father to move us out of Abadan. She was tired of living in an industrial port city whose oil refineries chugged out pollutants that tainted the local air and water supplies. In summertime, the temperature rose to as high as 120 degrees. The whole town stank. Heavy black tar seemed to permeate the air. We were all breathing it in. We couldn't help it.

"Nasser!" I recall Mom saying many times. "Nasser, we must get out of this town. It is no place to raise a child!"

She had a plan. The town due north of Abadan was called Khorramshahr—literally: "lush city." It was not a particularly large city. In 1975, it had a population of 150,000 or so. Still, relative to where we were living, Khorramshahr seemed like an oasis. Sprawled beside the Karun River, it boasted some of the country's finest date palm trees and supplied a fifth of the world's crop. It was cleaner and more developed, with better schools. In general, it was a much better place to raise kids. A lot of doctors lived there; many were my father's colleagues. Khorramshahr was also a bit more expensive than Abadan, but my mother had a plan for that, too. She would work a full-time job to help us afford a new place.

My father protested, of course. He said that a good Jewish wife shouldn't be working full-time as a lab technician; she should be home with her children. This was a losing argument from the start. By this point in their relationship, my mother couldn't care less about his opinions. Besides, in her view, my father had lost all moral superiority when he let his brothers squander the family's life savings. And so, at my mother's insistence, in March 1975, we moved from Abadan to Khorramshahr. My mom found a job as a lab technician in the same hospital my dad worked at. All in all, it was a good compromise.

The villa we bought was a large compound surrounded by ten-foot-high walls with a courtyard large enough to hold six cars. You passed in and out through a broad metal gate painted bright blue that was wide enough for two cars to pass through abreast. The gate had a smaller door cut into it so people could move back and forth without opening the big gate. Toward the back of the grounds, a grove of trees stood off to one side, then a separate grassy area big enough to hold another eight cars. We had a swimming pool, too, though it mostly stood empty. The house itself was fairly large, two stories, which housed five bedrooms. For that part of the world, our house was nothing unusual. The street we lived on contained many similar homes.

We now had more space than we'd ever enjoyed before. Under these conditions, my parents' relationship relaxed and stabilized. They had both worked hard to get us to Khorramshahr and I think they began to recognize each other's contributions to their partnership. The more they respected each other, the better they communicated as spouses.

Ramin and I were starving for attention from Dad, who was always working. We desperately wanted him to play soccer with us in the yard of our villa, or go on picnics with us with our friends, or hang out at dinner parties. It just never happened. He always left before we woke up and usually didn't come home until after we'd already gone to bed. Nor was he around much on weekends. It was Mom who was always there, Mom who made sure that our homework got done and our clothes were clean, Mom who made the food we ate beside her. Mom who disciplined us.

I have many vivid memories of childhood—birthday parties, school, playing in the big yard of our villa. In each of these memories, Ramin is right there beside me. We had become best friends, exactly as I had foreseen. But also, in a manner I hadn't predicted, we were adversaries. Brothers can be both and often are, I soon discovered. All that mattered was that, on the level of heart, the most important level there is, Ramin was mine and I was his. Only I was allowed to rough him up. None of my peers at school were allowed to lay a finger on him. Anyone who did would have to deal with me. I was very protective on this score.

Ramin felt the same about me. From an early age, he was the most loyal person in our family. He seemed to accept, for instance—much better than I—that we could be both idols and enemies to each other. If he hated it when I cheated him at a game or hit him for no good reason, he was still the first to come visit me after Mom punished me for mistreating him. While swimming together at the local pool, he hated that I was bigger, faster, more buoyant and skillful. But when he saw that I lost every race in my age group (he won every race in his own), he would share half his medals and prizes with me. The same went for the presents he got for his birthday and desserts served after supper. He shared everything and thought nothing of it. He does this even today.

By day, we'd fight like cats and dogs. At night, we'd hold hands while falling asleep. If it was just the two of us kicking a soccer ball in the yard, we were fiercely competitive with each other. If we played with friends, we were always on the same team, and woe be unto anyone who stood up against us.

In short, Ramin was a stronger, better person than me. He never lied, never cheated, never yelled. He was strong and ambitious and super competitive. To others, he was a cipher. He would lock his emotions in his small chest and never reveal his true feelings to anyone. However, to me, he was an open book, full of legible, powerful prose. As his brother, I could sense when he was sad or mad or happy or angry or jealous. If I attended a birthday party that Ramin wasn't invited to, I always picked up an extra Kit Kat bar or a take-home goodie bag for him. I never ate these treats until I got home so we could munch on them together. Today, some fifty years later, Kit Kats remain our favorite candy.

Even now, I'm not sure if our affection as brothers was something bestowed by genetics or built by the strong family bond Mom and Dad instilled in us. Whenever I ponder the matter, I recall how Maman Bozorg—the name we used for Sara, my maternal grandmother—would tell us biblical stories highlighting the need for brothers to be close and look out for one another.

"Now then," Maman Bozorg would say, pulling Ramin and me into her lap. "Today, we will talk about Cain and his good brother, Abel." Or: "Aha! I think the time has come to hear the story of Joseph and his brothers." And so on.

One time, Maman Bozorg took us out to the yard of our villa, where she gathered some sticks. "You see?" she said. "One stick is easy to break." She snapped one stick into two. "But two sticks? That is much harder." She showed us. Ramin and I both agreed it was harder to break two sticks.

"Now try three sticks. Try four," said Maman Bozorg.

In this way, her point became clear. Familial bonds have helped families survive since the time when human beings lived in caves. In the Jews' case, familial bonds were especially important since, often, the world seemed dead set against us.

Khorramshahr was a smaller community than Abadan. My family found that our Jewish life there was even more curtailed. Khorramshahr had no rabbi of its own. The entire town boasted only forty or fifty Jews, most of whom were secular, as we were. There were no other doctors among them and, since all worked hard to make a living for their families, we never had time to hang out with them. Our closest family friends ended up being other doctors in town, all of whom were secular Muslims.

When I say we were secular Jews, I mean that we tried to follow traditions but often fell short because of how hard my parents were working. For instance, it's customary for Jews not to work on Shabbat but my parents always did. We were diligent about keeping kosher—not eating pork, mixing meat with milk, and so on. But our town was too small to have its own kosher butcher. We got all our meat from a rabbi in Abadan who catered to Khorramshahr families.

It was not uncommon for one Jewish family in our community to buy a cow or a sheep that the visiting rabbi slaughtered according to ritual. Meat from this animal was then shared with the rest of the community. When it was our turn to purchase an animal, Dad took me with him to a nearby farm. Together we picked out a brown and white spotted calf, which I thought was adorable. In the back of my mind, I understood why we were purchasing the calf. But this was 1977. I was not yet seven years old and, like most children, I loved animals. Rather than focus on how the animal would become our food, I let myself become charmed by the largest, brownest, most peaceful set of eyes I had ever beheld.

On the appointed day, the calf was brought to the yard of our villa. I remember being so excited. It felt like we'd just got a new pet. I started to play with the calf. For an hour or so, I talked to it, feeding it treats with my tiny hands. The calf and I had just struck up a comfortable relationship when the rabbi hummed a few blessings in Hebrew. Pinning the calf's neck down to the earth, he pulled out an exquisitely sharp knife and slit the beast's throat with one rapid motion. Whereupon, kicking and thrashing, it began to bleed out.

I was stunned at first, then horrified. But the worst was yet to come. According to the ritual of *kapara*—a Hebrew word meaning expiation or atonement—blood from the calf must be smeared on the forehead of all present at a sacrifice.

The adults tried doing this to me but I ran away from them. Heartbroken and crying, I climbed up the tall loquat tree that grew in our backyard. Even in those parts, that tree was uncommon. I used to climb it often to gather the soft, yellow, apricot-like fruit that hung from its uppermost boughs. I never liked eating them but I enjoyed collecting them and giving them away to friends so they were not wasted. The adults chased me to the base of the trunk and stood there calling for me to come down but I wouldn't. I waited a couple of hours until everyone else had gone home before I descended. After that, my parents made a decision. They would never host such an event at our home again. They thought it would be cruel to put me through all that a second time.

Despite all this, my education as a Jew continued. In lieu of its own rabbi, Khorramshahr had a cohen, clergy of lesser status than a rabbi who are nonetheless deeply knowledgeable of Judaic tradition. During the old days of the Temple in Jerusalem, they were the *Kohanim* who performed the daily and holiday, or Yom Tov, duties. Our cohen had a large house with a large yard where he hosted all the Jews in Khorramshahr during Rosh Hashanah, Yom Kippur, and Passover. These gatherings became the primary venue at which I learned certain rites of Judaica. It was here, for instance, that I learned not to eat bread during Passover—only matzah would do for that. Where I learned the story of Moses and all he had done to lead our people out of Egypt. At age eight, I was fasting on Yom Kippur even though I wasn't yet thirteen and hadn't had my bar mitzvah. To me, it made no difference that I couldn't read a word of Hebrew. My mother and father were fasting along with the other adults so I thought I should, too.

What I remember most was the *feeling* of being Jewish, of being surrounded by people I considered family. We shared the same traditions, the same history, the same prayers, the same joy of eating challah bread or sipping wine, which I was allowed to do despite my age. Our conversations centered around the need to perfect ourselves because, by doing so, we could make our own tiny corner of the world a better place. This, to me, felt like a worthwhile endeavor. It felt less like an onus and more like a gift. And still does.

Once we moved to Khorramshahr, the tension between my parents abated somewhat. Likely this is because they rarely saw each other; they were both working hard to improve our financial situation. It didn't seem to hurt that they were each now further than ever from their respective families in Tehran.

This meant there were less opportunities for family members to intervene in their marriage. But no matter the reason, our family soon expanded again.

My sister, Romina, was born in October 1978. She was the most beautiful baby Ramin and I had ever seen and my parents gave us the honor of naming her—with one stipulation. We had to select her name from a short list of choices my parents compiled. In keeping with our family tradition, each choice began with an R. I remember my parents leaned heavily toward the name Roya, which in Farsi means "fantasy" or "dream." Ramin and I lobbied for Romina because we thought it sounded more like our own names. We thought this was the height of cool and something we could brag about to our friends. In the end, my parents relented.

"Romina it will be," my mother said.

From a practical standpoint, Romina was Ramin's little sister. They were closer in age to each other and they adored one another. Ramin was then five years old. He loved having a new companion. I had a harder time playing with Romina since I was eight years old and newborns were no longer so interesting to me. I had so much stuff going on at school—friends, sports, homework—that I couldn't see how a new baby sister complemented the growing complexities of my life.

Regardless, the family Tabibiazar had now grown to five. And all would have been well except for one thing. Though we didn't know it just yet, the Islamic revolution, which had been brewing for years, was about to explode.

CHAPTER EIGHT

EXODUS INTERRUPTUS

The Revolution Begins | 1978–1979

THE REVOLUTION BEGAN IN the summer of 1978, a few months before Romina was born. There had been open talk of the shah being forced to flee. People said that the borders were closing. This was a very uncomfortable time, particularly for an eight-year-old who was struggling to understand why everyone seemed so nervous. It would have been hard for me to understand that Iran's citizenry was then roiling with economic discontent. Outbreaks of violence were especially prevalent where my family lived. The Abadan/ Khorramshahr region played home to the nation's economic engine, its oil fields. Since we were right on the border with Iraq, we were also besieged by hardline Arab politics. All this would have been unsettling enough. But as Jews, we felt a particular dread. With the shah's power weakening, some Islamists were openly chanting, "Death to Israel."

I remember watching the TV, hearing the radio, reading the newspapers. Outbreaks of violence were mostly contained to Tehran and similar major cities but the balance of power was clearly shifting. The question was, toward what?

Many citizens were euphoric over the prospect of an Iran without the shah. My mother was one of them. "Democracy will replace autocracy," I once heard her tell my father. "The shah has been like a dictator here." She still resented how SAVAK had treated her older brothers, Jahangir and Elyas.

My father took a different stance. "Shah hasn't been so bad," he said. "Yes, there are problems. But let's be honest, he hasn't been so bad."

"So he's a *mostly benevolent* dictator," my mother sneered. "That still makes him a dictator. If he stays, I hope he conducts himself more like the Queen of England. Be a figurehead. Lead the parades but stay out of politics."

"That will not happen," my father predicted.

My mother ignored him. "Democracy must happen," she said. "Our people must form their own government. This is the way of the modern world."

But her hopefulness was short-lived. Very quickly, things took a turn for the worse. Fights began to escalate between opposing political factions. Chants of "Death to America" became routinely linked with chants of "Death to Israel." The murderous fervor that fueled all the shouting caused many people who initially supported the revolution to sour on it. Many Arabs who lived in our neighborhood started to identify with pro-separationist Arab groups whose stated goal was for southwestern Iran to join Iraq. This was met by a backlash from Iranians who considered themselves Persians. Many of them considered Arabs an inferior race lacking culture, class, and breeding while clinging to a religion that constricted rather than enlightened their thinking. These Persians would have been fine with Arabs joining Iraq but not if they made off with the oil fields and the rivers, which were so vital to trade.

"Let's just stay out of it," I remember my father telling my mother. "We'll wait and see what happens. When you don't know what to do, it's best to do nothing. Some condition will soon arise that makes it clear what needs to be done."

That summer, we went to visit my father's mother, Tavooz, whom Ramin and I called Nana, at her home in Tehran. She and my grandfather Ahron had moved there from Tabriz in the mid-1960s. But they'd only lived there a few years when Ahron, who had Parkinson's, fell and broke his hip. He died not long after that, leaving Tavooz alone. In the interim, she'd developed a mean streak a mile wide, particularly where my mother was concerned.

The two women had never gotten along well but the event that really drove them apart was the Very Expensive Fire Truck Incident. My mother felt we'd been wronged and that Tavooz, as the mother of all involved, should have ordered my uncle to give my father his money back. Tavooz, of course, did not want to get involved in her kids' private affairs. Her sons were grown men and grown men conduct their own business. Also, it was her understanding that money did indeed get lost when people started new businesses. Then she would say, "Besides, Nasser is a doctor. He can always make more money."

The two women never sat down to discuss their views. For one thing, they didn't speak the same language. For another, Tavooz was a Kurd who'd married a Turk from a small town while my mother was Persian from the nation's capital city. Tavooz thought my mother entitled; she felt that my mother should have been content being a doctor's wife. My mother felt that my grandmother was just another old-fashioned, illiterate woman who perpetuated the same kind of backward patriarchal attitudes that once led her sister, Farideh, to feel so hopeless and alone. They could never come to terms and so never resolved their disagreement. For years, there was never any fighting or shouting between them, only a cold and awkward silence, or sometimes eyerolls at larger family gatherings. I remember it was never much fun being in the same room as the two of them.

One day, Ramin and I were playing in Nana's bedroom, which had twin beds separated by a nightstand. Bored out of our minds, in a strange city we could not venture out in, and without any cousins to distract us, Ramin and I started leaping back and forth from one bed to the other, screaming and laughing until Tavooz burst into the room and started shouting at us.

In retrospect, I'm not sure what upset her more, the fact that two tiny barbarians had entered her home and were tearing it apart or the fact that we were somehow desecrating the memory of Grandfather Ahron by bouncing up and down on his bed. I suppose there was also the notion that we two tiny hooligans might injure ourselves by playing so rough. At any rate, she spared no energy scolding us.

Still stinging from the scolding and eager to show how mature I could be, I started listening to the evening news alongside the other adults in my family. Each night, the TV reported the shah was having trouble combatting the revolution. Then, on August 19, a Saturday, something terrible happened. The newscaster announced that, in my hometown of Abadan, someone had locked hundreds of people inside a movie theater called Cinema Rex and lit it on fire. Some sources pegged the death toll at 370. Others said it was likely closer to 470.

The political implications of the fire were huge. The movie being shown that night was *Gavaznha*, a word that means "deer" in Farsi. The film dealt with topics like crime, drug abuse, prison life, and the shifting allegiances of old friendships. Many considered it critical of the shah's rule. They said it showed how his White Revolution had driven many poor, uneducated Iranians into the cities. There, wholly unprepared for urban life, many turned to despicable means of survival while the elite grew richer and richer.

Nobody knew who set the fire. The shah's people called it the work of Arab extremists. Iranian Islamic revolutionaries claimed SAVAK had done it. I remember crying for two days straight. Who could do such a thing? Burn people alive? I couldn't believe it. How could anyone order the death of other people, my own neighbors?

The fire marked a turning point in the revolution. Public sentiment shifted suddenly and drastically toward the Ayatollah Khomeini. His popularity was bolstered when, the following month, armed forces loyal to the shah opened fire on a pro-Khomeini demonstration, killing hundreds and wounding ten times that number. New protests erupted all over the country. From his exile in Paris, Khomeini began demanding that the shah and his government be overthrown and at once, for the good of the country. Rioters began to attack what they saw as Western influences in Iranian society. This included financial institutions but also liquor stores and retail shops that sold Western-style clothing. Even automobiles made in the West were getting burned.

In the face of all this, I noticed my mother's pro-revolution sympathies starting to soften. She had once been adamant that a switch to democratic power would benefit the country. She still believed that the Ayatollah Khomeini would be a good spiritual leader for Iran. "Practically speaking, the Ayatollah will be the movement's figurehead, the same way the Pope is the figurehead of the Catholic Church."

"Ah," my father said noncommittally. "Is that how it will be?"

My mother nodded. "They're saying that socialist, Massoud Rajavi, will serve as president." At the time, this was one of the revolutionaries' primary talking points. "He is a good man, you know," my mother said. "With a socialist leading the country, Iran will have separation of church and state, the same as Western nations."

I remember my father said nothing to this. Looking back, that seemed like answer enough. I was then in the third grade. Young as I was, I still understood that our nation had a proud history dating back 2,500 years. The Persian Empire had once spread across what, today, we call India, Egypt, and Greece. It had survived the Mongol invasion and various wars among the Arabs. I remember telling my parents how confused and upset I was. I had nothing against the shah and I couldn't believe that he or anyone else in charge would burn their own people alive.

Was this what being a Persian meant? Were actions like these the legacy of our proud people? I remember my mind swinging back and forth along the pendulum path of uncertainty. Who was in the right here? Who was wrong? Who was the hero and who was the villain? For the first time in my young life, I had no idea.

Adding fuel to the fire, the newspapers kept running political cartoons of the shah dressed up like a vampire. Everyone knew that Muhammed Reza Pahlavi suffered from blood cancer. His illness required him to receive chemotherapy. *He requires the blood of young people to stay alive!* the revolutionaries said. *Is this not the height of evil? Has he not always been a puppet of the West? Did he not conspire with the Brits and the Americans to destroy our previous champion, Mohammad Mosaddegh?*

No matter how anyone looked at things, the shah was losing support. The final straw broke when, in December 1978, a group of the shah's soldiers turned on one of their officers and attacked him in the name of the revolution. Muhammed Reza Pahlavi saw the writing on the wall. He delivered a well-scripted, deeply compassionate speech about how he would rather relinquish control than see more people die. Then he fled the country for Egypt, leaving his prime minister, Shapour Bakhtiar, to govern a nation that was literally on fire.

Bakhtiar worked quickly and hard to make concessions but the situation only spun further out of control. Khomeini refused to parlay with the new prime minister. He declared Bakhtiar a traitor for working in the shah's government. Then, on the first day of February, 1979, Khomeini returned from exile in Paris on a chartered Air France jet. He touched down at Mehrabad International Airport in Tehran, where millions of Iranians turned out to greet him. To make his intentions clear, Khomeini moved quickly from the airport to Beshest-e Zahra Cemetery, where so many Muslim revolutionaries lay buried. Turning to the crowds, he delivered a speech that TV and radio carried all over the country.

Khomeini declared the current prime minister's cabinet both incompetent and illegal. Were he allowed to rule, all Iranians would be part of the new political process. He promised a separation of power in keeping with Western democracies to ensure that a new government would be run fairly. And he would support a socialist leader as president of the country. "I will strike the present government on the mouth!" Khomeini declared. "I will do this because the people have approved me!"

The spectators went wild.

Four days later, Khomeini announced he had chosen a new prime minister to replace Shapour Bakhtiar. Desperate to keep order, Bakhtiar attempted a series of crackdowns. It was a bad move. Khomeini's followers retaliated by seizing institutions they thought represented the shah. Like a tidal wave, they deluged police stations and government office buildings.

Things moved quickly after that. Days later, the nation's top military leaders withdrew their troops from quelling riots in the streets. They announced that, henceforth, Iran's armed forces would take no side in the conflict. After only thirty-six days as prime minister, Bakhtiar fled to Paris. There was no one left to defend the old regime. Within a few days, the shah's government had fallen. So had the all the social protections Iranian Jews had enjoyed for the last fifteen to twenty years.

For all their bluster and violence, the revolutionaries were deeply unorganized. It soon became clear they had no plan to govern the country they'd seized. Disorganized covens of rioters wandered the streets torching and beating whatever and whomever they pleased. Ramin and I watched this play out on the TV in our Khorramshahr home. It was all very shocking.

The Ayatollah began to reveal his true intentions. For instance, he soon reneged on his promise to support a socialist president. He made it clear that he didn't want a government where church and state were separate. Rather, he wanted to implement a Shi'a Muslim theocracy where church and state were the same entity and whose clerics imagined conquests well beyond Iran's borders. Khomeini then created a new paramilitary force, the Islamic Revolutionary Guard Corps, better known as the Pasdaran—a Persian term that means "guards."

Clothed in dark green uniforms, armed with guns and a violent ideology, the Pasdaran were rogue looters and extremists who now ruled the country. Prior to the revolution, its members had been part of the lowest socio-economic class. Under the shah's rule, they had felt slighted and powerless. Now that the tables were turned, they were ready to dole out cruelty with extreme prejudice.

A perfect example of this was the custodian at my father's hospital. Before the revolution, he'd been nothing, hired help. After the revolution, he gained incredible power by spouting pro-Khomeini slogans and ratting out counterrevolutionaries. The Pasdaran loved such firebrands. They were useful for advancing Khomeini's agenda, seizing media outlets and schools, while engaging in criminal enterprises like black marketeering, smuggling, extortion, and murder.

The Iranian Ministry of Health had appointed my father chief doctor at the hospital where he worked in Abadan. He got the position because he was the least controversial person they could find in a time when everyone was partisan. Dr. Tabibiazar was universally regarded as a quiet man. It was widely known that he didn't smoke, didn't drink, didn't have extramarital affairs or use prostitutes. He didn't steal, he'd never taken kickbacks from a pharmacy, and he'd never cheated anyone. He treated his patients with the utmost respect, often to his detriment. Also—to my mother's eternal dismay—he refused to take sides in a fight regardless of the consequences his neutrality might bring about.

People knew that my father was Jewish. They also knew he was honest. He refused to let politics factor into his thinking. His colleagues, who all took kickbacks and bribes, agreed that if anyone could steer the hospital through such turbulent times in the most neutral fashion possible, it was Nasser Tabibiazar, M.D.

In those days, Iranian doctors who worked for the Ministry of Health also worked dozens of side jobs. Many supplemented their modest incomes with real estate deals and the like. But my father did not. He would never "lower" himself to do anything he didn't believe in one hundred percent, and the thing he seemed to believe in the most was the practice of quality medicine.

My father, however, learned quickly that there is simply no way to please both sides of a revolution. As part of the Ministry of Health, my father's hospital displayed mandatory pictures of the shah and his wife, Queen Farah. The United States has a similar custom. When you walk into the Veterans Administration, the president's picture is right there, front and center, to greet you. One day, this custodian-turned-Pasdaran came to work touting pictures of the Ayatollah. Barging into my father's office, he demanded, "Take down those pictures of the shah and put up these pictures of our savior, Khomeini, instead!"

My father had worked with this man for years before these events took place. Only at that moment, however, did he understand the man's true mettle, the depths he would stoop to in order to gain favor with the revolution. In his Solomon-like fashion, my father ordered that pictures of the shah be taken down. But he refused to put up pictures of the Ayatollah in their place.

"What is this insolence?!" barked the custodian. "Do you not respect our leader, Khomeini?!"

"This is a hospital, as you well know," my father said. "The only power we respect here is the power of medicine to heal the sick."

"Do what you are told," the man snarled. He was not armed but he spoke with the authority of someone who was. "From this point forward, you will only treat those patients who support the revolution!"

My father just looked at this man. "I do not tell you how to run the revolution. You do not tell me how to run this hospital. Unless you would rather trade places." He waved an arm toward the emergency room, which, at the moment, was choked with people who, revolutionary or counterrevolutionary, had been wounded in various conflicts. "Suppose a man comes to me unconscious. What should I do? Not treat him until he wakes up so I can question his politics? If that's the case, scrub up, please. The wounded will keep piling up and we will require assistance in surgery. It's the only way your revolution will succeed."

The custodian blinked at my father. Like most revolutionaries, uniformed or otherwise, he was a poor, uneducated man whom circumstance had elevated to a position he was unfit to handle. On some level, he understood this, just like he understood that he needed my father. After uttering several more threats, he retreated from my father's office.

My father sighed, but any relief he experienced was premature. This was just the beginning. His colleagues and friends began pleading with him not to be stubborn. My mother joined this chorus as well. "These principles you harbor will get you killed, and perhaps us, too—your wife and children!" she said.

"I am a doctor," my father responded. "I treat the sick. All blood runs red regardless of politics or beliefs."

"This is exactly what I am talking about!" my mother shouted. "*I* know what you're talking about and *you* know what you're talking about. But you know how it is with the Pasdaran. If you are not friends, they count you as enemies! They write your name in their black book and—*poof!* One day you just disappear!"

But my father refused to change course. "The revolutionaries need me running the hospital and they know it. So long as I treat everyone fairly, we have nothing to worry about."

"But they can replace you!" my mother said. "Anyone can be replaced in a revolution!"

My father shrugged. "Perhaps the revolution will fail. Things are very uncertain right now. The situation could break either way. If the pendulum swings back to the shah, these Pasdaran and their black book will become meaningless. Let us see."

My mother and father fought constantly over this and other matters. In particular, my mother pointed out how people were saying the borders were closing. My father's two older brothers had already fled for the United States. They'd urged my father to follow. "Khomeini promises all these freedoms," they said. "Then he encourages his followers to behave like thugs. This will not end well. Nasser, you must leave at once."

My father then uttered a proclamation that has since become infamous in my family. "Don't worry," he said. "Whatever happens to the country will also happen to us."

He intended that to mean we should stop worrying, keep doing the right thing, and trust that everything would be well. Dad has always been a simple man whose good intentions lead to good thoughts that express themselves in good actions. According to his worldview, when a person propagates good, he cannot help but reap good in return. Any evil that arises is simply overcome by doing even *more* good. To be fair, this certainly worked in less turbulent times. But I noticed how quickly it broke down as conditions around us continued to worsen.

Dad kept insisting that we keep our noses to the grindstone and simply ignore what, to him, amounted to politics. Yes, Khomeini's forces were having their heyday. "Let them," I once overheard him telling my mother. "It's healthy."

"People are dying. How is it healthy?" my mother asked.

"The revolutionaries say there were problems with the shah's government. Well, I agree. And so do you. Those problems were like an infection. So now the country, like a human body, is heating up to fight the infection. But as with the body, it will pass. Things will return to homeostasis, at which point life will feel normal again."

My mother's silence told me she thought my father was being naïve.

Dad didn't notice. "In the meantime," he went on, "all I have to keep doing is run the hospital. If I do that, who can touch me?"

The custodian didn't give up. In what was a common practice back then, he had his committee—the local Pasdaran group—pay two hundred people about five or six American dollars each to stage a demonstration. Five or six bucks in Iran was good money back then. One day these demonstrators showed up in front of Dad's hospital chanting, "Death to Dr. Tabibiazar!" They called my father pro-Israel, pro-shah, and pro-America. They said he was anti-revolution. So much for keeping our noses to the grindstone.

My mom was at her job that day. One of her co-workers rushed to her saying, "Come quickly! There is a riot outside! They're going to lynch your husband!"

No one in Dad's hospital knew what to do. A few of the doctors called Dad's boss, head of the Department of Health for the State of Khuzestan. They begged him to intervene. "This is a government hospital," they said. "These people outside are going to kill one of your doctors. Call the military! You have to send troops!"

An hour or so later, two Mercedes flatbed military trucks pulled up and disgorged about thirty to forty armed soldiers. Pushing their way through the crowd, these men cleared an aisle that led to the hospital door by standing shoulder to shoulder, fifteen to twenty men to each side. Their bodies created a corridor that kept the rioters away. With the proper degree of gravity, their commanding officer walked down this aisle, went into the hospital, and spoke to my dad.

"Put your hands behind your back and grab your wrists as though you are handcuffed," he said. My father did not like this but he complied. The officer then draped a coat over Dad's hands to make it look like his hands were secured. "Very good," the officer said. "Keep your head down when we go out. Do not say anything. Do not show any emotion."

My father just nodded. For him, that last part at least would be easy. He could act normal.

"I will walk you out to the truck," the officer said. "You will climb in the back. Again, say nothing."

"Where are you taking me?" Dad asked.

"Good question," the officer said. "First, we will drive you around. This will give the crowd time to disperse. We want things to cool off a bit. Then, a bit later, we'll drop you off at the Pasdaran committee office. No, do not be alarmed. They just want to ask you a few questions and talk to you a little. In the long run, this is the best thing to do."

There were other doctors listening. They all knew what "questioning" meant. The Pasdaran were lawless. Odds were even they'd torture my father. A few of them started to protest. The officer held up a hand for silence. "This is how it must be," he said evenly. "You see how these people have worked themselves up. They crave a victory. The best thing to do is let them have one." He turned to my father. "But you will be safe. We are monitoring this situation very closely."

No one felt very convinced by this, my father least of all.

Dad was detained at the Pasdaran office for a few days, during which time no one had any communication with him. Mom tried to shield us from the details but Ramin and I were terrified for his safety. Mom became so frantic, she went to a neighboring family in Khorramshahr whose father was also a physician; he worked at the hospital with my father. This man gathered two other doctors and went to the Pasdaran committee office, where they begged for my father's release.

"Please," they said humbly. "We respect your decision. But we believe you have made a mistake in this matter of Dr. Tabibiazar."

"No mistake," one Pasdaran officer said. "This man is *shāhanshāh*." This word was used to describe anyone loyal to the Pahlavi regime.

"Not true," said this gaggle of doctors. "And let us be clear. Dr. Tabibiazar is not *shāhanshāh*; he is simply doing his job. He's not against the revolution, he is an honest man who loves his country. But he is also a doctor. It pains him to see anyone injured or ill. This includes your own men who show up wounded at our hospital. Please, you must reconsider. The hospital cannot function without him. If you deprive us of his expertise, it will have a detrimental effect not only on your own forces here in Khuzestan but the revolution at large."

Their plea worked. My father was released and sent back to run the hospital but he found someone else had already been put in charge. Also, someone had plastered pictures of Khomeini everywhere. There was now a picture of Khomeini hanging in my father's office. He just looked at it, said nothing, and went back to work. What choice did he have? By then it was clear that Khomeini's forces had prevailed. The revolution was there to stay.

More emboldened than ever, the Pasdaran began watching my father constantly, just as SAVAK had once watched my uncles, Elyas and Jahangir. Word on the street said that my father's name was still written down on the revolution's black list—their execution list. People said his days were numbered. Ramin and I did not know how long he had but we felt certain the time would come when he would disappear again, this time for good. And so we attempted to flee.

We were not alone. By the end of the Second World War, about 150,000 Jews lived in Iran. Most were clustered in tight communities throughout Tehran and other cities such as Shiraz, Isfahan, and Kermanshah. Once the revolution erupted in early 1978, that number decreased to about 100,000. A mass exodus had carried the rest—about 60,000 according to some estimates—to other countries. More than half went to the United States. About a third fled to Israel. The remaining 5,000 or so scattered across Europe, primarily in France, Germany, Italy, Switzerland, and the UK. My family and I hoped to join this exodus.

Days after Dad was released from detention, he ordered us to pack our suitcases. We were going for a little trip, he said. Unbeknownst to us children, he and Mom had booked us seats on a flight out of Abadan Airport, bound for Germany through Tehran. When Ramin and I understood what was going on, we got very excited.

I remember us boarding the plane and nestling comfortably into the seat. I remember being excited to finally meet our German cousins. I also wondered when food would be served. I had heard that flight attendants brought hot meals served in little tin trays that you ate from off your seatback tray. I thought that was cool. I'd also heard that children were sometimes given special treats if they behaved and I planned to behave. I advised Ramin to do the same.

Just before the flight took off, some Pasdaran officers boarded the plane. I remember trembling when I saw them standing up near the cockpit, wearing green uniforms with their rifles slung over their shoulders. One of them had a piece of paper in his hand, which I later learned was the flight manifest. Moving up and down the aisles, he asked passengers questions. Everyone shook their heads until at last he came to my family. "You are Dr. Nasser Tabibiazar?" the officer said.

I remember the look on my father's face. The tension he tried so hard to repress. "I am," he said.

"And this is your family?" The officer gestured at my mother, Ramin, Romina, and me.

"Yes," my father said tiredly.

The officer nodded. "Please come with us."

"Is there some kind of problem?"

"Come with us."

Back in the terminal, more Pasdaran showed up and surrounded us. They were accompanied by members of the local police, who explained that my father could not leave the country.

"We were just going on a little trip to see relatives," my father said.

The officer smiled as if to say, *Of course. Tell it to the committee. Now please come.*

"There is no need to be afraid, doctor," the officer said. "You are quite safe here. Everyone needs you back at the hospital. Just do your job and all will be well."

We begged to differ, of course. By that point, we understood perfectly well that my father's assessment was wrong. Keeping your nose to the grindstone and just doing well was not going to work. I was only eight years old and it suddenly was crystal clear to me that we had to get out of the country as quickly as possible. But how?

Here is a perfect example of why we were scared. Shortly after Khomeini took power, the anxiety of Iranian Jews was exacerbated by the death of a man named Habib Elghanian. A prominent, wealthy Jew from Tehran, Elghanian had been president of the Tehran Jewish Society throughout the 1970s. More than anyone else, he symbolized the success we Jews had obtained under the shah's rulership. And yet, Habib Elghanian was no friend of the throne. In 1975, as part of a crackdown on business corruption, the shah fined Elghanian stiffly for perpetrating "illegal activities," after which he threw him in jail.

With this sort of anti-shah pedigree, one might have assumed that El-ghanian was safe in the new regime. Not so. Three months after Khomeini returned, Elghanian was arrested and hauled before an Islamic tribunal loyal to the revolution. He was found guilty of various charges, including corruption in his business dealings and, tellingly, "friendship with the enemies of God"—a term that meant Zionists in general and Israel in particular. As far as the Ayatollah was concerned, Elghanian represented everything the revolution hated. He was a landowning Jew in a country Khomeini hoped would become the next crown jewel among Muslim nations.

The trial reportedly took twenty minutes, at the end of which the tribunal sentenced Elghanian to death. He was executed by firing squad the next morning. Since the revolution deemed that having money was sinful, the entirety of Elghanian's wealth was confiscated by the new Islamic state and distributed among the most powerful mullahs. It's hard to describe the shock wave this sent off among the Persian Jewish community.

Immediately, Jewish leaders sought an audience with Khomeini. A meeting was set up in the Shi'a holy city of Qom. During this meeting, the rabbis expressed their distress over Elghanian's death. They told Khomeini they were Persians first and foremost, that being a Jew did not automatically equate with being a Zionist. Khomeini made a big show of listening. Then he promised to protect the Jews so long as they kept a low profile and refused to move against him. Famously, he referred to passages in the Quran that represented Moses, a figure deemed holy by all three monotheistic religions. He called Moses the "Speaker-to-Allah," who "represented pharaoh's slaves, the downtrodden" of his era. Khomeini then said: "We recognize our Jews as separate from those godless, bloodsucking Zionists." Immediately after which, he issued a fatwa, or holy decree, protecting Iranian Jews from attack.

All this did little to placate a stunned community. By that point, everyone recognized Khomeini as a shrewd man who was comfortable going back on his word. He was also a shrewd tactician. He knew that open prosecution of Jews would draw fiery criticism from the international sphere, which, for the most part, already condemned his revolution. His fatwa was therefore more about him flexing his muscles for the benefit of his Islamic followers than helping the Jews he claimed to value, Moses or no Moses.

Few Iranian Jews were placated by Khomeini's actions. They began leaving the country in droves. Once the revolution found its feet, there were less than 10,000 Jews left living in Iran.

My family wanted to leave too but, for the moment at least, we would have to stay put and see what life brought our way.

CHAPTER NINE

THE REVOLUTION'S YOUNGEST LEADER

The Revolution Continues | 1978–1979

HOW DOES A SOCIETY function without Twitter, Instagram, or Facebook? Back then, we had no internet, cell phones, or social media. The best ways to check on friends or family were to write them a letter or call them by telephone, but we had to be careful. The Pasdaran were tapping the phone lines. Mail was being opened and read by Khomeini loyalists. It became quite common to call someone you knew and have them not answer. Their phone would just *ring, ring, ring* each time you would try them.

What did this mean? Had they fled? Were they lying murdered in a ditch somewhere or thrown in jail? Or were they part of the revolution now, unwilling to talk to anyone they considered against Khomeini's values? Nobody knew who they could rely on anymore. Friend and foe became virtually impossible to distinguish from one another. Order had almost completely broken down. The revolutionaries' fiery rhetoric and willingness to use violence mixed badly with their almost complete lack of organization. These people had taken over a country they had no idea how to run. It was all a big mess that was getting worse fast.

My parents began arguing more vociferously than ever. Was this awful situation temporary? Would the shah come back? Would somebody else from the royal family take his place on the throne? Should we leave the country but keep our house until everything blew over? Or should we sell the villa? And if that was the case, who exactly would we sell it to? Who would buy it? And what would we do once they sold it? Where would we go and how would we live?

Through all this, Ramin and I were still in school and this was a blessing, of sorts. I was nine years old. Being a fourth grader made me feel like some things, at least, were still normal. But after the incidents at the hospital and the airport, our father gave us strict instructions. "At school," he said, "you must say nothing about the revolution. Nothing at all, do you hear me? If anyone says anything negative about the revolution, turn away as though you did not hear. Pretend to be deaf, if you must."

Ramin and I vowed to comply. We understood that our father's life was at stake. Even so, I confess I had great difficulty keeping silent. I was also the best student at my school and had a large following of other kids who took me for their intellectual gang leader. I tended to be very outspoken about my views, except in one case involving my first crush on a girl.

Her name was Azadeh, which means "freedom." Even today, I can still see her face; I hear the sound of her voice when we talked or her laughter. She was a Muslim girl. Of course! I was my father's son, after all. Azadeh reciprocated my feelings even though we never spoke to each other out loud and certainly never held hands or anything like that. In fact, we hardly saw each other since, when I started fourth grade in September 1979, our classes were no longer coeducational. Under a new structure demanded by the revolution, boys would go to school in the morning while girls attended classes in the evening. This schedule alternated week after week. I was not pleased with the new arrangement but, again, my parents sat down with Ramin and me to explain what was going on.

"Go along with whatever they say," my mother said, to which my father just nodded. "And now, more than ever. . . no mention that you are a Jew. Do you understand?"

Both Ramin and I looked at our father, who just nodded again. Those nods of his could say a lot.

To overcome the split classes, Azadeh and I worked out a system where we communicated by writing messages to each other on the blackboard in an abandoned classroom on the fourth floor of our school. The messages we left were innocent, nerdy, and always super brief. "How you do you like school?" I would write. Then, after sweating with anticipation for twenty-four hours, I would return to the room and see characters written in her lovely hand. "I like it a lot," Azadeh replied. "How about you? What do you like most at school?" I nearly swooned.

We asked each other about grades and tests, which subjects and poets we liked, which teachers were our favorites, that kind of thing. At one point, Azadeh asked me, "Who are your friends?"

I hedged on this answer because I thought it would take too long to describe. I was palling around with three other boys. Emad was a heck of a soccer player who also happened to be an Arab. We didn't get on so well at the start. During a match, he headbutted me in protest over a bad call. Headbutting was one of Emad's signature tactics. He used it on anyone who dared challenge him or offend him. Everyone was afraid of Emad. I wasn't. Instead of slinking away, I headbutted him back, even harder than he'd hit me. I remember him blinking the tears from his eyes. Then he told me, "That really hurt." From that point forward, he and I were friends.

Zahir was my best friend, a chubby Muslim boy who reminded me of an ox. He was so big and his eyes were a calm liquid brown. Had he wanted to, he could have used his size to inflict terrible damage on other children—yes, even Emad. But nothing could have been further from his mind. He was the nicest kid I knew. He had a very even temper and was always fun to be with. His family was wealthy but Zahir did poorly in school. Each day after classes, I would help him with math while our other friend, Amir, helped him study the rest of his subject load.

Amir was a very small boy who wore perfectly round glasses. He was a Bahá'í and nice to everyone he spoke to, which is why he got bullied a lot. Emad, Zahir, and I made it our job to look out for Amir. Many times, we protected him from other kids who wanted to rough him up because he was little and they were jealous of his good grades. Amir was smart and I liked him a lot, though at times I worried that bad things would happen to him if he didn't learn to look out for himself.

Emad, Zahir, and Amir were the only friends I trusted enough to admit that I liked Azadeh. Their reactions were mixed. Emad thought the whole thing about writing notes on the blackboard was stupid. "Why don't you just go up to her and talk?" he said. "I mean, I know it's difficult with the boys and girls being separated but I bet you could make it happen somehow if you really wanted to."

"Oh, leave him alone." Zahir tipped me a wink that Emad couldn't see. "I bet Ray already has a plan to do just that. Don't you, Ray?"

I kept silent rather than admit that I had no such plan up my sleeve.

"I think it's nice," said Amir. "If two people like each other, they should be allowed to say so."

"And if they hate one another?" Emad asked. "Does that work the same way?"

Amir didn't reply to that.

For weeks, Azadeh and I continued to trade notes on the blackboard. Then one day I went home after school to find my mother waiting for me in the kitchen. She didn't look pleased. "Your school called today." She nodded at the phone hanging on the kitchen wall.

"Oh?" I froze in place, wondering what I had done.

"Who is Azadeh?"

"Azadeh?" I made a big show of thinking this over. "I don't believe I know anyone named Azadeh. That's not a boy's name, you know."

My mother arched one eyebrow at me. "It's a girl's name," she said.

"Oh?" I made another big show like this was news to me.

"Farzin, you have to stop writing notes to this girl on the blackboard."

"I don't know what you're talking about."

"Farzin!" I was alarmed at how serious she became, and so fast. "Listen to me. Azadeh is a Muslim girl."

"So?"

"Don't play stupid, Farzin. It doesn't become you. In case you hadn't noticed, there are tensions right now with the Islamic community."

"I know what's going on," I said, though perhaps a bit too sulkily. Because the next thing I knew, my mother was giving me a stern lecture about how sensitive conditions were, how it wouldn't take but the slightest provocation for a young Jewish boy to be expelled from school. How my being expelled from school could impact my father's already tenuous standing in the community. It all made perfectly logical sense, though it felt pretty awful.

"So." My mother folded her arms. "Now you know it's the best thing to do. You must stop talking to this girl immediately. For her sake and yours. Promise me, Farzin."

I refused to look her in the eye. "Promise you what?"

"Farzin. . ."

"I'm just asking a question."

"Farzin!"

"Okay!" I said.

"Okay what?"

"Okay, I promise."

"Promise what?"

But I wouldn't say it. It hurt too much. I left the room quickly and didn't talk to my mother for days after that. I was frustrated and angry with her, with school, with the world, with life. I wanted to talk to Azadeh and though I understood why I could not, I sure didn't like it. Not in the least.

I never went back to that abandoned classroom on the fourth floor again so I don't really know if she kept leaving notes. I just know I felt a little broken inside. But such was life. When I told my friends how I felt, their reactions were mixed once again.

"Your mom is right," said Emad. "Quit whining. It's for the best. Who cares about girls anyway?"

"Not to worry." Again, Zahir winked at me. "I bet Ray's got a plan cooking to make everything come out alright. Don't you, Ray?"

"I still think people should like who they like," said Amir. "I mean, what's the point of liking someone in the first place if you can't do anything about it? That doesn't sound fair to me. It's like being born with a good singing voice but having no songs to sing. It's just sad."

It wasn't just boy/girl classes that changed at our school. A lot of our teachers weren't sold on the revolution. Knowing this, the Pasdaran installed new pro-revolutionary administrators across the country. They were to institute polices and standards aligned with Islamic revolutionary values. In other words, they functioned as the eyes and ears of the mullahs and all their supporters. Unfortunately, these new "educators" knew nothing about teaching. Rather, they kicked off campaigns that one would correctly term brainwashing.

One of my fourth-grade teachers was such an "educator." I remember the first day I met him. He was about five feet ten, rather thin, perhaps twenty-five years old. He had thick black hair cut short so it was wavy, not curly—like an Iranian James Dean—and a long, aesthetic face. His uniform, as I came to think of it, was a pair of beige pants worn with an off-white shirt that he kept unbuttoned and a pair of old Converse tennis shoes. Though he had an olive-skinned Arabic look about him, he was not an Arab. And he shaved.

Charismatic, ambitious, and very determined, this "teacher" believed wholeheartedly in the revolution. He spoke often and openly to us about how optimistic he was that Iran would become a fair and just society governed by its own people. Daily, he read us the newspapers. Daily, a group of nine-year-olds sat wide-eyed while this nice young man rattled off articles about rich people stealing from the common people, about how anti-revolutionaries should be purged from our society, about how the fate of every spy should be to die by firing squad lest they gain control of public office and thus pose a menace to all we held dear. Sometimes, he showed us pictures of men who had been executed. At that point, such pictures were plastered almost daily on the newspaper's front page.

This all made quite an impression on me. Evidently, I made a reciprocal impression on the teacher. He took me under his wing. I was flattered at first. Only later did I discover that this new teacher saw a chance to brainwash a promising young Jewish boy to become a future leader of the revolution.

One day, he asked me to stay after school. "We will go on a field trip," he said. "Just you and me. I am going to take you to a very special, very important event that will show you what this revolution is all about and the kind of leader you can be."

Together, we walked from the school for about an hour to the center of Khorramshahr. There was a roundabout there for cars coming over the bridge that spanned the Karun. At the roundabout's center stood a very tall, white marble column atop which had once perched a bright metal statue of the shah on his horse. I had seen this statue many times, but this time, when I arrived there, the statue was gone. The white marble column was all that remained. It was wide enough that thirty or forty people could encircle it if they held hands. In front of this column, a crowd now stood. The teacher and I took a position at the very front of the crowd. Everyone seemed to be waiting for something.

A massive commotion stirred the crowd. I remember not knowing what was going on. Some young revolutionaries appeared, along with Pasdaran wearing their light green uniforms, holding American-made M4-style carbines. They were leading an overweight, semi-bald man who appeared to be in his mid- to late forties. His eyes were covered by a black scarf and his hands were bound in front of him. I remember his shirt was half open, exposing his chest hair. His belly was big and spilled over his belt.

The Pasdaran brought this man to a halt not ten feet away from where the teacher and I stood. Turning to the crowd, they raised their fists and began shouting, "Allah Akbar! Allah Akbar!"

The crowd shouted back. "Allah Akbar!"

One of the Pasdaran, apparently an officer, turned to the blindfolded man, shouting, "Do you have anything to say?!"

The man said nothing. I thought he looked scared. His lips were moving but I couldn't hear what he was saying.

What is this? I wondered. *What's going on?*

The Pasdaran officer was now shouting over the crowd. I couldn't make out his words except for "traitor" and "thief" and "enemy of the people." He made some kind of signal with his hands and the other Pasdaran moved off, leaving the blindfolded man standing in front of the pillar like an actor about to perform some odd performance art piece.

Four of the Pasdaran backed up into the crowd and lined up. They were standing right next to me. While everyone kept shouting, they lifted their rifles and shot the blindfolded man.

What happened next is like something out of a dream. All action seemed to take place in slow motion. I remember the first bullets punched through the man's body and came out the other side, making bright red splashes on the marble and chipping away small pieces of rock, which flew at the spectators. I say "first bullets" because the firing squad kept shooting as though the first salvo wasn't enough to kill one unarmed man. One of their rounds struck his head, which jerked to one side. More rounds hit his belly, which sort of exploded. The man never shouted or yelled. He just sort of sagged and dropped so he was in a semi-seated position against the column while his blood and guts flowed out and he died.

Everyone started pushing, shouting, and screaming. The bullets that struck the marble column ricocheted, spraying the crowd with chips of stone and fragmented metal. My teacher grabbed my wrist and dragged me, running, out of the mayhem.

The excitement all around us was eerie and strange. I remember hearing those chants again. "Allah Akbar! Allah Akbar!" The people seemed happy. Elated. I didn't know why. I didn't feel scared or sad or anything like that. I felt puzzled, I guess. And numb.

Once we got clear of the crowd, my teacher started talking. His eyes were bright. He was very excited. He said that the revolution was going to be the most important thing in the history of our country and I would be a huge part of it. Not knowing what else I should say, I thanked him for having taken me to such a great experience. He seemed to like that. He beamed. Then I asked him to take me back to school because our housekeeper was due to pick me up there soon.

"Yes, of course," my teacher said. "But you must never tell anyone what you saw here today. Not your friends or your teachers. Not even your parents. This is what we expect out of our future leaders of the revolution. It is our honor code. Do you understand?"

I told him I did and we started the long walk back.

In retrospect, I'm fairly certain I was in shock. The only thing going through my head at that moment was a memory I had from first grade. Our school bus once struck a boy who ran out in front of it while chasing a cheap plastic soccer ball. I was sitting at the back of the bus. I remember the thump and the lurch of the bus as it hit something. I remember looking out the glass back door and seeing a small form lying still in the street. Its face had been flattened so the boy's eyes seemed to be looking up at me off the pavement. There was blood and his brains were outside his skull but the bus kept moving. The bus driver, a very nice man whom I trusted, was put in jail for two years. After that incident, I did not speak a word for two weeks. Words didn't seem to make sense anymore.

The same thing happened when I got home that night. My parents knew something was wrong. They asked me why I was so quiet. I just shook my head and went to bed early but when I closed my eyes, all I saw was that overweight, semi-bald man slumping against the marble pillar and bleeding all over the place.

The next morning, I picked up the newspaper and flipped through it, searching for the picture of the man I'd seen executed. There were a few pictures that day, I recall, all printed in black and white. Most had been taken posthumously. The men's eyes were closed and there were dark round spots marking the places where bullets had punched through their faces.

The articles I kept scanning said that the people from the financial services industries who'd been shot were all thieves. Such assertions were not uncommon back then. The revolution needed money and any financial gatekeeper who would not assist them was branded a counterrevolutionary who sympathized with the shah, Americans, and Zionists. Whether or not this was true seems hardly the point. Each killing was designed to send a message. There was a new sheriff in town and this sheriff ruled without mercy. I can't tell you how many financial professionals were executed back then but it was a lot.

Finally, I found the man I was looking for. The article said he was a city accountant accused of embezzling funds, though it didn't say why he had done this, who had accused him, or whether or not the man had stood trial. I remember the feelings that bubbled inside me, none of them good.

My parents saw me reading the paper. My mother took it away from me. "That is not for children," she said. "Why are you looking at that?"

"Why are people getting killed?" I said.

I remember the look my mother and father shot each other. A look I wasn't supposed to see. "Why do you care?" my mother said, as though I had just commented on the weather.

"Because," I said, "yesterday my teacher took me to see a man get shot." I pointed to the newspaper. "That man right there."

You would have thought that somebody'd slapped her. "Saw *who* get shot?" my mother said.

"When?" said my father.

I told them what happened. They were furious but I understood at once that they weren't mad at me. They were mad at the teacher.

"Who else went on this 'field trip'?" my father demanded.

"No one," I said. "Just me and the teacher." I paused, recollecting. "He said it was a special lesson for me because I am a special student. Someday, I will be a leader of the revolution, he said."

My parents began to argue. Though livid, my mother proposed that maybe the teacher had spoken the truth. Maybe he'd taken me to the execution because he truly believed I was special. My father, however, saw darker designs. He thought the trip was intended as a subtle hint to a Jewish family whose father ran the local hospital. The message in this seemed clear. Know your place in the new order or suffer the consequences.

That day, my mother drove me to school and burst into the principal's office, ready to shout herself blue in the face. The principal was an old friend. Our families knew each other. When she saw the state that my mother was in, she shut the door quietly, asking what happened. My mother was practically spitting when she repeated what I had told her.

"I want that man's job!" she shouted. "How dare he do that to a child? *My* child!"

"Sit down," the principal told her. "And be calm. Let us talk for a moment."

"Did you not hear me?" my mother shrieked. "Did you not hear what this arrogant bastard just did?! You must punish him! Fire him! Get him out of here at once!"

"I cannot," the principal said wearily. "He has more power than me or you or any of us."

"This cannot be allowed to stand!" my mother shouted.

"Ghodsieh!" The principal used my mother's Islamic name on purpose. It got her attention. "You need to keep your mouth shut!" When my mother stared at her, speechless, the principal shook her head sadly. "Don't you see? Even if I could discipline this teacher, it will mark us all as anti-revolutionaries. We could all be killed like the man Raymond saw die in the square."

My mother shook her head, terrified. "No. That cannot be."

"It can and it is." The principal folded her hands on her desk and looked out the window at nothing in particular. "As one mother to another, I promise you I will do my best to shield Ray from further interference. But if this teacher likes Ray, as he seems to, you should count this a blessing. Let Ray be his project. That should at least keep him safe for a while."

"What do you mean, for a while?"

"That teacher is on his way out," the principal said. "I just got word. The local revolution committee wants him to run a much larger school in a different region."

By then, we all understood what was meant by the term "revolution committee." They were the most ardent—one might say fanatic—supporters of the Ayatollah. Ruthless men who would soon graduate to become the Islamic Revolutionary Guard Corps, they were charged with ensuring the conformity and sustainability of the revolution. Khomeini's patronage had placed them above the police, above the military, and above the law.

Quietly, uncharacteristically, my mother let the matter drop. I was told to return to my classes. We never discussed what happened again.

CHAPTER TEN

CHAOS, INSURGENCY, WAR

The Start of the Iran-Iraq War | 1979–1980

THINGS GOT WORSE VERY quickly. Political tensions continued to erupt but the conflict soon expanded to include the ancient, ethnic grievances between Iranian Persians and Arabs.

Prior to the revolution, Arabs and Persians had lived together in relative peace. Most Persians supported Khomeini's regime but some Arabs—at least in our southwestern province of Khuzestan—were not sold on the mullahs' idea of Shi'a Muslim rule. Talks began to escalate of Khuzestan seceding from Iran to join the more pro-Arabic nation of Iraq, which lay just downstream of the muddy Karun River and across the Shatt al Arab.

The Iraqi government helped stoke these intentions. It knew that Khuzestan was rich in oil while also providing access to the warm waters of the Persian Gulf. Saddam Hussein saw the revolution's chaos as a potential opportunity to finally fold Khuzestan and its assets into Iraq. At the same time, he was trying to fortify his position against forthcoming conflict. Khomeini had always insinuated that his Iranian revolution could expand westward into Iraq. Eventually, these two nations would clash. Far better, Saddam Hussein must have thought, to gain the upper hand now rather than wait around, hoping for the best.

In April 1979, skirmishes broke out all over Khuzestan. The first few conflicts were inconsequential, nothing organized, mostly neighborhood fights as local tensions boiled over, causing bloodshed. But these skirmishes soon progressed into all-out war that consumed the province. The violence became so pronounced that the Ayatollah's new regime sent trained military forces to suppress the fighting. As April rolled into May, the streets of our town literally ran with blood. Today, the history books call this the Khuzestan Insurgency.

Our Jewish family was considered Persian but a lot of our neighbors were Arab. So was the nanny we'd employed for two years at that point. Her name was Sakineh but we children called her "Naneh." She was an honest woman whom Ramin, Romina, and I adored. She lived in the Khorramshahr slums with her daughter, a girl about Ramin's age, named Shirin, which in Arabic means "sweet."

One day, my mother took us to Naneh's house and saw it was made out of mud with a plastic tarp for a roof. "Oh, no, no, no," my mother told Naneh. "This will not do. You must pack your belongings at once. From now on, you live at our villa."

When Naneh protested, my mother got firm. "Do you not take care of my children?" my mother said. "Yes? Then I will take care of yours. From now on, you live with a roof over your heads. You will have clean clothes and your daughter will be educated. No! There will be no discussion on this! Get moving now. Do it fast!"

Naneh and her daughter became part of our family and we were part of hers. She was so protective of her new family, she put her life in danger on more than one occasion to ensure our safety. It never mattered to her who the perpetrator was. Arab or Persian, if they were trying to harm us, they were Naneh's enemy.

For instance, months before all the fighting broke out, a Persian thief entered our home and Naneh attacked him. Chasing him out of the house, she seized his leg when he tried climbing up over the wall. Naneh bit his calf while the man howled and kicked at her. Police later used her bite mark to identify a suspect and arrest him for trespassing and attempted larceny.

Naneh wasn't the only Arab my family was close to. The neighbors we used to get fresh milk from were also Arab. I remember this because their house had a cow in it. That's how poor they were. They had no barn to separate the animals from the house. The cow lived right there with them in their small backyard. They treated the beast like a member of their family.

Before the insurgency really kicked off, I used to visit that house quite often and collect fresh milk to bring back to our villa. One time, I went on this journey but never made it there. A group of Arab kids started following me, shouting taunts. I tried to walk away but they followed me everywhere. A few of the older boys cornered me in an alley and started pushing me, calling me names. They said they would break all my bones, then murder me because I was Persian. I tried to run but one of the bigger boys seized the back of my shirt and hauled me backward, into their mob. The next thing I knew, they were punching me, kicking me, spitting on me. I went from nervous, to scared, to panicked.

I was always a scrappy kid who gave as good as I got in a fight. I also knew I'd been left with no choice. Turning, I threw a few punches that pushed the line back until one of the bigger kids stepped in and clocked me hard with a closed fist to the side of my head. I remember my knees buckling. I dropped to the ground, huddled in a fetal position with both hands covering my head while the Arab boys kicked me, limb and spine.

That's it, I remember thinking. *I'm dead.*

Then Naneh showed up. Screaming in Arabic, waving her arms like a dervish, she attacked. The boys fled from her, flapping and cawing like crows who'd been shooed off a corpse they'd been feasting on. Once they were gone, Naneh scooped me up off the ground, threw my arms around her spindly shoulders, and helped me limp back to our villa, where she tended my bruises and scrapes.

From that point forward, I never went to get milk again. Naneh told us that duty was hers now. I would be wise to stay off the streets, she said. My parents concurred. The thought of getting jumped like that again kept me constantly on edge.

In an odd way, all this upheaval turned out to be beneficial for my family. Despite having spent time in jail, despite the likelihood that his name was still on the Pasdaran's execution list, my father kept running the hospital in Abadan plus several clinics in Khorramshahr. Any doubts about his loyalty to the revolution had been put on hold. The skilled hands of Dr. Nasser Tabibiazar were needed to stitch the Pasdaran's wounded back together. I remember feeling relieved by this but also very uneasy. My family and I understood that the Pasdaran's favoritism was temporary. They could rescind it at any moment, at which point, once again, we'd all find ourselves plunged into jeopardy.

May wore on and the fighting intensified quickly. Khomeini's regime ordered Pasdaran soldiers to dig in at Khorramshahr's city hall. That building stood at one end of the same street our house was on. At the other end of the street, a group of Arab irregulars had bunkered behind sandbags. When the two groups started shooting at each other, our villa was literally caught in the crossfire.

Day and night, the machine guns would chatter. Now and then, mortars would roar, the earth would shake, and a nearby house would shiver, then sigh as its roof or its walls collapsed. We were scared half to death but my father kept typically stoic. He pointed out that our villa had very thick walls, which were ten feet high. Almost nothing could pierce them, he said. Also, the doors of our main gate were solid metal and constantly locked along with the smaller pedestrian door set inside it.

"We will be fine here," my father said. "We just have to wait things out."

We ended up being stuck in our house for days. Pinned down might be a more accurate term. Dad snuck out to go to the hospital but even this wasn't possible at times. The whole situation felt very erratic.

When Dad wasn't home, Ramin and I slept in my parents' bed with Mom and newborn Romina. On the nights Dad was with us, we still wanted to sleep in the bed all together. We felt safer like that while, outside, the machine guns continued their arguments. I remember how, to amuse himself, Dad would reach under the bedcovers with his foot and pinch Ramin and I with his big and second toe. To this day, I have no idea how he did that. His feet were practically prehensile. I've never met anyone before or since who could do that. We thought it was equal parts disturbing and hilarious.

It was especially hot that spring. The red mercury line of our kitchen ther-mometer kept creeping past 110 degrees Fahrenheit and we had no air condi-tioners. I remember how, following local custom, my father had built a massive, dark yellow, hard plastic canopy over our entire backyard to provide shade.

The unseasonably hot weather gave my mother an idea. Down at city hall, the Pasdaran forces had erected their own courtyard canopy, only theirs was hedged with sand bags, which had armed men hunkered behind them. "Far-zin," my mother told me. "Take this jug of water, some ice, and this food to the soldiers. They will think better of us and your father if we show solidarity during this fight."

I got very excited by this. I was nine years old and I'd been given an important mission! Leaving the house through our metal pedestrian door, I jogged down the street toward city hall, moving in zigzags, sidewinder-style. I'd watched soldiers do this in war movies and they never got shot. I thought, *If I do the same thing, nothing can touch me.*

The Pasdaran welcomed me heartily. They called me "water boy" and "our new little friend." I remember how proud this made me.

On my second trip out, thinking I deserved some kind of reward, I asked one of the soldiers to show me his gun. He and a bunch of his friends let me fire their pistols, which I thought was the height of cool. I was part of the revolution now. I was one of them. It made me feel proud, belonging to something so important.

The third and fourth time I ran supplies to them, bullets whined down the street by my sneakers. The Arabs were shooting at me. I was astonished! *No problem*, I thought. *I'll just keep moving sidewinder-style.*

By some miracle, I made it to city hall, where a Pasdaran officer gravely accepted the water jug and the basket of food I had brought. Then he gave me a stern lecture. "Tell your parents we are grateful for their support. But do not return here again. The streets are too dangerous now. We all like you and we want to see you grow old. Do you understand?"

I thought he was being absurd. I began telling this ignorant officer how I'd seen a bunch of old war movies. I wanted him to know all about how to move sidewinder-style. If he and his soldiers didn't know how to do it, I'd be happy to teach them, I said. The look he shot me was so flinty, I shut my mouth at once. Fearful I'd made a mistake, I left their encampment using the alleyways, slinking along like a dog in the night.

I never went back, and just as well. Not long after that, we heard that several families, including some children, had been caught in the crossfire and killed.

They say that God loves a fool. Now that I've lived as long as I have, I'm convinced this is true. On that occasion, like so many others, I think I simply got lucky. I do not know why but I remain thankful.

A few days later, the fighting abated. The air stood heavy and still. The streets were quiet. Our house had become so oppressively hot, we were sitting outside near the empty pool, under the canopy, fanning ourselves with whatever flat implements we could find.

I remember my mother saying she wanted to see what was going on. Getting up, she walked to the gate and opened the metal pedestrian door. My father snapped out of his heat stupor and shouted, "No! Don't! Close it!"

Mom slammed the door shut. The moment she did so, the metal plate shivered and clanged like a gong. We dashed inside the house, where we stayed through the rest of that day and the evening.

The next morning, moving gingerly, my father went outside. Approaching our gate, he eased open the pedestrian door. A sniper's bullet had dented the metal precisely where my mother's head had been. I guess I wasn't the only fool getting lucky back then.

As if it had been waiting for this discovery, a new phase of fighting kicked off. The machine guns started to chatter again. Mortars thumped the turf. This time their commotion was augmented by the overhead whine of military helicopters and fighter jets.

I remember seeing my parents turn pale. My mother looked at my father, who nodded. "Farzin," my mother said. "Take Ramin. Go into our bedroom and close the door."

My parents' bedroom was toward the back of the house, furthest from the street. They walked us back there, getting us settled. Ramin, I recall, wanted to get under the bedsheet.

"Why under the bedsheet?" I said.

"It will protect us," he said.

Again, I saw that look pass between my mother and my father. "Yes," my mother said. "Right. Get under the bedsheet. That's where it's safest."

This didn't make sense to me. How could a bedsheet ward off bullets and bombs? When I asked my parents, they just winked at me.

"It is magic." My mother shrugged. "I don't know how it works, I just know that it does. Now do as I say."

Ramin was six years old at the time and far more inclined to believe such pronouncements than I was. He went willingly under the sheet, where he told me proudly that nothing could harm us. The bedsheet magic would keep us safe, he said. I did nothing to disabuse him of this notion. He seemed happy enough in his ignorance. Being under the sheet made the stifling bedroom that much hotter. But hotter was better than dead, I supposed.

We were both too excited to sleep so I focused my energies on teaching Ramin something useful. He had never learned the Shema Yisrael, that quint-essential affirmation Jews have made about our faith since the first millennium, BCE. At nine years old, I knew the prayer well, having studied it in temple. To say it correctly, you lift your right hand in front of your face so your pinky rests on your closed left eye and your thumb rests lightly on your closed right eye while your middle three fingers, extended like a W, rest on your forehead. The letter W in English looks like the letter for "Sh" in Hebrew. So making your fingers like a W is a way of honoring the first letter of the first word of the prayer: Sh'ma.

While keeping your hand in this position, you chant a prayer whose three verses are taken from three separate biblical passages, two from the book of Deuteronomy, one from the book of Numbers. The first verse begins like this: "Sh'ma Yisra'el, Adonai eloheinu, Adonai echad!" Loosely translated: "Hear, O Israel! Yahweh is our God, and Yahweh is One!" In other words, the Shema Yisrael reminds us of the power behind monotheism: that we commit ourselves to one all-powerful and ever-living God, and so we are all under God's protection. This belief unites all Jews. From personal experience, I can say that praying the Shema Yisrael makes you feel stronger, as if bullets have no power to strike you and death itself must relinquish all claims to you. These feelings come over me even today when I utter the prayer. Back then, it was the perfect device to help two small boys fall asleep peacefully in a war zone.

Each evening before Ramin and I went to bed, I would lead him through this prayer. He did not understand what it meant. "It means that God is always watching us," I explained. "We are never really alone so we never have to feel weak or afraid. God's love will never fail us."

Regardless of sentiments like this one, the violence in Khuzestan soon took on international tones. On April 30, half a world away from our villa, six armed men stormed the Iranian embassy in London. They took twenty-six people hostage, including embassy staff, some local police officers, and a few innocent bystanders. These men claimed to be part of a group called the Democratic Revolutionary Front for the Liberation of Arabistan. Reading from a statement they had prepared for the press, the militants insisted that Western corporate petroleum interests backed by the shah had crippled Iranian society. These interests, they said, had deprived the people of Khuzestan from participating in the massive profits reaped from the oil fields they called home. Over the next week, the hostage takers demanded the release of several Arabic prisoners who were languishing in Khuzestan's jails. They also called on the world to recognize Khuzestan's autonomy while insisting that all six hostage takers be granted safe passage out of Great Britain.

The British government responded by having its Special Air Services mount

Operation Nimrod. During a daring seventeen-minute raid, small teams of highly trained operatives rappelled through the embassy's windows. Hurling stun grenades, they shot five of the six hostage takers dead. One hostage was killed during the rescue. When all was said and done, the incident did little to further the interests of Khuzestan separatists. If anything, it further galvanized the West against what it conceived of as Middle Eastern extremism.

Back then, I processed exactly none of this. All I knew was that, on my home street in Khorramshahr, the shooting eventually stopped. We were told that the Pasdaran won. They had lost only a dozen soldiers while more than a hundred Arabs had died.

Again, we breathed a sigh of relief. I remember telling Ramin and little Romina, "Well, good. We might have peace now. Let us see."

Once again, I could not have been more wrong.

In October 1979, Shah Muhammed Reza Pahlavi went to the United States to undergo cancer treatments. People were saying he couldn't last long. His detractors said that his illness was now so grave he had nakedly dropped all pretenses and called his American puppet masters for aid. It was hard to argue against this. The news dashed any hopes we had clung to that the shah would return someday to restore our country's peace and prosperity.

The following month, on November 4, a group calling itself the Muslim Student Followers of the Imam's Line raided the U.S. embassy in Tehran and took fifty-two Americans hostage. The episode seemed like a dour copy of the incident that took place in London the previous spring. With Khomeini's apparent approval, the hostage takers demanded that the shah be returned to Iran. They wanted him to stand before a revolutionary tribunal for what they called "his crimes." The U.S. refused to comply. They maintained that the shah had come to the U.S. seeking medical treatment. This was true. Following his exile from Iran, the shah began a meandering tour that took him to Egypt, Morocco, the Bahamas, Mexico, then the U.S., after which he continued to Panama and back to Cairo, all in a bid to cure his cancer.

The hostage takers also demanded that the U.S. government apologize for its interference in Iran's internal affairs. They cited the overthrow of Mosaddegh in 1953 as an example and insisted that Iran's frozen assets in the

United States be released. This kicked off what became known as the Iran hostage crisis, which, when all was said and done, lasted 444 days. My family and I watched tensions escalate through the unblinking eye of our television screen. But we didn't have time for concern because conditions at my dad's job were getting worse.

It was now mid-May 1980. The ambitious custodian-turned-Pasdaran-officer who'd insisted my father post pictures of the Ayatollah was still causing trouble. Now he wanted my father eliminated. He wasn't shy about expressing this view.

My mother had taken a new job as a lab technician in the same hospital my father helped administrate. One day, some colleagues sought her out. They looked badly shaken. "Ghodsieh!" they said. "They are going to kill Dr. Tabibiazar!"

My mother nearly dropped the glass slide she was holding. "Who is?" she demanded.

"Who do you think?" they said. "That Pasdaran *pedar sag* who caused all the trouble with those photos of Khomeini!" In Farsi, *pedar sag* means someone whose father is a dog. The best translation I know is "son of a bitch." "He's been stalking around the other end of the hospital, compiling the committee's execution list. Ghodsieh, we read the list. Nasser's name is on it."

Frightened to her bones, my mother left all the blood samples she was working on, got up from her lab bench, and went to my father, who hadn't yet heard the news. Closing the door of his office, Mom told him everything she had heard. She later told me this was the first time she'd ever seen my father truly scared. He turned pale and sweat broke out on his balding forehead.

"We have run out of time," Mom implored him. "We cannot stay here any longer."

Ever the stoic, my father shook his head and said nothing.

"No!" my mother railed at him. "Do not do that!"

Dad threw up his hands. "Do what?"

"Do *not* fall silent. Do *not* look away! I tell you we have no choice. We have to leave now!"

"And where will we go?" Dad murmured.

I like to think, in that moment, he was grimly aware of the precedent we would follow by fleeing. At that point, we Jews had been hot-footing it from one area of violence to another for more than two millennia. Hadn't Dad's great-grandfather Avram come over the Caucasus fleeing Russian persecution? And for what? So that three generations later, Dad's father, Ahron, would uproot his family and flee from Miandoab to Tabriz? *Where will it stop?* my dad must have wondered. *And suppose we flee. Who will take us in? How will the children fare? And how can we smuggle out enough wealth to start a new life?*

Mom shot a glance at the door and lowered her voice in case someone was listening. "We go anywhere!" she seethed at him. "Your brothers have already left. My own brothers left for Germany long ago. Now Sima and Saeed are planning to leave."

This was true. My father's sister and brother-in-law had gotten word to us about their plans. They said that their son, Sasan, was planning to fly out of the country anytime now. Thinking there is safety in numbers, they'd approached us, suggesting that we leave with him.

"Nasser, we have to come up with a plan! Unless you want your children to see you shot by a Pasdaran firing squad as a Zionist spy!"

That evening, my parents decided to sell our villa. They set up the listing, then began the process of selling off our furniture. But word got out about this and the Pasdaran once again detained my father for questioning at the local committee office.

"Why are you selling your furniture?" they asked.

"We're buying a bigger house," my father said.

"That doesn't make sense," said one of the Pasdaran. "A bigger house needs more furniture, not less."

"Ah." My father smiled pityingly at the man. "I see you are not married."

The man looked stung. "What has that got to do with anything?" he said.

"If you were married," my father said, "you would understand the position I'm in. When a wife wants furniture sold, a wise husband allows her do as she pleases. Trying to stop her will only cause problems."

A few of the other men in the room nodded quietly. Soon after that, my dad was released. He went home directly and told my mother to stop selling furniture.

"They are watching us," he said. "From here on out, do nothing out of the ordinary."

"But what will we do about all of our goods?" my mom asked.

"Leave that to me," Dad said.

About a month later, in late June or early July 1980, Mom and Dad contracted with another family to buy our villa. They only got half their asking price but that was no matter. We all knew that speed was of the essence. For a little more money, my dad threw in everything that we owned—our furniture, carpets, draperies, cookware—everything in the house would transfer to the new owners. Finally, and perhaps most important, the new owners consented to let us stay in the house and rent it back from them during the summer and autumn of 1980 while we looked for our "big new place."

I remember this time quite well because in late July—on the twenty-seventh to be precise—our streets were set afire with news. After moving again to Egypt, Shah Muhammed Reza Pahlavi had finally succumbed to his illness. He would never return to reclaim the country he'd fled. The line of Pahlavi— indeed the very concept of the shah and all it stood for—had come to an end.

Not two weeks later, in August, my parents told us we were taking a trip.

"Fantastic! Where are we going?" I said.

"It is summertime. We will visit family," they said. "This is a fine time to go since you and Ramin are out of school. But you can only pack one suitcase."

I thought that was odd but I went along with it. When the time came, we took a train to Tehran, where we met with my father's mother, Tavooz. Uncle Saeed, Aunt Sima, and our cousins Sasan, Soheil, and Sohrab were also there. It was like a big party.

I remember a lot of hushed talk taking place among the adults. It was the kind of talk that stopped whenever Ramin, Romina, or I walked into the room.

We were only in Tehran for a day and a half when my parents brightly suggested another idea. "Since we're already on vacation, let's take a week and visit our relatives in Germany."

"Who's we?" I asked.

The adults shot looks at each other. Though I didn't know it at the time, they had decided our family should leave first. Sima, Saeed, and our cousins would follow us quickly.

We went to the airport and were about to board our plane but the immigration police stopped us. They also had my father on some kind of list. I remember my father insisting we were just going to visit relatives in Germany. What was the problem with that?

"You do not have a permit to leave," said the officer who stopped us.

"Since when do people need a permit to go visit relatives?" my father asked.

But the look the officer shot him announced that the matter was now closed.

Reluctantly, Dad herded us out of the airport. "This is no big deal," he told us. "We still have three weeks before school starts up. You all stay here with your grandma and grandpa."

"What about you?" I said. "Where will you be?"

"Back in Khorramshahr."

We children did not like this at all. My mother liked it less. She told my father as much in no uncertain terms. "Perhaps it would be easier for you to escape," she said, "if you don't have the kids and I with you. Why don't you and Sasan try sneaking out of the country first? The kids and I can follow you once you're safely over the border."

My father rejected this notion. "What if I am out of the country and something happens to you and the kids while you're getting ready to leave? I will not be able to help you." He shook his head. "No. We are not going to separate."

"Then you must stay with us!" my mother said.

"Flora, think this through. I told the hospital I was going on vacation for a week. If I don't show up for work, the Pasdaran will know that we fled. They will track us down here."

I noticed he did not elaborate on what would happen after that.

"Just take a few days here," he said. "I will go home ahead of you. By the time you arrive, I will have a new plan. Do not worry. I promise you, all will be well."

I remember I had an eerie feeling I'd never see him again. Despite that he was so rarely around, he was still my father. My family. And it turned out I was right. When my father left Tehran, I didn't see him for two more years.

Once Dad left, Mom decamped us to her own mother's place. She felt more comfortable staying with my Maman Bozorg than with Dad's mother, Tavooz. We kids were thrilled by this. We were getting to visit more relatives than ever. It felt like a lark. A couple weeks later, my mother rallied my brother, my sister, and me to make another trip. Saeed and Sima drove us to the airport. We were just about to board our plane and fly back to Khorramshahr when an announcement came over the loudspeakers.

"BE ADVISED, BE ADVISED. ALL FLIGHTS ARE NOW CANCELLED. THE COUNTRY IS NOW AT WAR. ALL AIRSPACE IS CLOSED."

We had no idea what to think but we also didn't have time. The airport was evacuated immediately and we headed back to the parking lot.

During the car ride back, more news came over the radio. "THE IRAQI ARMY HAS JUST ATTACKED OUR NATION. KHORRAMSHAHR HAS BEEN

HIT BY A SERIES OF AIR STRIKES. MANY PEOPLE HAVE DIED ON THE WESTERN EDGE OF THE CITY. IRAQI TANKS ARE INBOUND. IRAQI PLANES ARE TARGETING TEHRAN AIRPORT AND OTHER MAJOR CITIES. PLEASE RETURN TO YOUR HOMES. GO NOW! RETURN TO YOUR HOMES!"

For the sake of expediency, Sima and Saeed took us back to Tavooz's house. She was not pleased to see us on her doorstep once again. This had little to do with the war. To this day, I think she couldn't bear the thought of Ramin and me jumping on her late husband's bed and ramming around her house like a pair of young bulls. But she took us back in.

We were all pretty frightened and confused. My mother went straight to the phone and tried to reach Dad but he wasn't picking up at home. She tried the hospital but no one picked up there either.

After about the twentieth call, my mother cradled the receiver and stared at it like it might start telling her secrets.

Tavooz walked into the kitchen. "Well?" she said. "Did you get hold of him?"

My mother said nothing.

"Flora," my grandmother said. "Where is Nasser? Where is my son?"

Mom just looked at her. She had no idea.

Later that afternoon, we left one grandmother's house for another's. I remember being afraid that my father wouldn't know which house to call us at. At Maman Bozorg's house, Ramin and I sat by the phone for hours and willed it to ring with all our might but it never did.

Those were some of the longest and worst hours I can remember.

The war took everyone by surprise, though in retrospect it seems clear why it happened. In Khuzestan, the Shatt al-Arab serves as the border between Iran and Iraq. Prior to 1975, lands along the river's east bank had been part of Iraq. The Iraqis only ceded control as part of the Algiers Agreement, a set of accords drawn up to end the second Kurdish War. That wasn't the end of the matter. Iraq kept encouraging all Arabs living in Khuzestan to rebel against the shah. As I mentioned, Khuzestan's oil fields were some of the richest in the Middle East. Baghdad hoped to reclaim them some day.

Saddam Hussein, who later played such a large role in the Gulf War and Iraq War, became president of Iraq on July 16, 1979. He'd seen Khomeini's revolution, and the Khuzestan Insurgency in particular, as opportunities. Under the shah, Iran's military was counted as the fifth most powerful in the world. Without the shah, chaos reigned. Hussein also knew how deep Arab sentiments ran in the Khuzestan region. If the Iraqi military crossed the Shatt al-Arab, they would not be treated as invaders. Tens of thousands of indigenous Arabs would greet them as liberators—and join their war.

On September 22, 1980, Iraqi forces launched air strikes that took out Iranian airfields followed by a ground assault. The incursion captured territories across Khuzestan with relative ease. It was creeping closer to Khorramshahr, where our villa stood.

Later that day, we got the first call from my father. He had been gone a couple of weeks and we were elated to hear from him. But I could tell by the way my mother spoke into the phone that Dad was badly shaken. I remember her telling him to secure a few keepsakes from our house. "The family photo albums," she said. "And the Persian carpets." She meant two identical silk carpets made in Tabriz. They held sentimental value—one had been purchased for me, the other for Ramin. But they were also worth a lot of money. If push came to shove, our family might be able to sell them, and we needed cash quite badly to make our escape.

I remember Ramin and I clamoring about Mom's waist. We wanted to talk to Dad and make some demands of our own.

"I want my bicycle!" Ramin said. "Save my bike!"

"Can you get my stamp collection?" I shouted.

The line went dead in my mom's hands. She stood there a moment, staring at the receiver.

Ramin finally broke the silence. "What happened?"

As if it was answering him, the TV set in Maman Bozorg's living room broke into a special report. "We interrupt this broadcast," the announcer said, "to report that Khorramshahr on the southwestern border of our country is under attack. The Iraqi military has. . ."

Terrified, we looked at my mother, who put the receiver back on the phone. Her face had gone ashen.

"Mom?" I said. "What does that mean? Is Baba. . .?"

"It's nothing," my mother said stiffly. "Everything is fine. Your father must stay where he is. He must work at the hospital. He said he will try to get all the things you requested out of our house and bring them somewhere safe but he can't go there now. There are too many bombs."

"Will he be alright?" Ramin pressed.

"Yes, of course he will be alright," Mom snapped. "He is in the hospital now and even Iraqis do not bomb hospitals. Now get your feet off the table."

"Why can't he come here and live with us, though?" Ramin asked.

My mother wheeled on him, angry. "Did you not hear me? I said he must work at the hospital and take care of his patients. There are probably lots of wounded your father needs to help. Where is your sister?"

"I don't know," Ramin said.

"Go find her. Play with her. Then you must all go to bed. Tomorrow we will have much to do."

She was right, because my mother understood that we four—her, me, Ramin, and Romina—were probably not going anywhere. Not for a while at least. We children would have to start school in Tehran. My mother would have to look for some kind of job to support us. We would also have to find someplace to live since both my grandmothers' houses were simply too small for us to stay in for any extended period. All this on top of the fact that we had no idea if Dad was alive anymore. We never heard from him after that.

A few days into the war, I noticed my mother was listening to the radio a lot. When I asked her why, she said, "Shhhh. Be quiet. I can't hear the news."

A couple days later, I asked her the same question. This time, she seemed even more distracted. I heard her mumble, "They read off the names." After which she looked up suddenly. I saw her realize she shouldn't have said that. That's when I figured it out.

"The names of the dead," I said. "You're waiting to hear them say Baba's name."

Her eyes never left me. She nodded.

From that point on, Ramin and I took over this daily chore. Before school, every morning, we took shifts at the radio while my mother looked after Romina and made daily trips to the Ministry of Health to press for information about my father.

Six to eight weeks went by like this. We kept hope alive but it cost us dearly. Sometimes the faith we place in other things takes everything inside us to maintain and it still feels like a lie, like we're just trying to deceive ourselves so everyone around us will turn a blind eye to what the universe is concocting. True hope requires that we live in a tremendously strange in-between space beyond the certainty most people live in. At its worst, it feels like a ruse you're perpetuating through nothing more than sheer willpower. Until, that is, something happens that confirms you were right all along.

One day, the phone rang. My grandmother picked up, said hello, and listened to the voice on the other end of the line, after which she handed the receiver to my mother. I remember Mom listening carefully. For a while the look on her face was that of a graven idol in some ancient temple of mourning. Then her features lit up and she began spouting words of thanks and praise.

Farsi is a particularly eloquent language, full of poetry and multiple levels of meaning. In increasingly extravagant terms, Mom used all the tools at her linguistic disposal to tell the person on the other end of the line how she felt about what she'd just heard. She praised the Lord above. She praised the ground beneath the feet of the person calling. She praised the messenger doves of heaven for bringing her this incredible news. She wished a thousand blessings upon all who had contributed to this information reaching her humble ears. Then she hung up, bowed her head, and wept with joy.

The person who'd called was a doctor at my father's hospital, a friend of my dad's. He was calling to say that everything was okay. Dad was alive but he had been injured. He was gaining strength rapidly now. "Very soon, he will call you," this friend said. "I just wanted you to know you have nothing to worry about. All is well."

From that moment forward, someone always stayed by the phone in case it rang and my father was calling. A few days later, this happened. Everyone crowded around my mother to hear Dad's voice.

I thought he sounded weak and tired. He asked how we were all doing. We assured him we were fine. Then he told us our villa was gone. It had been one of the first ones hit by the air strikes. Bombs had leveled it. Boom! From one second to the next, everything we owned, everything we once thought was so important, disappeared.

Years later, he told us what happened to him. In the wake of the bombings, when the Iraqis began their ground advance, my father got an order to evacuate the hospital. Ship all patients and personnel to the next big hospital in Mahshahr, the orders said. So that's what Dad and his colleagues set about doing.

Mahshahr was about a hundred kilometers east of Khorramshahr. It was out of the fighting at that point. Moving everyone out there was a Herculean task, not to mention so quickly. My father rushed throughout his facility, squeezing everyone into ambulances, cargo trucks, and employees' personal automobiles—whatever vehicles could run. He made sure that everyone got in a car and drove off. Then, with a core group from his staff, about eight to ten people, he made a beeline to the last car left in the lot.

These holdouts had figured they could all squeeze inside but at the last moment one of the hospital's janitors appeared. He had been locking some doors in the hospital before he realized this was stupid; his life was worth more than some locked door. So he'd hightailed it out to the parking lot, hoping for transport out of the region.

"Please let me go first," the custodian begged my father. "You are a doctor. They will send a car back for you but not for me."

"*Pedar sookhteh, yadet nareh,*" my father responded. In Farsi: "You bastard, don't forget."

In his mind, he had no choice. He was head of the clinic. He couldn't drive off and leave his custodian there. That wouldn't have been honorable. So he gave up his seat in the car. As the custodian climbed in, Dad again made him promise to send a vehicle back once they'd reached the hospital in Mahshahr.

"I will!" the custodian told him. "Thank you, thank you, doctor! Bless you!"

The car drove off.

It was the end of the summer, blazing hot, about forty-five degrees Celsius, and humid. For a moment, my father stood there, dripping sweat on the asphalt, watching the car disappear in the east. Then, alone, he went back inside the empty hospital and listened to the radio. Hour after hour, increasingly urgent broadcasts reported that Iraqi ground troops were advancing on Khorramshahr. But the car he'd been promised never came. Then the phone lines went dead. Dad had no way to contact anyone.

Finally, concerned that if he waited any longer, the Iraqis would completely surround the hospital and lay siege to it, Dad decided to press his luck. Mahshahr was a full day's walk but he thought he could make it if he left immediately. He exited the hospital with only an apple he'd found sitting on a countertop and a sponge he had dipped in water to ward off the heat. With these, he began to walk east, toward Mahshahr and away from the fighting. He knew the highway well enough; it was basically a straight shot to where he was going. Also, given that he was then on the eastern flank of Khorramshahr, he reasoned that he had a pretty good chance of fleeing the war zone before the Iraqis cinched their noose on the city.

So he walked. And he walked. And he walked—like Avram, his great-grandfather before him. There were differences, of course. Avram never walked past burnt cars and cars that were still burning or dead bodies that littered the road like so many dolls cast aside by an angry child. Soldiers, civilians—it made no difference. The broken forms of men, women, and children alike, of every age and variety, lay twisted in contortions of violent death.

Through all this, through fire and smoke, through the moans of the mortally wounded and the lacerating heat of the sun, my father kept walking. Soon, his apple was gone, devoured and discarded. The sponge he had brought was bone dry. And still he kept walking.

To this day, he doesn't talk much about what happened on that road. In his typical way, he brushes the matter aside. "I remember feeling faint," I once overheard him telling my mother. "I remember looking ahead and seeing heat waves writhing like angry snakes off the pavement. Then the horizon, it just sort of. . . tilted. And I was falling. That was the last thing I knew."

"Was it hard?" I asked him once. "That journey?"

"Not really." He shrugged. "What choice did I have?"

"But it must have been hard," I pressed. "Weren't you afraid?"

Again, he shrugged. "Fear is irrelevant. Like the weather, it comes and goes. You still need to do what needs to be done."

Later, some of his doctor friends pieced together what happened. Dad must have passed out from heat exhaustion. He fell on the side of the road where he lay very still, like the corpses littered around him. Sometime later, a bunch of trucks rolled up the highway. The soldiers who drove these vehicles were tasked with the grisly work of gathering bodies and bringing them north to the hospital in Mahshahr where my father had been headed. He rode the rest of that route piled among the dead.

It was only by sheer luck that, during the offloading process, Dad was recognized by a hospital intern. This young man had been charged with learning the identities of the dead. He was compiling a list of names so it could be read over the airwaves—the same list that had kept Ramin and me glued to the radio, to hear if our father had died. Shocked to see Dr. Tabibiazar among the dead, this intern checked his vitals and found that, amazingly, he was still alive. This intern saved my father's life.

The hospital staff rushed my father into a room, where he was treated. For the next six weeks, he languished in a coma. When he woke up, the first thing he said was, "Where is that *pedar sag*! Where is he?" Dad was looking for the custodian he gave his seat up to in the car.

The hospital staff who'd cared for him told him that car and everyone in it had never arrived. Years later, they learned the Iraqis captured it. Rumor had it that everyone riding inside had become a POW at a facility outside Baghdad.

"That's why they never sent the car back," said one of Dad's colleagues. "Listen, Nasser. Focus on yourself now. How do you feel?"

My father nodded weakly. Translation: not bad for someone who, by all rights, should be dead.

His colleague nodded back at him. "Good." Then he held out a white lab coat and clipboard. "Then I hate to say it but the time for lying about has passed. The war has progressed while you slept. We are choking with wounded. We need you to work. Can you do this?"

Gingerly, my father swung his legs over the side of the bed. "How bad is it?" he asked.

His colleague shook his head sadly. "Worse than you can imagine. Come see for yourself."

CHAPTER ELEVEN

NEW CITY, NEW WAR

Tehran | 1980–1982

FOR THE NEXT TWO years, my family lived apart. My mother, brother, sister, and I stayed with Maman Bozorg for about four months, camped on the living room floor of her apartment while the country plunged into mayhem. We had no money, no income, no school to attend, and only the clothes on our backs. My mother went out every day to look for new means by which we could make ourselves at home in a city under attack.

Practically every night, air raid sirens would blast and we'd all run down to huddle in the building's basement. There, bereft of electricity, clustered by candles, flashlights, and makeshift lamps, we listened to battery-operated transistor radios, seeking reports on the Iraqis' progress. We were joined by other residents from the building plus other neighbors whose homes featured no place for them to hide. Often, we stayed holed up all night while the Iraqis launched air strikes at Tehran's military bases.

Though it was terribly dangerous, Ramin and I sometimes snuck out to watch the blasts from anti-aircraft guns blossom like white orchids in the blue-black sky overhead. Their brilliance was all the more startling because the army had ordered all lights in the city extinguished. Often we heard and saw old U.S.-built Phantom fighter jets, a staple of the Iranian military, screeching low over the city, intent on defending us. I remember there was a certain beauty to all this, an eloquence and a poignancy that resided amidst the insanity of war. But we had little time to ponder it.

Food became an issue almost at once. The government was rationing everything. No one had enough to eat, let alone access to kosher foods. But here we got lucky. As a long-standing member of her community, Maman Bozorg could pull certain levers that most of her neighbors could not. She knew a local butcher with whom she'd shared food for a number of years. Every time she cooked a big feast, she'd take some of the meal to this butcher, who loved her cooking. During the war, at irregular intervals, he made a point of smuggling cuts and scraps, whatever he could spare, to Maman Bozorg.

My mother got a job as a biotechnician at a laboratory in our neighborhood. Of course, she did. She'd always worked to support us, why should things be any different in times of war? Each day, while she went to work, Ramin, Romina, and I would stay in Maman Bozorg's care. One day, Maman Bozorg served us beef kabobs. It had been so long since we'd last eaten beef, we couldn't believe it.

I remember my mother coming home from work that day. Stopping dead in her tracks, she sniffed the air. "Is that meat?" She gaped around at the kitchen. "That's actual meat I smell. Where did you get it?"

Maman Bozorg washed the grease off her hands while explaining about her friend the butcher.

"Is there any left?" Mom said.

Maman Bozorg picked a towel up, shaking her head. "For you and me? No. Meat is only for people who are growing. The kids need it more than we do right now."

"Oh." In that one little word, my mother managed to convey both her immense disappointment and the fact that she understood. Maman Bozorg was right, of course. But—"Is there anything else I can have?"

"Of course." Maman Bozorg smiled. "Adults get yogurt and rice."

I watched Mom's face fall. We'd already been living off rice and yogurt for months. "Okay." Sighing, she took a seat wearily at the table.

The rationing began to get worse. Yet somehow small brown eggs began to appear on our breakfast table. Also, once in a very great while, we began having chicken kabobs. Intrigued, one morning I asked Maman Bozorg, "Grandma, where do these eggs from? Where does the chicken come from?"

"Yes." Ramin was curious, too. "Did you get it from your friend the butcher?"

"No, sweetie," Maman Bozorg said. "I made it myself."

Ramin and I looked at each other, confused. So Maman Bozorg took us down to the basement of her building where we were astonished to see a line of chicken coops. The smell was atrocious, I recall, like a mix of ammonia and cardamom spice. Smiling, Maman Bozorg explained how she'd started raising chickens and pigeons to help offset the food rations. Opening a coop's door, she reached in and pulled out some eggs, which she passed to me gently. "Be careful. Don't break them," she said.

Then, reaching back in, she seized a pigeon by its neck, jerked it out, and snapped its neck in half. The pigeon's feet and wings kept kicking and slapping. One of its dead black eyes stared accusations at me from the new, impossible angle its head had tilted toward. I had never seen anything like this before, let alone in such close proximity. Even my run-in with the butchered calf wasn't quite so traumatizing as watching that chicken continue to writhe. And I remember feeling sad. At that point, despite how hungry we were, I'd have rather played with the pigeon than eat it.

Eventually, my mom, Ramin, Romina, and I moved out of Maman Bozorg's house and got an apartment on the first floor of the same building my father's mother, Tavooz, lived in. The vacancy opened because so many people were fleeing the country. In those days, a lot of families left on "vacation" and simply never came back. The city was emptying out at an astonishing rate but we still couldn't leave. So long as my father's name was on the Pasdaran's execution list, he had to stay in Khuzestan, working at the hospital where he tended a constant flood of war wounded. My mother refused to entertain any notion of fleeing the country without him.

Our family's separation was merely one swatch in our quilt of misfortunes. The matter of our bombed villa kicked off a legal disagreement. The people who'd bought the property claimed they had never taken possession. They wanted their money back. My father, being a fair-minded man, made several attempts to reconcile with the buyers. I suppose it helped matters some that, at that point, we'd already lost so much. Losing more couldn't hurt very much. Dad finally cut a deal where the buyers got most of their money back and we were returned the two luxurious Persian carpets my parents had bought years earlier for me and Ramin. Incredibly, my family still owns them. By mustering various connections, my father had the rugs shipped out of the country to one of his brothers, who lived in the States. Dad also gave his brother what amounted to most of the rest of our wealth—about $50,000—this time with the explicit order that his brother hold on to this money until we arrived to claim it.

There was also the fact that my father was serving on the front lines of the Iran-Iraq War. It was a horrible, bloody conflict that he bore witness to firsthand. Both sides committed atrocities. The Iraqis used chemical weapons that scalded the skin of anyone who came into contact with them and seared a person's lungs with every breath they drew until they lay dead. The Iranians did something equally awful. Knowing they didn't have enough tanks, the more theocratically minded among them began drafting twelve-year-old boys as mine sweepers.

The process went something like this. A mullah, or clergyman, would instruct the boys on how honorable it was to be a *shahid*, a martyr for Islam and their country. They would give each boy a ceremonial key, saying, "This is your key to heaven. Now make us proud and go do the work of Allah." Ignorant of the consequences, inspired by men who praised them and said kindly things about their families, these twelve-year-old boys would run into the minefields, clutching their precious keys in their fists. Time and again, my father saw what remained of them afterwards. These children were the exact same age as his own kids. And I think it not unlikely that, each time he saw one of the victims, he thought about me and Ramin. Later, he confessed to me that the images of children—legless, agonized, howling as they died, or already dead—had been seared in his brain for all time. I was shocked by this announcement, shocked by the image of what he described but shocked, too, that he'd told me at all. As long as I've known my father, I can count on one hand how many times he's spoken of the war.

Regardless of how it happened, the man I once knew—the kind and gregarious man who smiled a lot and was unfailingly kind—vanished. Two years after we were separated, when I finally met my father again, he'd become like a shell of himself. His eyes were haunted. He rarely spoke, and then only when absolutely necessary. Though never a tall man, he seemed to have shrunk, as though, like a tortoise, he'd pulled back into himself, hoping to gain some protection. In those days, we had no name for what Dad was suffering from. Today, we would call it post-traumatic stress disorder.

With the war raging, Dad had no time to tend to his emotional wounds. If I'm being honest, I'd have to admit that at least some of his discomfort was self-inflicted. Consumed by despair and helplessness, shaking with moral rectitude, Dad started writing long letters to various Jewish federations worldwide. Time and again, he detailed the horrors he'd seen. He closed each letter by asking what on earth could be done about this awful predicament. Children, he insisted, should not be in war zones at all, let alone used as human sacrifice.

His letters were intercepted, of course. I sometimes imagine the reaction they caused among censors in the Khomeini's regime. Who was this man who would write such things? What was his name again? No! Surely, this couldn't be the same Dr. Nasser Tabibiazar who'd been at the top of the Pasdaran's execution list prior to the invasion. Didn't he know he was already marked for death? Now, on top of that verdict, here was evidence—in the good doctor's handwriting—that proved he was also a Zionist spy.

It was a ridiculous conclusion. My father had sought the Iranian government's help all along to find ways to stop the atrocities. However, in keeping with the realpolitik of the day, the Iranian war machine needed to threaten people like my father so they could continue sending children up to the front lines to run over land mines. Perhaps even more sad, the global geopolitical environment never sought to intervene against Saddam's atrocities in the war. The West and several other, more localized powers seemed to consider Khomeini the bigger threat.

I ended up suffering my own losses during the war. One day, we received a call at my grandmother's house. It was the mother of my old friend, Amir. Turns out she and her family were war refugees, like us. Also like us, they had fled to Tehran. Amir had enrolled as a student at a different school, which is why we had never run into each other. Amir's mother bumped into a mutual friend who told her we were in Tehran. My mother moved at once to set up a playdate.

I was so excited; I thought it would be like old times. But Amir had changed. He was still small, still bespectacled, still quiet, still gentle and smart. He was also more serious than ever, which is saying something. Sitting in his presence, I couldn't help feeling like I was talking to an impossibly tiny old man rather than another ten-year-old.

"Have you heard from anyone back home?" I said. "Like Zahir? Or Emad?"

Amir looked down at the book he had taken off my shelf and opened. "Dead," he said.

I felt my guts contract. "What?"

"They died. Emad in the bombing, Zahir in the ground attack. Or that's what I heard anyway."

"No," I said, shaking my head. "No, no, that can't be."

To which Amir said nothing.

I cried for days after that. The deaths of Emad and Zahir brought the impossible realities of life into a collision course with my youthful fantasies.

Zahir could not be dead. He was simply too kind, too friendly, too good to be dead. Why would anyone hurt such a person as he?

I did not understand.

I have yet to understand.

Since Mom worked every day, our neighbors or Maman Bozorg would take care of Romina while Ramin and I were at school. Because of his age, Ramin attended a Jewish school while I completed fifth grade at a school run by Muslims within walking distance of our new apartment.

Almost immediately, I faced discrimination. My math teacher in particular was very anti-Semitic. Though I quickly distinguished myself in his class and got every answer right on his tests, he never credited me for my work. He would often ask questions in class. My hand would go up and he would ignore it. I was a nonentity to him. This only made me try harder to get his attention.

One time, he assigned us a geometry project where everyone had to build a three-dimensional structure. Some students were assigned cubes, some cones, some tetrahedrons. I was told to build a pyramid. The teacher made this lesson into a contest. The student who built the most interesting structure would win a colored pen, he said.

I spent a lot of time on this project. My pyramid structure was the most beautiful thing I was then capable of imagining, let alone building. I spent time painting each side different colors and even went so far as to rig up a string so someone could hang it from the ceiling like a mobile. When I brought it into class, everyone agreed I had made the most interesting structure. Everyone but the teacher, that is.

He sneered at my project. "This?" he said. "This isn't interesting, I think it's crap." Whereupon, seizing my pyramid, he threw it out the window.

I went home that night and bawled my eyes out. I'd never reacted this way over something school-related but I thought what had happened was so unfair. My grief inspired my mother to go into the school the next day and speak with the principal. He repeated the same routine that my previous principal had when the young revolutionary took me to witness the execution.

"I understand you're upset," this principal said, "but I can do nothing in this case. That math teacher is a revolutionary. You know there's a war going on, right? You know what the attitude is toward Zionists."

"We're not Zionists, we're Jewish," my mother protested.

The principal waved his hand as if this were a mere technicality. "Look," he said. "This is a Muslim school, that's the long and the short of it. If I were you, I'd tell your son to be a little less proud. Keep a low profile. Just do the work and know what's good for you, that's what I'd tell him."

My mother came home and explained this to me. "He is right. Just do as he says," she implored me. "You'll only be at this school a few more months. Next year, you move to Alborz and things will be different there, you'll see."

Alborz was one of the top schools in Tehran, an all-male institution of three or four thousand students that I had qualified to attend due to my grades. When I finished fifth grade and finally started taking classes there, Mom told me again to keep a low profile.

"They will have you take courses in the Qu'ran and calligraphy. Five times a day, they will have you face their sacred Kaaba in Mecca and tell you to pray. Do everything they tell you to do. Do not mention that you are Jewish. If someone should learn you are Jewish, tell them you are excited to learn all about their religion. Do you understand what I'm saying, Farzin? Do you see how important this is?"

I did as she asked. At Alborz, it was an open secret that I was Jewish. Still, each day I would unroll my little carpet several times and pray as everyone else did. I learned to write verses from the Qu'ran in beautiful calligraphy and I studied the mullahs on TV, how they sang their prayers in rich baritones, giving performances worthy of the opera singers. I mimicked their style as best I could, though my voice broke over and over again. Unbeknownst to my teachers, each day after school I attended a Hebrew class to prepare for my forthcoming bar mitzvah.

Around this time, I developed a keen interest in philosophy. To be clear, at that age, I had no real understanding of what philosophy was. It just struck me as odd, for instance, that if monotheism is a correct premise, if there really is only one god, how come Muslims, Christians, and Jews saw this figure so differently? I was also taking gymnastics and competing in local competitions. I wanted to study karate but Mom nixed the idea. She thought karate was too violent a sport. She also pointed out that, under the current circumstances, my learning to fight could be potentially, even fatally, incendiary.

Ironically, my efforts to keep a low profile brought me increasingly to the attention of school administrators. They must have been very impressed that this little Jewish boy was so observant of Islamic rituals. Within a few months, they asked me to sing prayers for the whole school each morning over the loudspeaker system while all the other students were lining up, getting ready for class. I was happy to do this since the assignment kept me from having to chant "Death to Israel! Death to America!" as all the other boys did.

Being the Qu'ran reciter made me quite popular at school. It also carried unexpected consequences. One was the letter I received one day toward the end of my sixth-grade year, hand-delivered to me in class by the principal of Alborz school. This letter praised me for doing a good job reciting Muslim prayers at school each morning. It said the entire community was very proud of me and looked forward to the future role I would play as a leader of Iran. It was signed by none other than the Ayatollah himself.

I brought this letter home to my mother. She read it, spat on it, tore it to pieces. "*Yimakh Shemo!*" she hissed.

The phrase was familiar to me. It's one of the strongest curses in Hebrew, reserved for the greatest enemies the Jewish people have ever known, such as Adolf Hitler. *Yimakh Shemo* means "May his name be erased off the face of history."

Whatever trials I faced at this time, they were nothing compared to Ramin's. Though he attended a Jewish school, its revolutionary headmasters also made their students stand in line and chant, "Death to Israel! Death to America!" This made Ramin so uncomfortable, he tried running away every morning. Each time, however, they caught him and doled out some punishment. Once, they smacked the backs of his hands with a ruler. Another time, they stuck a pencil between his fingers and squeezed them until he shrieked in pain. He was eight years old and so terrified of getting our family in trouble, he never told us what was going on until months after these punishments began.

When my mother found out, she went straight to the principal of Ramin's school. "How dare you treat my child this way?" she demanded. "How dare you treat any child this way?"

This principal was less sympathetic and more direct with her than any other school administrator had ever been. "Pipe down," he said. "How dare *you* speak to *me* in this fashion? You will tell your child to do everything we tell him to do or I will personally add all your names to the local Pasdaran's execution list. Now get out of my sight."

Mom came back to our apartment heartbroken and scared. That night, she begged Ramin to follow the rules. "Just for a while," she promised him. "Until we find you another school to attend."

She eventually did this but it was tough going. Ramin was quite stubborn. Honorable to a fault, he refused to say anything he didn't believe in; he would never go along just to get along. We tried solving the problem by having Ramin report to school late. We made up a ton of excuses. *He's seeing a doctor, and yes, unfortunately all his appointments are during the morning school sessions.* Or: *He keeps missing the bus.* Or: *We had transportation trouble.* Again and again and again.

To me, these episodes show off an essential difference between myself and Ramin, one that still informs our behaviors and therefore the paths our lives have taken to this very day. Ramin is loyal to his family. He remains adamant about his beliefs even at the risk of personal injury. Whereas I, for some strange reason, call it fear or obedience, learned the benefit of compromise and assimilation if they could further my own ends and those of my family.

Again, the Talmud allows for a Jew to renounce the Jewish faith if it saves a life. And if there's any gray area there, remember: all sins against God can be forgiven in Yom Kippur.

During the second year we lived in Tehran, my father's sister, Sima, and husband, Saeed, moved back to the city. They still had their three boys with them—Sassan, Soheil, and Sohrab. They took an apartment on the second floor of the same building we were living in. Up until that point, they'd been living in Kermanshah, to the southwest. Their home wasn't exactly in a war zone, like Khorramshahr. Still, they were close to the border with Iraq and therefore close enough to the fighting to make them uncomfortable.

They told us they planned on leaving the country as soon as possible. Tavooz had just left, which is something we were all very grateful for on more levels than one. Sima and Saeed were aware that their own escape would prove more difficult. While they weren't on an execution list like Dad, the time had passed when citizens simply went on vacation and never came back. Also, Sassan and Soheil were approaching the age to be drafted into the army. The revolution's leaders needed a strong military. They prohibited children of a certain age from leaving the country under any circumstances.

"It's not impossible," I remember Sima telling my mother. "Maybe we can smuggle the boys out separately, either east or to the south. We'll figure something out. But we must be careful."

Difficulties cropped up in every direction we turned. For instance, toward the end of 1982, my father was visited by his friend and colleague, a man I'll call Masoud Kashani. Kashani was then serving as the nation's Lieutenant Minister of Health. Ostensibly, he visited my father's hospital on a routine inspection tour. But while there, he drew my father into an empty room and closed the door.

"Are you out of your mind?" Kashani demanded. When my father asked what he was talking about, the bureaucrat laid things out. "Nasser, these things you have written, these letters. If there wasn't a war going on, you would be dead right now. Do you know this?"

My father just shrugged. "If there wasn't a war going on, I would never have written those letters in the first place."

Kashani slapped a hand to his forehead and groaned. "Please, just stop."

"Stop what?"

"Stop writing the letters!"

Again, my father shrugged. The way he did it must have signaled he had no intention of doing any such thing.

"Fine." Kashani threw up his hands. "Fine! I will do what I can. I have already done so much to keep you safe. But, Nasser, let me be clear. You are only alive because you are a doctor, and doctors are needed right now. That could change in the space of a heartbeat. When it does, I cannot stop what follows."

Here my father spotted an opportunity. "You know," he said. "I have worked on the front lines for two years now without cease. Perhaps if I took some time off, I might be under less stress."

His implication must have been clear. What if he up and collapsed one day? Could the front lines stand to lose a doctor of my father's quality? How many wounded soldiers might die if Dr. Nasser Tabibiazar was not at the hospital, functioning at his best? Kashani saw the wisdom in this. He signed an order granting Dad a couple of weeks' vacation so he could visit us back in Tehran.

It was a fortuitous turn. Earlier that week, my mother's workplace had been visited by the Paksazie, Khomeini's culture police. Even back then, with a war going on, the Paksazie made it their business to inspect local businesses to make sure that everyone working there followed the rules of revolutionary Islam. One such officer accosted my mother. He claimed she was not wearing her hijab properly. Apparently, a few locks of her hair were showing. He ordered her employment terminated.

This was done on the spot. Mom's employer looked miserable about it; he liked my mother and especially liked her work in the lab. The poor man's hands shook badly as he told her to pack her things and get out. He didn't want to fire her but what choice did he have? What choice did *anyone* have in those days?

Hearing that Kashani had been so helpful protecting my father, Mom called on him, hoping he could intervene on her behalf. Kashani received her graciously—at first. To hear Mom tell it, he brought her into his office, closed the door, and sat her in a chair before his big desk. He began to celebrate himself as her benefactor.

"Are you here to thank me?" Kashani asked. "I suppose that must be the reason you've come."

"Thank you for what?" said my mother.

"Why, for interceding on Nasser's behalf! For granting him vacation!"

"Oh, yes," my mother said. "Thank you for that."

Kashani perched on the edge of his desk. In this position, he was looming above my mother, looking down at her. "You are welcome, of course. So, what can I help you with now?"

"I need your help getting my job back!" Mom laid out her case. She said that, after the Khuzestan Insurgency, our entire family should be considered *jangzadeh*—war survivors. She also explained that were she allowed back to work at the lab, she would keep her hijab on properly at all times.

Kashani kept silent a moment. Then, after making a great show of considering his option, he said, "I can do this for you." Leaning forward, he put his face close to my mother's. Mom just stared at him until, finally, she had to look away. She told me later she thought he couldn't be serious. What had she gotten herself into?

Kashani saw her reaction and pulled back. Smugly, he said, "You will be back in this room very soon. Nasser's life depends it. And next time, you will be begging me."

I remember the moment Dad arrived at our apartment to start his vacation. We were so happy to see him! The mood darkened, however, once Mom told him what had just happened. Not only had she no job but Kashani could no longer be relied upon to protect Dad.

At that point, it was clear that we had no choice.

We had to flee.

CHAPTER TWELVE

FLIGHT

Iran-Turkey Border | 1982

"DON'T TAKE ANY BAGS," Dad told us. "It looks too conspicuous."

The next day, we went to the bus station with nothing but the clothes on our backs, some jewelry my mother had chosen, and a tiny parcel of cash and other valuables my father had cobbled together.

No one stopped us at the station and so, from Tehran, we went to Tabriz, where we changed to another bus bound for Azerbaijan. Skirting the southern shore of Lake Uremia, this bus deposited us in the city of Uremia at the foot of the mountains of West Azerbaijan, near the borders with Turkey and Kurdistan.

It was November 1982, very cold. I remember we weren't dressed warmly enough but this, it turned out, was the least of our worries. Almost the moment we arrived, my father began making calls. He'd grown up in these parts. He spoke fluent Turkish and Kurdish, which helped him navigate a complex web of contacts until, finally, he was speaking directly with the head of a group of smugglers.

"Please help us," Dad said. "My family and I need to leave the country as quickly as possible."

The Kurds seemed all too willing to help. They had no love for Khomeini's regime. One of our contacts brought us to a white marble house with two Mercedes-Benzes parked out front. We were taken inside, seated, and served tea.

About two hours later, another car pulled up. Ramin and I ran to the window to see who it was. A man got out of this third car and came inside to speak with my father. Later, I was told that all these people we had communicated with were just handlers. The smugglers were careful. They knew about spies and they knew what would happen if a spy caught them hustling people out of the country.

The handler that spoke to my father was very respectful. He did not stay long. He left with a curt nod. We waited. The evening wore on and we grew tired. That night, we slept in the white marble house. The next morning, the handler came back. Apparently, he had confirmed that my dad was the son of a Kurd, also a doctor who had worked in the army and now ran a hospital.

"Where are you headed?" the handler asked.

"To America," my father replied. Because that was our dream at the time.

"Very well," the handler said. "We will get you a car and come back tomorrow. But you must understand that you cannot take much."

"We have only what you see here." My father gestured toward us.

The handler nodded. "Tomorrow you meet the smugglers. Do everything precisely as they say, and may Allah be with you."

The next day, a new batch of Kurds showed up in yet another Mercedes. We all piled in and they drove us west, over dirt roads that looked as though no one had used them in ages. They dropped us off in an area where men with machine guns waited with horses.

My father translated what was being said to us. "They want us to get on the horses. I will take Romina on one. Your mother will ride with Ramin on another. The other two horses, the smugglers will ride."

I looked around. "What about me?"

"You ride with a smuggler. Okay? In the back."

In the back meant "off the saddle," basically clinging to the horse's ass. The moment I saw what this involved, I lodged a protest, which my father ignored. "Go on now. Up you go."

"But where are we going?" I asked.

"Up there." Dad pointed toward the looming Zagros Mountains, like a high purple wall in the distance. I remember thinking it impossible we could get up there. I'd grown up in cities, so naturally I wondered, *Where are the roads? Where are the buses? For heaven's sake, where are the people?*

This was my very first trek on horseback. I'll never forget it for dozens of reasons, least of which was the impact it made on my buttocks and thighs. I had never imagined that riding a horse demanded so much from the human groin. I learned very quickly how slippery a horse's ass can be, particularly when it's been walking all day and sweat starts to lather its coat. Each time we climbed up a hill, I would slide like an eel off the horse's thick buttocks. Each time we went down a valley, I'd bump up and down, bruising the parts of the body a twelve-year-old boy is still exploring. The whole ordeal was so painful, I told my father that I preferred walking and he acquiesced.

The higher we got in the mountains, the more the terrain turned arid and gravelly, dry as old bone and peppered with silt. Wherever I turned, things looked yellow and gray. The day wore out fast and we camped in a place where the sunset hung like a bright orange ball in the sky, hurling shadows on valley and dell.

I had never been on an adventure like this and it shocked me, almost, how magical everything seemed, how much fun I was having. But then, I would look at my mother and father. Their stern faces reminded me what was at stake, all the things we were leaving behind, plus the fact that our journey was shrouded in darkness. The higher we got in the mountains, the more we knew that our crossing was imminent. Once we crossed the border, nobody knew what would happen to us.

In the first village we came across, we stopped at the house of a tribal leader, who invited us in. The house's interior was covered in Persian rugs. They seemed to function both as decoration and insulation. The house had a *korsi*—what in Persian we called a *sandali*, a low table with a brazier full of heated coals on top of which blankets were arranged. You put your feet under the blankets, which trapped the heat and warmed your toes. Already we had reached a substantial altitude, so this was important.

There were pillows all over the place. The tribal elders sat on them, in a circle. They kept very still. None of them blinked or seemed to be breathing. Almost everyone carried a rifle. A teapot was set in the middle of the circle. The man who seemed most senior among the elders took a shine to Dad once he realized that he was a doctor. I remember the two of them talking in Kurdish. They smiled and laughed and I thought everything would be fine.

Then the tribal leader said something else. He made a gesture. I saw my dad stiffen as one of the other elders dug in his vest and pulled out a pouch, which he passed to my mother.

"What does he want?" Mom asked.

My father was already digging into his pockets. "Put all your valuables into the sack. Do not hold anything back."

"Are they *ransacking* us?!"

My father maintained his smile. When he spoke, he kept his voice calm and never broke eye contact with the leader. "Just do as he says. And make no sudden moves."

"But this is all we have!" Carefully, almost with shame, my mother produced a number of buttery yellow gold Persian bracelets, the kind called *alango*, which she had hidden under her clothes. "Nasser, without these to sell, how will we survive over the border?"

My father did not reply. Once the bracelets went into the sack, he gave the sack to the leader, who nodded and slipped the sack under his robe. He said something in Kurdish.

"What was that?" my mom asked.

"He said now we can cross the border. But we have to wait for a moonless night or we will be seen and Pasdaran scouts will shoot us down dead.'"

"Like that matters now!" my mother hissed. "Without our valuables, what will we be in Turkey? Penniless! We will be destitute, Nasser!"

My father kept grinning at the elders. "Lower your voice, please, Flora. And smile. They have all the horses, they have all the guns. We will do what they say."

A bit later, the leader of the Kurds gestured at my father and led him outside so the two of them could speak in private. Night was coming on fast. Ramin and I were tired. We went outside and spread blankets out under the stars, looking up at the bright silver moon. Again, we performed the Shema Yisrael.

Keep us safe, I said to the God of my people. *Keep all of us safe as we cross, pretty please. I am asking you this with all of my heart.*

When my father at last came back to us, he pulled out the same sack of valuables the tribal leader had taken from us. "Hide that." He gave the sack to my mother.

Mom was astonished. "Where did you get that?"

"He gave it back to me."

"Why?"

"Turns out he's a very good man. He explained that some of the other smugglers might try to kill us if they thought we had anything valuable on us. Thanks to that little bit of theater, everyone thinks that we're destitute. Now do as I say, please, and hide that. Let nobody see it. It's all we have left and we must keep it safe."

The next day, we began passing primitive Kurdish villages nestled deep in the sheltered ravines. There were a lot of them. The most lavish structures I saw were tiny one- or two-room hovels whose thick, stubby walls had been fashioned from large stones and mud. Normally, an animal pen was attached like a two-car garage in Western homes. Other houses were smaller, more like cabins built for nomads who followed their sheep through grazing season. Chickens, goats, and sheep abounded. Once in a while, a prosperous villager might have a horse or a couple of mules tied up in his yard. I saw no cows.

The smugglers directing our ragtag group would lead us into each village and up to a house they knew would accommodate us. Sometimes we slept under the sky on blankets laid out in the yard. I liked when we did that. At night, the stars glittered like diamonds that someone had tossed on the black velvet curtain of night. There were no man-made lights in the mountains so the galaxies swirled like tides overhead and the cosmos laid itself bare as the universe beckoned with mysteries deeply complex.

I remember telling my mother, "I had no idea."

"No idea about what?" she said.

"How many stars are up there."

She looked at the heavens, silent a moment. "Yes," she finally said. Nothing more. That one word captured it all.

Sometimes our hosts put us up in the stables but this, it turned out, could be dangerous. The first time we did it, I broke out in hives. I had no idea I'm allergic to hay and discovered this the hard way. Stables are also notorious breeding grounds for insects that delight in human misery. Bugs would attack our bodies, biting us everywhere. Poor Romina got the worst of it. She was only three years old. After only one night, her smooth pink skin was a horror of welts. Her thick hair was teeming with lice.

The next morning, we went to a nearby creek and washed her as best we could. One of the elders in that village felt so badly for her, he gave us goat's milk, sheep's cheese, and eggs to eat but Romina wouldn't stop crying. So the elder brandished his old Russian bolt-action rifle. Smiling at us, he chatted in Kurdish. I was frightened. My parents had gone off someplace to speak with some smugglers. We were alone with this man with no one to translate for us.

Eventually, I convinced myself that this grinning, chatty man could be trusted. He seemed to enjoy the company of children, which I believe speaks volumes about a person. *Perhaps he has kids of his own*, I thought.

For the rest of that day, this man became our guardian, guide, and playmate. Language barrier or not, I began to understand why he kept waving his rifle at us. He wanted to teach us to shoot, so that's what we did. I remember him showing me how to hold the long gun, pressing its stock up tight to my shoulder while taking aim. He had set a big rock way out in a field, which we used as a target. I recall how the rifle bucked when I pulled the trigger, the loud report it made. Young as I was, I could see that the weapon was ancient. After each shot, you levered the breech, which popped the cartridge loose, at which point the Kurdish man passed me another. The whole day passed like that. Point, shoot, reload. Point, shoot, reload. I never hit the rock but the man seemed pleased with the progress I'd made.

Romina was still feeling poorly, so this very kind man slaughtered a chicken and a goat for us. I was later told that such extravagance was unheard of in these tiny hamlets where meat was a valuable commodity. Most of the people we'd met on our journey ate yogurt, rice, potatoes, and cheese, so we did the same. This menu grew boring quite quickly. Today, as a doctor, I'm willing to bet that it also didn't meet the nutritional needs of growing children.

But this very kind man had given us meat! I remember him chopping the meat into little chunks, which he added to a cast-iron pot with some water, carrots, potatoes, and local herbs. I still remember the taste of that stew. The goat was gamey and chewy but, on the whole, we found it delicious. We had so much stew left over, we took it with us as we trekked through the next few villages.

By this point, we had spent weeks in the mountains. Our progress was slow. The rough terrain contributed to that, as did the fact that we were constantly being handed from smuggler to smuggler in village after village in what amounted to a vast network of human traffickers.

Wherever we went, word seemed to have gone ahead of us that Dad was a doctor. This may have slowed us down further but I also think it eased our way through the mountains. Sometimes, during the evenings, Dad wandered off. I don't know where he went but I suspect he might have been calling on sick members of this tribe or that tribe. A couple of times, I was present when men asked Dad's opinions of things in Kurdish. I noted they always did so with great respect. We were being treated far better than some of the other refugees we saw.

From time to time, we ran into people like us, those who were also hoping to cross into Turkey. One such person turned out to be a fighter jet pilot with the Iranian military. He was fleeing the country for fear of his life, he said.

"But aren't you part of the army?" I said. "Surely a jet pilot would be valuable to the regime?"

Very patiently, this pilot explained how the shah had forged close ties with Israel, so close that their militaries often trained together. In the revolutionaries' eyes, this meant that the pilot, trained by Israelis, was really a Zionist spy.

"But you're *not* a Zionist *or* a spy," I said. Then I thought about it. "Are you?"

The man shook his head. "No, of course not. But whether I am or I'm not is really irrelevant. All that matters is that the Pasdaran hate anything Israel's touched. They would shoot me just for having touched Israeli soil." He held up his hands to show how simple this was. "A lot of people like me fled through Afghanistan and Pakistan. I chose Turkey. I thought it'd be easier." The look he cast about at our poor circumstances told me he was having second thoughts about that. Eventually, this man parted ways with us. He was nice and I thought it sad we would never see him again.

I remember two other refugees, a nice young man and his very pregnant wife. Try as I do, I cannot recall what propelled them to risk everything and attempt the crossing. I only remember that they were kind and they seemed to like children. They played with Ramin, Romina, and me, for which we were grateful. Due to the wife's pregnancy, the couple was slower to move than we were. They fell behind us on the trail.

Up to this point, our trip had been very exciting. But now—with the border and freedom so close—we began to feel afraid. What if something went wrong after all we'd been through? It would hardly seem fair. To make matters worse, we were told we could only cross the border on a moonless night that never seemed to arrive despite how we waited. And waited. And waited.

Ten days ticked by. To Ramin, Romina, and me, this felt like an eternity, but my father kept telling us what the smugglers said. Conditions had to be just right. The Kurdish smugglers assured us again that Pasdaran spies were everywhere. They knew people were crossing the mountains into Turkey and they were shooting to kill.

Finally, the hour of our exodus arrived. I remember being incredulous.

Moonless? Overcast? This night was a chamber of absolute darkness. I literally could not see my hand in front of my face. To make matters worse, that night we were not allowed to take what the smugglers called the main path. It was too heavily guarded. We would find another way by walking along the edge of the mountain on a trail only wide enough for us to walk single file. To our left, stretching high, was a sheer stone wall. To our right, past the edge of the narrow trail, a sheer drop plunged hundreds of feet to the bottom of a gorge. The path itself was gravel, easy to slip on, especially if you weren't wearing good hiking boots, which we weren't.

The Kurdish smugglers jabbered instructions at my father.

"What are they saying?" I asked.

"Do not fall off."

"I do not like this," Mom said.

"Liking it has nothing to do with it," Dad snapped. I could tell the ordeal had unnerved him. "Just do what he tells us, please."

The Kurds came back to us, snapping more orders. One of the smugglers gestured. Another ducked behind trees and returned gripping a short hank of rope. Hooves *clip-clopped* on the hard-packed earth. My mother moaned, "Let me see that. Shine that light over there."

The leader, the big one with the flashlight, moved toward one of the mounts so its glow could wash over the horse.

"No!" I heard my mom gasp.

We were looking at four albino mountain mules, dead white with eerie, sickly-colored eyes.

"Ghost horses," I heard my mom moan. "I am *not* getting up on that thing!"

The lead smuggler spoke in broken Farsi. "Quickly! There is no time! Cars will be waiting. They take you to the bus station. You go to Istanbul!"

"I will not." Mom turned to my dad. "Nasser, I told you, last night. I had a dream. My father, Mirza Agha, came to see me. 'Do not ride the ghost horse,' he said. 'The ghost horse is death!'" Wide-eyed, she pointed at the bone-white mules. "Now what does that look like? Huh? I'd call that a ghost horse, wouldn't you?"

At that point, I can't honestly say who was more frustrated and confused, Dad or the smugglers. The smugglers argued among themselves while my parents got into a hissing match in Hebrew. Through all of it, I watched little

Romina's eyes popping wide and white in the flashlight's glow. She was paralyzed with fear. She made no sound while my parents kept raging at each other.

"I don't care about your damn dreams!" my father said. "I care about getting us over the border without getting us all killed!"

"You worry about getting killed? Then do not ride a ghost horse after my dead father said they would kill us!" Mom said.

The lead smuggler finally broke. "Doctor," he said to my father. "The mules know the path. They are steady and fast and you have to get going. The cars that await you will not be there long. They cannot be seen and will not drive in daylight. You must get on now!"

When again my mother refused, the smuggler exploded. "Fine! You walk. But the trail is too dangerous for this one." He pointed at little Romina. "She comes with us."

My father lunged forward. "No!"

"There is no other way," the smuggler said. "She is so small, she will not be seen. We keep her safe on the other side until you arrive. Or you get on the mules and take her like that. Either way."

"You take her." My mother had turned to the smuggler, looking him dead in the eyes. "Take my daughter."

"Are you mad?!" My father raged at her in Hebrew. "Are you out of your mind?"

"The rest of us walk. We will not ride these death horses." Mom pointed at the white mules, then looked at Romina. "We will see her on the other side."

"We can't just *give* these bastards our daughter. What if they sell her into slavery? Is that what you want?"

"She will be fine," my mother told him. "So long as we follow the message of Mirza Agha—"

"Superstitious woman!" my father exploded. "You pick up your daughter right now and you get on that horse!"

My mother turned back to the smuggler. "Go now."

The lead smuggler was tired of all this. Picking my sister up, he moved toward the car. Romina stayed silent and staring as these strange men took her away from us. She had been told not to make a sound under any circumstances. She did her job well that night, though I saw in her eyes that she was terrified. I caught one last glimpse of her face before she was gone, swallowed up by the dark.

I will remember that look on her face until the day I die.

"You have lost our child," I heard Dad moan. "We will never see her again, you stupid woman. Because of your dream."

That was the first time I saw my dad cry. I remember it startled me. How could it not? He was our rock. If that rock should crack, what on earth would become of him then? Or us?

My mother turned away from him. "Romina will be on the other side. We will see her. She will be there. But that man was right. We need to get moving right now."

She did not mount a mule. She started walking instead and the rest of us followed suit.

CHAPTER THIRTEEN

THE PROPHECY
OF MIRZA AGHA

Turkey to Israel | 1982–1983

THAT LEG OF OUR journey was like nothing I had ever experienced before or since. Like walking through an alternate universe where illumination is a figment of your imagination. Like walking through a black hole far out in infinite space or the sunless, pressurized depths of the sea.

Mom led the way down the path with one of the smugglers walking beside her. Ramin and I were behind them, then my father, then a few smugglers leading the white mules. I remember the path began undulating almost at once. The dips became sharp and the inclines steep. The gravel was treacherous under our feet, so were the stones lying about. Some of them were as big as softballs. They could easily twist your ankle.

Since it was dead black, we all held hands as often as we could. I remember Ramin and I scrambling over various objects—tree stumps and boulders, it felt like. I remember thinking the lead smuggler had been right. Mules were essential for anyone who wanted to make this trip easier and quicker. And there was no way Romina could have made that trip without them. No way.

At one point, I overheard more Kurdish being rattled off. My father offered translation. "Everyone listen to me." He sounded agitated. "They say up ahead, the trail gets very narrow. We must pay attention. On the right, there is a sheer drop. Do not go near it. Stick to the left and hug the mountain. Do you understand?"

We told him we did.

"This time, I will go first. Ray, I want you up here with me. Your mother I want with Ramin."

We all held our breaths as we shuffled around in the black. Dad came forward and groped in the dark till our hands touched. "Good," he said. "Now everyone move very carefully. Stay to the left, like I said. Hug the stone."

I could tell once we rounded the corner that this was absurd. I felt a blast of cold wind in my face, then the yawn of infinite space on my right. A vacuum crouched there, dark and cold. I could feel its emptiness filling my pores and it terrified me.

"Be careful, Ray. Pay attention," I remember Dad hissing at me. A wind kicked up and he quieted, waiting. When it passed, he hissed again. "I feel loose soil. This next part is slippery. Tell your mother."

I did as instructed and passed the news back through Ramin. My mother did not respond, which made me wonder how she was doing. Had Mirza Agha, in her dream, told her all this would happen, too? It was the first time during our entire flight where I got really and truly scared. The first time I realized what the stakes were.

This is not an adventure, I thought. *This is real. If one of us gets hurt out here, we could all die.*

We continued creeping forward then. Inch by blind-as-an-earthworm inch.

Dad said, "Ray, be careful. The path here is bad—"

Then he slipped. I felt his body go down and cried out. Letting go of Ramin, I grabbed my father's arm with both hands. His body felt like dead weight. I realized then he had nothing under his feet. He had slipped off the side of the path and was dangling now over infinite space with nothing but me holding him suspended between this world and the next.

I'm twelve years old and my father will die if I let go. I cannot do that. After all he has done for us, everything he has sacrificed. . . Please, God, do not let him go.

"Farzin," I heard Mom whisper. "What is it? What's going on?"

Then, from the utter dark:

"Ray." Dad was still whispering. Urgent.

"Hold on," I said. Grinding my teeth, I dug in with my heels, leaning backward. "Find your feet!"

My feet slipped out from under me and I landed on my butt, still gripping Dad's hand in both of my own. Now his weight was dragging me to the brink.

"Ray, what's going on?!" Mom said.

I could feel Dad writhing beneath me for purchase. Then his weight sort of shifted and stabilized. "Ray, I'm on something here. . ."

"I can feel it."

"Think I can. . . hold it."

"What are you *doing*?!" Mom hissed.

I heard mutters in Kurdish and told Dad, "I'm pulling you up."

Please God please oh please please please. . .

"Here we go. . ."

I heard Dad grunt. Then, working together—him pushing, me pulling—we levered him slowly, carefully, up a few inches and over the brink, where he sprawled himself flat on the gravel path. He was breathing, ragged and shallow, like some wounded animal who'd just run fast and far from something that quite nearly caught it and ate it.

When my mother found out what had happened, she refused to say another word about it. For a long time after that, we hugged each other tight in the dark. The muttering started in Kurdish again and my father, who'd just gotten hold of himself, said we had to keep going. The border was not far ahead and the smugglers kept saying we couldn't be late. Cars were waiting to take us to a bus station where we would depart for Istanbul. But the Turkish police were on high alert against refugees being smuggled over the border. That was the reason the smugglers would only drive us under the cover of night.

They had expected us to arrive by 2:00 a.m. I had no idea what time it was but I knew we were running late. Very late.

And Romina was with them.

"Be careful," I heard my father say. "Please, everyone. Be extra careful."

We moved forward again. Total blackness. The howl of the wind on my right was even more mocking now, as was that dead empty space. Foot by foot we proceeded, and sometimes down on all fours, keeping close to the earth lest it suddenly wash out from under us.

The trail kept arching and dipping. Behind us, the solid thumps of the mules' hooves kept up a counterpoint to our frightened breaths.

At one point, I heard more muttering behind us. Then a shuffling sound. Clatter of hooves against rock. A soft nicker. Then gasps. Muffled curses in Kurdish. A moment later, there was a high-pitched whine like a scream from below and what sounded like a giant wet bag of meat hitting the ground at high velocity. It took me a long moment to figure out what had happened. When I did, I inhaled sharply.

One of the ghost mules had tumbled over the edge.

No way, I thought. Then: *What should we do?* The child's part of my brain asked, *Should we go get the mule?* The adult part knew full well we could not. Moreover, it then understood how close we all were to death, how my mother and Mirza Agha had been right.

I remember my father reaching back and fumbling to grab for my sleeve. "Keep going," he muttered. "Grab hold of your brother and mother. We have to keep going."

That trip on the mountain trail should have taken an hour but, because we did not ride the mules, it had cost us closer to four. We were late to arrive at the rendezvous clearing. Two cars were scheduled to wait for us but there was only one when we got there. Two Kurdish men stood outside it, waving flashlights. In the wash of their beams, I saw a golden 1973 Mercedes-Benz. I remember because I was really into cars back then.

My mother called out for Romina and ran toward the car.

"Wait!" Dad called out.

He needn't have gotten upset. The Kurds who stood by the car opened one of the back doors and there was little Romina, curled up in the back seat, fast asleep.

"Okay," my father said. "Thank you. Now we come with you—"

The smugglers refused us. They said we had taken too long. They could not remain. The sun was about to come up and the other car had already left. When I turned around, the Kurds who had taken us over the trail had already melted off into the darkness, taking the remaining mules with them.

My father argued with the Kurds as they got into their Mercedes. "Are you kidding? This is outrageous! We are here now. My family is here! You take us to the bus station. That was our deal!"

The driver stuck his hand out his window and pointed. "Go that way. There is a road. Follow that road and you will be safe."

The car's engine revved. Its transmission slipped into gear. Its tires spat dust in the wan light cast by its taillights. A moment later, it was gone and we were alone then, lost in the dark.

"What do we do?" I heard my mother say.

For a moment, my father was silent. Then: "We walk. Everyone take someone's hand."

Scooping up little Romina, he tucked her against his shoulder and led the way.

Dawn broke not so long after that. I remember the rose-colored light creeping up from the horizon, the way it spread, lighting everything around us like a photograph being developed. It was December by then and the mornings were cold. Morning fog hovered over each patch of flatland. The trees all around us were dry, gray, and pale and completely denuded. Wherever I looked, the landscape was arid, flat terrain, like you see in Yosemite National Park.

The smugglers had shown us which direction to head in so we started walking that way. We had no food or water. It was just the five of us, shivering, terrified, miserable.

It took us about five hours to reach the first landmark, an asphalt road. By then it was closer to nine in the morning, or ten. The night was over. We could no longer hide in the dark. We stood by the side of the road until my father instructed us to keep walking. We had to reach town. He told us to walk without drawing too much attention to ourselves, as if such a thing were possible. We were a family of five, disheveled and filthy, walking on the side of an empty road with bags in our hands. An everyday thing.

A bunch of cars whizzed past us and at first nobody stopped. Then a broken-down pickup truck pulled off to one side. The driver leaned out, started talking to us. My mom told us to be quiet, let Dad do the talking.

My father went over to speak to the drivers in Turkish. A moment later, he waved to us to walk toward the car, so we hurried over.

"Get into the flatbed," he told Ramin and me. "Flora, you and Romina get into the cab."

"What did you say to him?" Mom demanded in Farsi.

"I told him we're tourists from Germany doing some sightseeing."

"That's the best you could do? Tourists from Germany with your accent? Did he buy that?"

"I don't think so." Dad pushed Ramin up into the flatbed and jumped in behind him. "Don't look a gift horse in the mouth. He said he'd drive us to the next town. Get in!"

Up the road was a place called Başkale, a tiny border town in the foothills of the Zagros. The driver dropped us off at a tourist hostel. We took a room on the second floor. After lecturing us again to be quiet and speak to no one, my father went off to get food and to call his brothers in Germany and the U.S. so he could ask them to wire us money. My father came back and reported excitedly that help was finally on the way.

But here things turned disastrous again. My brother, sister, and I were kids who had just spent the past weeks trekking through mountains, sleeping with animals, weathering bug bites. We hadn't changed clothes in all that time nor had we bathed. Being at the hostel was probably the first time in my young life that I really looked forward to a shower.

Ramin and I went to the shared bathroom on the second floor, took off our clothes, got under the water, and started splashing around. We thought our adventure was over. We were so excited, we made lots of noise. Too much noise.

My father asked us several times to be quiet. We came out of the shower and I kept teasing Ramin. Dad kept asking me to knock it off but I ignored him. He'd never been the family disciplinarian; that was Mom's job. Still, I could see him looking nervously out the window.

"Knock it off, Ray," he said. "Quit harassing your brother."

I ignored him and kept pushing Ramin around until a heavy hand landed on my left cheek.

The blow shocked me. Dad had never hit me before. The air stood still. The silence that ensued was the quietest I have ever experienced, accompanied by a little whistling noise in my left ear.

"Be quiet!" Dad whispered again. His face was bright red from tension. That's when we heard the sirens. Quickly, Dad grabbed Ramin and myself by the arms and led us back to the room but it was too late.

The police surrounded the hostel. Someone must have tipped them off. They came upstairs, moving from room to room until they found us. Their leader took my mom and dad. They told me that my brother and I would move with Romina to another hostel that held refugees.

"There are other Persians there," the officer told me. "They will take care of you."

That turned out to be true but the same thing couldn't be said for my parents. The Turkish police were not gentle with them. My father has never elaborated on this but I've always understood they demanded money from him—extorted might be a much better word—while threatening to send his children back to Iran as orphans. In the end, they took everything that we had. Dad let them. What choice did he have? He just wanted us to be safe. They let him go and he came back to the hostel where they'd moved us. Without my mother.

"Where is she?" we said.

Mom was returned to us later that evening. Something had changed. Her furious gaze was cast down as though she were shooting laser beams out of her eyes and she didn't want us to get hurt by them. I remember the great lengths my parents went to, deflecting the questions that Ramin, Romina, and I lobbed at them. It was only much later that I pieced together what had happened.

The police had been even rougher on Mom than they'd been on my dad. Perhaps they suspected that, as a woman, she'd be more vulnerable. Within a couple of days, once they realized they couldn't fleece us of anything, they transferred us from Başkale to a larger town nearby called Van, where the Persian refugees were.

Van is a quaint, small city on the eastern shores of a lake with the same name. We stood looking out at the beautiful lake juxtaposed against the backdrop of the Zagros range in the distance. Somehow the scene managed to convey the feeling of being in two areas at once. One foot in one place, one foot in another. It was the first time I remember feeling like I was straddling two different destinies. One lay behind me, the other before me.

I am no longer Farzin, I thought. *Farzin is somewhere back there. So who am I now? And where is my home?*

This feeling has never left me.

We ended up staying in that hostel for about a month. It was full of other Iranian refugees, all waiting to get their security clearance for a country that would take them in. Each day, my father went out and worked tirelessly, trying to arrange our refugee status. Later, I learned he called Israel, the United States, Austria, Germany, Italy. . . the list went on. Germany and the U.S. refused to accept us and I think this dashed his hopes for a while.

Meanwhile, the rest of my family was having an okay time hanging out with the other Persian refugees. The menfolk were always off doing the same thing Dad was, jangling phone lines, writing letters, doing everything in their power to find the next stepping stone in their lives. Ramin and I learned to play backgammon. We got pretty good at it, too.

Since we'd basically lost all our money, Mom began selling the jewelry she'd worn out of Iran. Day by day, more pieces vanished, replaced by small wads of cash whose sums were decidedly paltry compared to the actual worth of her bracelets and chains, her watches and rings. And while we were living like this we, of course, heard everyone else's stories.

At one point, we saw the fighter jet pilot again and he told us the fate of that pregnant woman and her husband. They had been caught while crossing the border. Pasdaran scouts shot the wife in the belly. She died almost immediately and her husband was sent back alone to Iran. I remember Ramin and I sat silent for a long time after we heard that. What could we say?

Ultimately, my father's efforts proved successful. He was able to reach several organizations, such as the Jewish Federations, both in the U.S. and Israel. He was also able to prove we were Jewish thanks to a letter from Rabbi Yedidyahu in Tehran. Armed with this, we were finally allowed to leave our "detention" at the hostel. Once we got the security clearance, we hopped on a bus that was headed to Istanbul.

We had left Iran in November 1982. It was now February 1983. Our plan was to hop a flight to Tel Aviv, where we could put the past behind us. And yet, as we quickly discovered, the tithe for our passage had not yet been paid in full.

Istanbul was nearly a thousand miles from Van on the country's western edge, where Turkey touches Bulgaria and the Sea of Marmara yields gently to the tranquil blue-green Aegean. We were told our bus ride would take twenty-four hours. I remember thinking, *So what? At least we're not being eaten by bugs, living on goat's milk, or freezing to death in the open. At least we're not losing Dad because he slipped off some bottomless cliff. Mom isn't being roughed up by Turkish policemen and pregnant women aren't being shot. How bad could this be?*

Turns out this was the wrong question to ask.

While staying at the hostel, I'd begun to feel pretty lethargic. I had no appetite. Very little thirst. I remember listening to my parents talking one night. They were very concerned.

"What's wrong with him?" Mom demanded. "He is not eating or drinking anything! Not even water!"

"The trip is catching up with him," Dad said. "The kids have been under a lot of stress. Let's wait and see."

I felt fine enough to climb aboard the bus by myself. Sure, I was a little dizzy but that made sense. I hadn't been sleeping so well.

We were deep into the trip when my parents offered me something to eat. I refused. The mere thought of food made me nauseated. I thought I was carsick from the bus driving the curvy mountain roads. Eventually, Mom got really mad and implored me to eat something, anything. When we stopped at a bus station for a short bathroom break, Mom and Dad forced me to eat something. I chewed it up and swallowed but then I puked it all right back up.

Mom was furious. She shouted at me to eat something. I told her I couldn't. It was hard enough just to keep my eyes open.

"Nasser, what's happening? Wait. Is he turning yellow?"

"No," I remember hearing my father mutter. "No, no, that's just the coloring of the light through the window."

"Nasser, Farzin is turning yellow!"

"Relax. He is fine."

"He is NOT fine, Nasser, he's *yellow*. Don't tell me it's light, Nasser, look at the sclera of his eyes!"

Dad took me under the light and looked into my eyes. I could tell right away he knew what was wrong with me. I saw it in his face. I also saw he was afraid to tell my mother.

"Well?!?" my mother demanded once Dad had finished examining me.

"Okay, it isn't the light," he sighed. "That's jaundice. Hepatitis."

"You mean his liver's inflamed?!?"

"That's what hepatitis is, isn't it, Flora?"

"What should we do?'

"It's one o'clock in the morning. We just passed Ankara. We'll be in Istanbul in just a few hours. We need to keep him hydrated until we get to a hospital in Istanbul."

I barely remember the rest of that trip or the refugee hostel we went to in Istanbul. By that point, I was so weak I couldn't move. My mother tried giving me water and food but I couldn't take anything. I was puking intractably, bringing up nothing but bile.

I remember feeling hot, like I had a fever, and my abdomen felt weird, like there was a balloon swelling up in my guts. It wasn't pleasant and I kept falling asleep.

"Let me have him," I remember Dad saying. "You stay with the kids."

Then he was walking me out of the hostel, out in the street, and waving his arm for a cab. He'd grown up speaking Turkish so he was able to tell the driver we needed to get to a hospital fast. Whatever was closest. We got in and the car roared off.

After what felt like only a few minutes, the taxi ground to a stop and my dad pulled me out. "Let's go." He tried setting me onto my feet but my legs were spaghetti. I started to go down but he caught me. "Up we go."

He picked me up, slung me over his shoulders like a sack of potatoes, and started jogging toward the emergency room. To the end of my life, I will remember looking down at the back of his neck. Despite the cold, I could see beads of sweat on his bald head. I started to cry. "Please, Baba! You are getting tired. Put me down. I can walk!" Every bounce sent jolts of pain ripping out from my distended belly but I was afraid of telling him that. I didn't want to worry him any further. I could already hear the fear in his voice. I could hear him breathing heavily. And yes, it occurred to me then that now he was carrying me. I'd saved his life once. Maybe now he was saving mine. But God did it hurt!

"Please, Baba!" I said. "Please put me down. I will try to walk."

He did. But the moment my feet took my weight, I collapsed. Dad scooped me up and we entered the hospital.

We were clearly refugees, and just as clearly I was tremendously ill. We had no money to pay for my treatments. In the end, the hospital only admitted me because Dad was a doctor.

Later, the doctors told my dad I wouldn't have survived another hour. I was completely dehydrated. The labs that came back on my kidneys, liver, and other internal organs showed they had all begun to fail. I could not leave the hospital and Dad didn't want to leave me alone to go get Mom. There were no cell phones back then and Mom had no idea which hospital Dad had taken me to.

Initially, they put me in a long room that held about thirty other children. But my father argued that I couldn't stay there. I'd get an infection, he said. So the hospital cleared out a janitor's closet and wheeled my gurney in there with an IV hooked to a pole. To this day, I'm not really sure why I got this treatment. It might be because they didn't want me to infect other kids. Maybe it was because Dad was a doctor. Or maybe I was just too sick. Whatever the reason, I got a janitor's closet as my luxury private room in a foreign country where we had no money and no family or friends to reach out to.

I remember that room like I'm in it right now. The staff had cleared out all the cleaning supplies. My cot was pushed against the right wall, opposite the janitor's slop sink. There was so little space that my head was right next to the back wall with my feet touching the door. There was only a small window in the room. It was located somewhere behind me, high on the wall. There was a closet next to the sink. They both smelled like ammonia and scrubbing detergent. There was so little room that only one or two other people could visit at a time, and whoever came visiting had to sit in a folding chair set right against my head that barely left any leg room. When it wasn't being used, you had to fold the chair up and put it away.

Three weeks went by. Whenever I was awake and turned my head, Ramin and Romina would be there, looking through the door, which was always left cracked. They were checking on me the only way they could because they weren't allowed to see me. Hepatitis is a food-borne viral disease with a forty-day incubation period. It's also highly contagious. The best guess we can offer is that I picked it up shortly after we boarded the bus in Tehran that ferried us west, toward the mountains. To this day, we have no idea why no one else in my family contracted it.

Mom and Dad were allowed in my tiny room, one at a time. During the day, I was told, they were splitting their time between staying with me and traveling around Istanbul, preparing for us to leave Turkey. Thanks to their efforts, Austria, Spain, and Israel granted our family asylum.

"Which should we choose?" I heard my mother and father debating.

They were still hoping to get us to the U.S. Mom had heard that going to Spain and Austria was the best way to get U.S. visas but Dad didn't want to go to countries he didn't know without any money and no guarantees we could eventually get to the States. Also, by this point, his brother had told him he'd lost the $50,000 Dad had given him for safekeeping just a couple of years earlier.

In retrospect, this is understandable. My uncle, like many immigrants recently arrived to a new country, struggled financially. He had his own family to provide for. He saw an opportunity to invest in a restaurant and he had

$50,000 just lying around, inert, in an account. I'm sure he thought he could invest our money and repay our account once the investment matured. But the restaurant tanked and he ended up losing everything.

It was hard to get mad at him for this. He was a good man trying to raise his kids and make a living in a foreign country. He did what he thought he had to do and was deeply apologetic about what happened. He told Dad that the U.S. is not a good place if you have no money but Israel would certainly take care of poor families.

"We go to Israel first," Dad said. He wanted to visit his family whom he hadn't seen for years and see his mother, Tavooz, now living near Tel Aviv. "We can always go to the U.S. after a layover there."

Once I no longer needed an IV drip and could eat and drink on my own, I was allowed to leave the hospital. We went to the Israeli embassy, which issued us permits. Since we had no money to pay for plane tickets, my uncle in Germany bought them for us. But then, because of my illness, we had to wait another month because, as a matter of public health, the airlines wouldn't allow us to board a plane. In total, we stayed in Istanbul a little over two months.

We finally flew to Tel Aviv in April 1983. We arrived at the tail end of the Lebanon-Israel War. The country's economy was in shambles. Inflation was up 300 percent, we had no money, and none of us kids spoke Hebrew.

"None of that matters," I heard Mom say on more than one occasion. "At least we're still together."

I will never forget being welcomed at the airport by Uncle Elyahu and his three sons. It was such a relief to see friendly faces. To know that, for the first time since 1978, we were free, we were safe. Better than that, everyone around us was Jewish so there was no need to hide anymore.

I remember driving back to Uncle Elyahu's house. Everywhere I looked, the streets were well-lit—and so clean! The sidewalks were clearly marked. There were no air raid sirens screaming, no anti-aircraft guns going off. There were even caution signs posted here and there. *Caution!* I thought. *What a novel idea! What kind of society is this that people advise caution rather than, say, shooting at children, running them over with motorbikes, or blowing their homes up?*

It was the middle of the night when we arrived at Uncle Elyahu's place. Despite the late hour, our hosts asked Ramin, Romina, and me if we wanted anything special to drink. I told them I wanted a juice. They took us outside to a local store and spoke to the owner, who smiled at us and rolled up the corrugated metal shutter that protected his store when it was closed for the night. Uncle Elyahu bought us grape and cherry juice boxes made by Capri Sun. They were the kind of drinks whose straw you jam into the top of the package before you drink them.

Today, some forty years later, I still remember the taste of that juice. To me, Capri Sun will always be the taste of freedom.

CHAPTER FOURTEEN

THE LAND OF MILK AND HONEY

Israel | 1983–1990

That first night, we all stayed at Uncle Elyahu's place. The next day, they moved us in with Tavooz, who was sharing a two-bedroom apartment with another elderly woman. We camped out on their living room floor, where we would remain for the next eight or nine months. There were seven of us, all fighting for space and time in the apartment's single bathroom. Not exactly what you'd call an ideal situation, especially for Tavooz, who, whenever she looked at me, seemed to fear I'd start bouncing off the beds. I mentioned to Ramin that we should not do this under any circumstances, and he agreed.

We had no money, no income, no prospects, and only the clothes we had managed to smuggle over the mountains. No one in my family spoke Hebrew beyond the most rudimentary phrases. But life went on.

My bar mitzvah was scheduled for August and nothing could stop that. Someone gave my parents enough money to buy me a fresh pair of pants and a shirt that were Carolina blue. I tried them on and thought I looked ridiculous, but what could I say? We were in no position to argue.

On the plus side, my bar mitzvah was held in Jerusalem—right at the Western Wall, in fact. My mother and Tavooz weren't allowed to come since only men are allowed in that district. But my cousins all came and Uncle Elyahu led the ceremony. Holding my hand, he chanted the ancient prayers. I remember thinking, *Now I am a man. This is what it feels like to be a man.*

By the end of that year, once Mom and Dad learned enough Hebrew and each found jobs, we got our own tiny apartment in the beachside town of Bat Yam on the southern outskirts of Tel Aviv. In Hebrew, Bat Yam means "Daughter of the Sea." I'd never seen anyplace like it. We were right on the Mediterranean. Looking north, or so I was told, you could see the island of Cyprus squatting emerald green and bright on the shimmering water.

I loved Bat Yam at once although, in my memory, it was a poor place. Mostly working-class people lived there, packed tight into five- or six-story multiunit apartment buildings that were not well kept. The streets were narrow and cramped. The cars I saw everywhere were old; they slouched on their tires like exhausted metal alligators. Everyone had solar panels mounted on their roofs to heat their water tanks.

Most of the joy in Bat Yam was up by the shoreline. The seediness sort of gave way there to a beautiful promenade lined with shops overlooking the water. If you've ever been to Brighton Beach out in Brooklyn, New York City, it was that kind of atmosphere. If we wanted to see something fancy, we just hopped a bus north into Tel Aviv, where they had ritzy hotels, boutique shops, and fancy villas like the ones you see in Miami these days.

We lived near Uncle Elyahu. He became like a second father to me. I thought he was the kindest, most wonderful person I'd ever met. He was selfless and thoughtful, like my father, and I enjoyed his take on religion. Though he maintained all Jewish customs—Shabbat, Yom Kippur, going to synagogue, and so on—he was not a *haredi*, meaning not Orthodox. As an educated man, he seemed willing to keep his mind open to influences both traditional and new.

My parents immediately enrolled Ramin and me in school even though neither of us spoke a word of Hebrew. I finished seventh grade by the end of that school year, May or June 1983. Ramin was supposed to be in fourth grade but they held him back a year so he ended up finishing third grade during those first few months in Israel.

There was no vacation once summer arrived. Instead, each day I took a bus north into Tel Aviv, where I went to an Ulpan school to learn Hebrew. The Ulpan schools are set up as a joint venture by the Israeli government and the Jewish Agency. They offer a very effective system for learning the Hebrew language. Practically all new immigrants attend Ulpan to get themselves up and running.

I began to pick up Hebrew rather quickly. I found it a very straightforward language. It's rules-based and very mathematical. Each word has a different three-syllable root. Overall, the language has seven tenses. Once I felt comfortable with these elements, speaking Hebrew was plug-and-play. I could mix and match words and meanings as I needed, making sentences and, of course, committing plenty of hilarious errors early in the process.

Unfortunately, there were no classes available for kids who were Ramin's or Romina's ages. That whole summer, my cousins and Uncle Elyahu taught them informally when I got home from classes. The effect was startling. Ramin did so well that, the following year, he jumped past fourth grade and started fifth grade.

This isn't to say that Ramin had it easy. I mentioned how, back in Iran, he'd taken a lot of grief for being a Persian Jew who wouldn't chant "Death to Israel." Now, in Israel, he got beaten for being Iranian. We discovered the hard way that many Israelis didn't look kindly on Jews from Iran. There were many reasons for that. The general sentiment was that Persians were poor and stingy. That we had only come to Israel because we had no other choice, not because we loved the country or were Zionists through and through. Many times we heard rhetoric amounting to "When Israel was first formed or at war and we needed your help, you Jews stayed in Iran. But now that your country has fallen apart, you come here? And so what? We should just drop everything to accept you? Why?"

Ramin had a particularly stressful time going to school in Israel. He was often called Parsi-Parsi, a derogatory term in Hebrew referring to Jews of Persian heritage. Calling someone Parsi-Parsi was tantamount to calling them "poor and stingy." I would face similar discrimination a bit later when I went to high school. But at that point, at least, I was spared.

My school made a point of pairing all incoming immigrant children with an Israeli buddy to help them acclimate to the new school and society. In eighth grade, my buddy was Yehuda. He was a gangly, funny kid who wore glasses and had a crooked smile. He could be very sarcastic but I always knew that his heart was in the right place. It was a good match. Apart from keeping a lot of the school bullies off my back, Yehuda helped me work on my Hebrew until, by the end of that year, I felt comfortable speaking the language. I reciprocated by helping my buddy with his math homework.

In the summer of 1984, I was thirteen years old. My IQ tests qualified me to attend Boyar, a coed high school regarded as one of the best in the country. It was located next to the Holocaust Museum in Jerusalem and it welcomed about a thousand students, grades seven through twelve, from all over Israel and the world. The curriculum was interactive and focused on science, which I excelled at. But there was a problem.

Boyar was a boarding school. To attend, I would have to leave my family and move to Jerusalem, about forty miles east from our home in Bat Yam. To get there, I would have to take the red Number 405 bus out of Tel Aviv, driving through seared lands that lay baking and shimmering with heat waves in the Holy Land's sun. Alone. I would be given only one weekend every two months to visit back home.

The more I considered this prospect, the more I realized how attractive I found it. Any chance I had to get out from being cooped up in a tiny apartment in Bat Yam sounded fine to me. But my mother had serious reservations about letting her thirteen-year-old son go off alone in a strange country. "Family comes first!" she said. "We do not separate, not after all we've been through!"

She forbade me from going. We fought a lot about that until Uncle Elyahu interceded on my behalf. He explained to my parents what a privilege it was to study at Boyar, how my doing so would be a great advantage not only to me but the entire family. Mom relented after that and I was allowed to attend Boyar. To my surprise, however, I spent almost as much time getting in fights there as I spent studying.

Mostly kids bullied me about my language skills, or lack thereof. I was still not adapted to Israeli culture, still learning the nuances of Hebrew. They also called me a nerd because I was great at math and sciences but not so good at playing the games that keep socially anxious teenagers in step with one another. And of course, I got made fun of because I was Persian. This was the worst part of all and the reason I once got in serious trouble with an older student named Yosi.

Everything about Yosi was big: his height, his shoulders, his attitude, his nose. He picked on everyone. He was the bad apple that no school likes but every school has. I believe he was very intelligent but he came from a pretty bad home, or so we heard.

The first couple times he tried picking on me, he cussed out my mom and my dad for being dirty Persians. This was actually no big deal. As I said, at the time it was common for kids in Israel to use rhetoric like this. But after all my family had been through, I wasn't about to let anyone bully me or besmirch my family name. I would defend myself with my fists, which for me was also quite common at this time. Mostly, these fights took place quickly and under the radar. The teachers never saw them and the kids who got involved seemed to know instinctively when enough was enough. Once a fight was finished, a sort of silent truce was declared and everyone simply moved on. But the fight that got me in trouble was hard to brush under the carpet.

One day in the dining hall, Yosi approached with his tray of food and sat directly across the table from me. "So, Raymond," he said. Opening his napkin, he paused and scoffed. "That's a stupid name for a Jew but I guess you know that already, don't you?"

I kept my head down. Saying nothing, I put all my focus on eating the pasta the kitchen had served that day for lunch.

"I guess Raymond's not a Persian name either. Huh? Is it? Dirty, filthy, Parsi-Parsi? Huh?" Yosi lowered his face so it was close to the tabletop. He wanted me to look at him leering at me. "You Parsi are just trash that washed up on our beaches. You know that don't you, Parsi-Parsi?"

The other kids around the table chuckled a bit but then they began asking Yosi to knock it off. I remember chewing my food and thinking the pasta sauce could benefit from a pinch of pepper and salt in equal proportions. That's when Yosi said—

"So when is your mom gonna visit? I hear she's a whore and I want my turn with her. I could use a good turn with a Parsi-Parsi whore. I'll show her what a real Israeli man is—"

He hadn't finished his sentence when I stood and jerked up the table with one hand. The trays sailed off and food flew everywhere. Whipping my other hand out, I grabbed the front of Yosi's shirt and pulled him toward me and into an uppercut that I rammed into his nose. Under my fist, I felt cartilage crunch and snap like an old dry twig being crushed. His nose broke and blood exploded all over his face. Then there were hands on my shoulders, my arms, my neck. They pulled me backward and people were shouting.

I remember looking at Yosi, seeing the shock on his bleeding face. To this day, I'm not really sure if he was surprised by the fact that I'd punched him or by the pain of his broken nose. Strangely enough, I felt calm at this point. I knew he had learned his lesson. So had everyone else who, up until then, had called me Parsi-Parsi. More importantly, I'd made it clear that no one could call my mother a whore.

Unfortunately, the vice principal of our school happened to be sitting two tables away when this incident happened. He saw the whole thing and he had me hauled out to his office, where he made it quite clear that my time at Boyar had come to an end. After which he called my parents and told them he was sending me home.

Neither my mother nor father spoke Hebrew well enough to intervene. Uncle Elyahu went to Jerusalem and negotiated a second chance for me. I remember him speaking brusquely but also quite sternly in eloquent Hebrew. He knew exactly the right tack to take. Rather than focusing on what I had done, he took the vice principal to task for allowing an environment to exist where the children of war refugees could be accosted in such a fashion. Elyahu was a kind man whom even strangers warmed to. His quiet, gentle demeanor was able to calm the angriest of people. I was the beneficiary of his kindness in more ways than one. Before I knew what was happening, I was told the good news. I could stay at Boyar so long as nothing remotely resembling what had happened took place again. As in ever. If it did, my expulsion would be automatic. Quietly, with my eyes downcast, I assented and went back to class.

Yosi was eventually expelled from Boyar for a double whammy. The police caught him shoplifting at a local store. He'd also been accused of assaulting a female student who went to Boyar's day school. Basically, Yosi had other issues he was dealing with that likely affected his behavior. But then, I suppose, the same could be said about everyone. About me. My tussle with Yosi was not the first fight I'd ever been in but it was the last time I've broken someone's nose. To this day, I'm not proud of it.

While I was in ninth grade, I took three academic tests. Their results showed that, while I hadn't exactly mastered written Hebrew, my scores in math and physics allowed me to skip high school and go directly to university. Somehow, word got out. The phone at our home in Bat Yam started ringing off the hook. My math teacher at Boyar called my mother about a wonderful opportunity that existed where I could study advanced math and physics at Hebrew University.

"But he's still just a kid," my mom insisted.

They agreed to give me a trial period. During my second semester of ninth grade, I started taking classes at Hebrew University in Jerusalem, which was a thirty-minute bus ride from Boyar. I liked the idea of skipping high school. I loved math and science, and I was excited to follow those disciplines wherever they led me. But the moment I got to campus, I felt out of place.

My mother, it turns out, was right. I was only fourteen and still in the process of finding my feet in this brand-new country. Emotionally, I was not as mature as my university classmates. This was partially due to my age but also partially due to the fact that all Israeli citizens must undergo compulsory military service. Girls must serve a minimum of two years while boys serve three. Because of this, the vast majority of my classmates were seven or eight years older than me. A few were former officers in the Israeli military and more than a few of the oldest were combat veterans. I understood that I'd been given a fantastic academic opportunity. But just as man cannot live on bread alone, I couldn't live on academics alone. I needed a social life and so I returned to Boyar.

By this point, midway into my ninth-grade year, my father had flown to the U.S. on a visitor visa, which was the best he could get at the time. He had a goal for this trip. First, he would get himself settled, secure himself work, then apply for a green card. Once that was done, he would initiate the much longer process of bringing each family member over one by one. Our dream of going to America would finally be realized. Dad decided to live in Los Angeles because his brothers lived there. They would help him find his feet.

My dad's sister, Sima, and her husband, Saeed, were also there with all three of their sons. During the craziness of the war, knowing their two older sons were approaching the age to be drafted, they sent them over the southeastern border with Pakistan. From there, the boys were able to book passage to the U.S., where their uncles took them in. Sima, Saeed, and their youngest son left Iran later by exploiting a loophole for medical emergencies. With the stated purpose of visiting their ailing mothers, they flew to Austria and never went back. In 1984, they arrived Stateside, where their family joyfully reunited.

It's hard to underestimate my father's amazement as he landed in LA. Even back then, the entire north-central neighborhood of Westwood was packed with so many Iranian Jews, the area was comically referred to as "Tehrangeles." Picture the gorgeous architecture and deep ethnic flavor of Chinatown in any major U.S. city. Now change the writing so everything's written in Farsi rather than Han logograms.

Many a Persian Jew who fled Iran became a Shah of Sunset Boulevard. Since then, Iranian Jews in LA have carved out brilliant careers as lawyers, doctors, and engineers. Their ranks contain some of the shrewdest businesspeople on earth. They all send their kids to Beverly Hills High School while encouraging them to become dentists so they can open a chain, or business lawyers because everyone's in business and everyone needs a lawyer, or plastic surgeons because... well, for obvious reasons. Alternatively, kids are encouraged to get a civil engineering degree and go into real estate, since civil engineers have the perfect expertise to renovate and flip houses. For all these reasons and more, it's no wonder that Beverly Hills was the first American city to officially celebrate Iranian New Year.

To be clear, Dad was not among those wealthy Iranians who'd escaped Iran before the revolution and brought their wealth with them. Rather, Dad was a refugee with nothing to his name but his family and the clothes on his back. When he got there, he lived with Sima in Encino in the San Fernando Valley. And though he felt quite at home in this new community, Dad encountered work difficulties.

He learned that, to practice as a doctor, he first had to pass the United States Medical Licensing Exam. This was a huge problem because he didn't know enough English. And so, though he continued to study for the exam each night, he took a day job as a physician's assistant.

Working as a PA helped Dad tremendously when he applied for a green card. At that time, very few physicians' assistants were multilingual. Whereas Dad spoke Farsi, Turkish, Kurdish, and some Hebrew. Working as a PA without a green card paid so little he couldn't afford an apartment on his own. But Sima and Saeed said he could stay at their house as long as he needed to get on his feet.

Every night after work, he came home to his empty room, where his only company was the two silk rugs made in Tabriz, one for me and one for Ramin. The same two rugs that survived the war and were sent to his brothers after selling the house before the war broke out. The rugs that had made it all the way to America. Now, taking the place of his actual children, the rugs were with him, waiting it seemed for their namesakes to arrive.

Meanwhile, back in Bat Yam, my mother had again found a job working as a microbiologist in a clinic. She was basically a single mom, working hard to not only provide for us kids but to prepare us for when our own visas cleared and we'd fly out to be with our father.

Since I wasn't around much back then and Mom always worked, it fell to Ramin to care for Romina. His natural family inclination made him the perfect person for this job. Each morning, he'd tie up Romina's hair in a ponytail and take her to school. After school, he would cook for her and help her with her homework—all while attending to his own chores, his own schoolwork, his own interests.

Ramin's grades were good enough that he too got accepted at Boyar. But he refused the invitation. "Someone has to stay here," he said. "To look out for Mom and Romina." As a result, Ramin, Romina, and my mother share a very special bond. They were there for each other while Dad and I were away. They propped each other up whenever one of them needed it and took care of each other as families should.

They never had any money and so, for one of my mother's birthdays, Ramin wanted to do something nice for her. He found a cake recipe, got all the ingredients together, mixed them, and put the batter in the oven. It came out syrupy and flat. Ramin went over his process again and again but he couldn't figure out what had gone wrong.

My mother came home and saw the big mess in the kitchen. She probably wondered, *Now what?* Instead, she cleared her throat and asked Ramin, "What are you doing?"

He was angry with himself. He shook his head.

"We're making you a cake!" Romina explained. "Happy birthday, Maman!"

"It's not baking," Ramin grumbled.

Setting her bag down and dropping her keys in a bowl, my mother went into the kitchen and checked Ramin's work. "Flour?" she said.

"I started with that."

"Eggs?"

"They're in there."

"Butter?"

He nodded.

"Baking soda?"

He stared at her. "What?"

My mother repeated, "Baking soda."

"Hang on, hang on, let me see. . ." Ramin picked the recipe up, reading it thoroughly, knitting his brows. Then he said, "Oh boy."

"Did it tell you to—"

"Yes."

"So maybe you—"

"Right. I get it. I missed it."

My mother just smiled. Opening her arms, she pulled Ramin and Romina into a hug. "Never mind," she told them. "It's the best cake anyone ever gave me."

When I was in tenth grade, I had an experience that cemented my cultural identity as a Jew. That year, I took part in an academic and cultural exchange with high school students from Germany. About seven German students came to Israel, where they were hosted by students like me. They stayed at our boarding school. We showed our German counterparts all around Jerusalem, Haifa, and Tel Aviv. They got a chance to see how Israelis lived, how we ate, and the unique culture that had taken root in the less than three decades since the country established itself. Toward the end of that year, the program switched and the Germans reciprocated. About seven Israeli students went to Germany. I was one of them.

It was my first time in Germany. The host family and the host school were exceptionally nice. They showed us around Munich, the parks, and the hiking trails. I remember enjoying the culture and the food. Everything was going really well until we toured the concentration camps.

Nothing affected me more than the traces of mechanized death I saw at Dachau. Train tracks fed right into the place. Each day, we were told, new freighters arrived, with more and more cargo. Read: Jews. These people were led through a camp divided into two main parts, the camp where the prisoners lived and the crematorium where many of them died. Along the way, they were worked until they broke and dropped. Some became the subjects of outrageous medical experiments. Every so often, a group would be marched to the center yard, where they were summarily executed.

I stood in the middle of all this, trying to process it, but I couldn't. I got this feeling like somebody had just balled up a fist and punched me hard in the gut. The next thing I knew, I was bent over, weeping so hard it surprised the

Israeli teachers who'd accompanied our party. My classmates were as stunned as I was. I tried but I couldn't stop crying.

It would take me a few years to figure out what had caused this reaction in me. Suffice it to say that seeing Dachau was a moment where many parts of me suddenly clicked into place to create a fuller, clearer picture of the world. At once, I understood the full arc of my family's journey. The history of my ancestors who settled in Kiev and had to flee from that place. My great-great-grandfather Avram's crossing of the Caucasus Mountains. His settling in Miandoab but also the way that, generations later, his ancestors fled to Tabriz.

I understood as never before my own family's life in Iran and our flight from that country. *It's all part of the same pattern*, I thought. *The fact that we Jews hadn't had a home for so many centuries, had been persecuted for generations on end.* The weight of the Jewish community's suffering and joys, losses and triumphs hit me like no other force I had ever experienced, and all in the space of a second or two. With it came a broader understanding of humanity.

I also felt terribly guilty and this part gets tricky. Part of me felt like I wasn't allowed to grieve for the Jews who had fallen at Dachau. How could I do such a thing? What right did I have? Khomeini's regime had been brutal but no one back in Iran, not even the Pasdaran, had ever sent mass quantities of Jews to die in concentration camps.

After my visit to Dachau, I had a difficult time socializing with my German hosts. The father of the family that hosted me was the principal of our counterpart school. Over dinner one evening, he revealed to me that his father had been an agent of the SS. He said he regretted the history of his family and the history of his country, that his father's generation had killed my father's generation. He said what an awful mistake this had been, then he rushed to assure me that that shouldn't stop us from being friends.

Looking back, I appreciate that he was trying to be forthright with me. It must have been an act of profound vulnerability for him to admit such a thing. What he was saying made perfectly logical sense. My brain understood it completely. My heart, however, did not. Despite how I tried—and believe me, I tried—I could not disassociate from what I had seen at Dachau. It had been an institution established for one reason only: Jewish extermination. After seeing the camp, I found that no apologies could suffice.

While I was in Germany, I found time to visit Uncle Jahangir once again. This was the occasion when I saw the scars on his back. It was 1986. He had married a German woman named Ursula, whose family disowned her because she had not only married a Jew, she'd converted to Judaism. As part of her conversion, she took a new name, Rachel.

Rachel adored my uncle. In fact, when Jahangir passed away a few years later, she insisted on staying in the same town so she could put a fresh flower on his grave every day. Her one daughter moved to Heidelberg while her other children moved to Mainz and Hamburg. Years later, she rekindled her relationship with her sisters but she never left Jahangir's side. Eventually, she was even buried beside him.

Arriving back in Israel, I appreciated the Holocaust Museum in Jerusalem more than ever. Perhaps especially so since the mid-80s saw an explosion of Holocaust deniers.

At this point, along with other students at Boyar, I volunteered to help elderly Holocaust survivors. Though they were individuals, they fit certain patterns. All were old men and women with numbers tattooed on their left forearms. Most were childless. Many had changed their names to hide or at very least mute their Jewish identity. All had lost family members. A disproportionate number, I noticed, were shut-ins who never left their apartment or room and hadn't formed any new social connections in almost forty years. They found it too difficult to reintegrate into a new community.

My colleagues and I would bring food to them. Many, we found, were existing on rudimentary diets of cottage cheese, eggs, and bread. We made sure they got the medicines they needed. Then, as part of our volunteerism, we sat and listened to their stories.

This last part was done under an initiative to capture the oral histories of those who'd survived the Nazi campaign of Jewish extermination. To give voices to those who'd been voiceless and make sure humanity remembered how deeply inhumane it can be. I recall this was delicate work. We would prompt our new friends with questions like "Where were you during the war? What happened to your family? How is it you came to be here?"

The more questions I asked, the more stories I heard, the more I discovered eerie similarities between the survivors' tales and my own family history. Each story I heard highlighted a different aspect of my own. But again, I felt the gut punch of Dachau ball up its fingers and slam them into my gizzard. The only saving grace to this mission was the new insight I received.

I was a Jew. That identity meant more to me than ever. But now I could see something else, a detail that somehow I'd missed before. I realized I wasn't alone and never would be. There were others who'd lived through their own fires, far worse and more destructive than my own, and if they had found the courage to live, what right did I have not to honor them by doing the same?

The following year, the German exchange students came back to Israel. They did so on their own this time, not as part of the formal exchange program. I'd become friendly with two of them, Andreas and Brigette, who were due to stay for a month. But I found that, emotionally, I was still dealing with all that I'd learned. I want to be clear: this has nothing to do with their behavior or intentions. My wounds, I now must admit, were simply too raw for me to pretend that everything was okay. Rather than take them on tours around Israel, I gave them a map and wished them well on their own. Then I buried myself in my schoolwork, of which I had plenty.

It wasn't until years later that I was able to use the medicine of logic against my acute emotional inflammation. Eventually, I realized that people like Brigette and Andreas might be the best friends I could make because they challenged me to rise above my pain and embrace life in daring new ways. This is the way the healing process works, I've found. The disease is sometimes the cure. Every patient is different and all of us operate on our own timetables.

Money was tight when I was a student and so I took work wherever I could. I would do anything that paid. The first job I got was cleaning toilets. I didn't like that so much. Very soon, I upgraded to a gardening job. I liked that better since I found it fun to tend things as they grew. I even pulled a short stint working in a morgue, washing bodies in fulfillment of Jewish traditions for handling the dead. But that work wore on me quickly and I left it to keep peace of mind.

After a school trip to the King David Tower Museum in the Old City of Jerusalem, I asked the staff there if they needed new guides. Luckily, they did. After a short training period, I began leading my own tours through the Old City of Jerusalem.

The Old City is divided into four areas: a quarter for Jews, a quarter for Muslims, one for Christians, and one for Armenians. Old City was probably built in 3000 BC but these regions weren't set up until the nineteenth century. My home base for the guided tours was the King David Tower Museum next to

Jaffa gate on the western side of Old City, the Jewish area, next to the Old City Market and the Arab's Quarter, where the Jewish and Muslim quarters abut one another. I loved steeping myself in the history of the place and communicating what I'd learned to tourists and religious seekers who came from all over the world. Very often, I worked with school groups who came from all across Israel. But of course, it being Jerusalem, there were frequently moments of strife.

One day in 1987, while in twelfth grade, I was on duty leading a tour when a blue and white Citroën four-door roared past me, not ten meters away. I remember catching a glimpse of the men packed inside the car. At first blush, they didn't look any different from any other men driving a car on that street. I watched the men on the passenger side pull out Kalashnikov machine guns, which they stuck out the window and started firing indiscriminately.

I dove for the children who were with me, grabbed as many as I could, and dragged them down to the pavement, screaming at them to lie flat on the ground. The fury of so many chattering rifles was deafening. I say "so many rifles" because all at once the Israeli Border Police and some soldiers who usually gathered in front of Jaffa gate rushed to the street and returned fire immediately. The air overhead seemed to hiss and sizzle with flying rounds. The entire exchange lasted less than a minute but felt quite a bit longer. There were shouts. There were screams. The children were terrified. So was I.

When the smoke finally cleared, I looked up and saw what was left of the Citroën. Glass shards painted with blood were spread on the blacktop all around us. The car had hit a bollard and stopped. Its metal doors were pockmarked from bullets. A dead man drooped out the passenger-side window, his gun still hanging from a sling around his neck, while the driver sat like a mannequin, staring ahead through the spider-webbed windshield. This was nothing children should see. Telling them to turn their heads, I herded them into the museum while police arrived and a news van came to a stop by the curb.

As it happened, back in Bat Yam, my mother was watching TV and she saw me. One of the news crew's video cameras must have captured me in the background when they were filming. She was scared but also outraged. She called the principal of my high school to complain. "Why is my son not at school?!" she demanded. "What on earth are you thinking, letting him go to such a dangerous area of the city?!"

To this day, I wonder what the principal thought of such questions. This was an era before cell phones so it was natural that my mother wouldn't know much about what I was doing. But: *Dangerous area of the city? Of course, it's dangerous. This is Israel. We live with certain tensions here, in case you haven't noticed. What do you want me to do about that? Run for office? Make peace with the Palestinian Arabs?*

On some level, my mom understood how absurd her complaint was. She understood well the environment we lived in. Years later, in July 1989, I was no longer in school having graduated the previous summer. She called me up after the red Number 405 bus from Tel Aviv to Jerusalem—the bus I had ridden countless times to visit my family or return to Jerusalem—was targeted by an Islamic Jihad suicide attack that killed sixteen civilians and wounded twenty-seven others.

"Farzin," she told me. "You have to be careful!"

"I'm as careful as anyone can be, Mom," I said.

The unspoken truth in my comment was something we both understood. No matter how careful you are, how smart you are, how prepared you may be, life—especially where our family was concerned—seems to throw its monkey wrenches at you for its own purposes and pleasure. Knowing this, the best anyone could ever do is roll with the punches, spot opportunities, and try to make the most of them.

Stating this outright came as a kind of setback for my mother. She'd never wanted us to come to Israel. Like my father, she preferred that we go directly to the U.S. so her kids could avoid such obligations as compulsory military service plus the constant fear of terrorist attacks and war. But this simply hadn't happened. Not yet.

"Just keep an eye out, Farzin," Mom said. "Always be aware of your surroundings. You never know when things will happen."

I told her I would. What else could I say?

By this point, my father had been gone for over four years. Living in Los Angeles, he'd worked tirelessly with the American immigration system so the rest of us could join him. Now, like a magic wand being waved or a long-shut gate swinging open, he called to say that our immigration visas were coming through. Mom emigrated first with Ramin and Romina. I was the last to go because, as the oldest son, I was able to take care of myself while everyone else went overseas. But truth be told, I had deep reservations on the subject.

It was 1990. I was nearly twenty years old and considered myself an Israeli. Why shouldn't I? Israel had welcomed us after our escape from a deadly revolution. I'd spent seven very formative years of my life there. Within three months of arriving to the country, I'd been bar mitzvahed, before I could even speak Hebrew. Many times, I'd gone to the Western Wall and spoken the Shema Yisrael. It occurred to me that, to the rest of my family, Israel had been an extended stopover on the way to the U.S. Not to me. Despite a few ups and downs, I'd fallen in love with the country. I struggled with the notion of leaving it.

Israel wasn't just a Jewish nation providing a home for all Jews everywhere, it was my home. My personal home. Uncle Elyahu had been like a father to me. His children, my cousins, were brothers. They had cared for me and protected me like I was their own. They were family, and family's not something you easily leave.

But then I thought of everything my parents had sacrificed to get us out of Iran to what we hoped would be a more prosperous, safe, and fulfilling life. My father hadn't gone to the States so he could abandon being a doctor to work as a physician's assistant. He hadn't worked as hard as he had to lose everything for nothing. He'd done this for his children. For our well-being, our prospects, our future. He'd done it to diminish the likelihood that one of us would one day wear a uniform, carry a gun, and die in a war.

So now I had this dilemma. Who did I owe my allegiances to? My immediate family or my extended family? To Israel or America? To the ancestral land of the Jews or the land of the free and the home of the brave? To the present I'd created through my actions or the future I might create if I chose to start all over again? To the vision I had of myself or to my family's vision of me?

Looking back, this was a very hard time for me. The fear that I might betray the beautiful country that took my family in and gave us a home was profound. But this is the nature of choice. If a choice is ever worth anything, it must be measured by what one will lose as much as how much one will potentially gain.

In the end, I chose to join my family in the United States.

CHAPTER FIFTEEN

TEHRANGELES

Los Angeles and Boston | *1990–1998*

AT THIS POINT, ELIANA cuts in. "This is the part I really want to hear about," she says. "How you came to America and everything you did once you got here."

Addie nods. "Pappy, from what you're saying, you were. . . I don't know. . . conflicted. When you got here. Is that about right?"

I glance at Kelly, who shrugs like, *What can I say? We raised bright kids.*

Slowly, carefully choosing my words, I say, "Yes, I think that's a good way to say it. It's always difficult for an immigrant to adapt to a new culture."

"But you *did* adapt," Liam says. "I mean, you're here. *We're* here. So it worked!"

"It did," I say. "But it sure wasn't easy."

"What happened?" he says.

So I tell them.

I'll never forget my arrival at Los Angeles International. Once again, I had nothing but the clothes on my back plus an old Israeli military duffel bag stuffed with some keepsakes and $5,000, which I'd managed to scrape together by working odd jobs. I remember feeling deeply insecure. My anxiety had nothing to do with money or where my life was going or anything like that. It was more personal, related to my identity. Once again, I was ready to build a new life but I felt a bit confused about that essential question: *Who am I?*

Am I Raymond now? I wondered. *Am I Farzin? Am I Persian or Israeli? Or am I American now? Who will I fit in with here? Or, more importantly, who will fit in with me?*

In some ways my worries were all for naught. I was welcomed by half my extended family who'd already moved to LA. Both my dad's and mom's brothers and sisters turned out to meet me. It seemed like everyone was thriving in their new home. They were all nostalgic for the old days in Iran but they were also excited to make their new beginning in America.

I had difficulties adjusting. In the back of my mind, I kept expecting the Pasdaran to show up and haul Dad to detention. Or that an improvised explosive device might go off in a crowded town square, as happened so often in Jerusalem. No question about it, the U.S. was the safest place I'd ever been. As best I could tell, none of our neighbors were spying on us and reporting our activities to the local committee office. No one I met had had their home leveled in an air strike or razed as part of a ground assault while removing settlers. The likelihood that my family and I would again have to flee with nothing but the clothes on our backs felt low. What a radical shift this was.

The more I looked around, the more I started to like California. The weather was fine, the people were mostly laid-back, and the city was grand. There was something for everyone. I began to meet people from a wide variety of backgrounds and cultures. I liked being close to the Pacific Ocean and drove there often to look at the waves and watch the sun setting deep in the west.

I began to appreciate all the sacrifices my parents had made to get us there. Tired of the low pay he was getting as a physician's assistant, my father and his brother started a jewelry business with their brother-in-law, Saeed. Saeed had also been a doctor back in Iran. He had also given up his practice due to problems with medical licensing. Dad had no interest whatsoever in jewelry. Neither he nor Saeed had more than two or three ounces of business acumen between them. But they were Persians who spoke excellent Farsi. In downtown LA—"Tehrangeles"—a man could go further with a lot less. Their connections within the Persian and Israeli communities of downtown Los Angeles paved the way for that business to flourish. Any opportunities they missed out on due to their underpowered business skills, they made up for by having integrity. People trusted my father and Saeed. They recommended their business to friends who all insisted on calling them "doctor" out of respect.

My mother faced similar challenges. Her lack of English and lack of credentials relegated her to working within the Persian community but she too found a niche. Having worked as a phlebotomist for so many years in various medical labs, she was excellent at handling needles. She figured the best way to parlay such skills was to train as a cosmetic technician specializing in permanent makeup applications and hair removal via electrolysis. Being naturally personable, she grew her business quickly. Dozens of clients returned to her over and over. And Mom has always been smart with money. She saved portions of every paycheck she earned with an eye toward earning her real estate license. That didn't turn out as planned.

The problem, again, was her English. It just wasn't facile enough to communicate trust in the highly selective, fast-paced real estate sector. Once she understood this, Mom gave up that plan and settled instead on pooling her funds with other family members to invest in real estate. She handled each transaction herself. My father, recognizing that she was the better business person, simply supplied her some funds from out of the modest sums he made.

The first years after my arrival, we were all living in the tiny apartment Dad had rented near Sima and Saeed's condo in Encino on the corner of White Oak and Ventura Boulevards. Our living circumstances were challenging at best. Once again, our whole family was packed together like smelts in a can. However, by letting Mom work her magic, collecting a little bit more from every check, my parents at last put down a deposit on a house they could call their own.

Ramin and Romina were still just kids when I first arrived in LA. Too young to work, they focused on school and perfecting their English. I, on the other hand, was old enough to contribute. And so, at my father's insistence, I bought a car.

"Farzin, this is LA," Dad told me in Farsi. "You can't take a bus in LA to get from place to place."

"And you sure can't walk," my mother added. "Walking gets treated like witchcraft here. People think you're evil for walking."

"Exactly," my father agreed. "So you must have a car."

I researched the situation and found a used car I thought looked sturdy enough. It cost $1,500. But Dad shook his head. "Don't get a used car. That's begging for trouble. You never know where a used car has been or what's wrong with it. Used cars conk out on you at the worst possible moments. No, you need a new car."

"How am I going to buy a new car?" I said. "I only have five thousand bucks!"

You know what they say. Ask, and you shall receive. In 1990, the only new car you could buy for so little money was the basic model Korean-made Hyundai Excel. I'm not defaming that company. In recent years, it's come a long way. However, back then, the Hyundai Excel was basically a glorified, gas-powered, box-framed golf cart whose cheap plastic interior, crank-down windows, and lack of power steering—power anything, for that matter—made it the vehicle of choice for people of limited means. The Hyundai I bought was white, which made me think of a blank page on which I could write whatever I wanted.

"I hope you're ready for a great adventure," I told my car the first time I filled it at a gas station. "Because you and I have places to go."

The Blank Page didn't appear to have heard. It sat silently, waiting while I dug in my pocket for the spare change I'd scraped together to pay for three gallons of regular unleaded. The guy who accepted these funds was also an immigrant—Pakistani or Indian, I thought. He made no comment when I dropped my coins in his palm. I got the feeling that he understood my circumstances perfectly.

"Okay?" I said.

The guy nodded back. "Okay."

This is how one communicates when you basically speak no English. And that, I knew, was my next major project.

I'd arrived in the U.S. speaking excellent sixth-grade Farsi, good Hebrew, plus a smattering of Turkish, Arabic, and other languages that were all mostly useless in this new country. But no English. This did not bode well for me getting a job. Hoping to get on track both educationally and vocationally, I signed myself up for English classes at a nearby community college called Pierce, due west of Encino down the Ventura Freeway in Woodland Hills. I also signed up for a typing class, thinking I could perhaps get a job doing secretarial work. Quickly, however, I learned that a) by and large, young women were getting hired as secretaries over Persian dudes, and b) it's hard to type up a proper business letter when you barely understand what the letter is saying. Once I understood this, I gave up trying to be a secretary. I began driving the Blank Page all over the San Fernando Valley searching for other work opportunities.

I tried to get work as a gardener but that industry was dominated by Mexicans who had no use for a Persian/Israeli kid who spoke barely any English and no Spanish whatsoever. That led me to try dishwashing, which made sense on paper at least. The San Fernando Valley was chock-full of eating and drinking establishments from upscale dinner venues to funky, down-and-out coffee joints. What I soon learned about dishwashing, however, is that it's hard work that pays very little. Also, the Mexican contingent practically owned that particular sector, too.

At one point, a friend in the Persian community told me that I had the chutzpah to work as a waiter. "It's really great money," he said. "I know a woman who works as a waitress. She hustles her butt off but she's smart and friendly like you. She rakes in excellent tips."

"It can't be that different than leading tours through Old Jerusalem," I said. "And I probably wouldn't get shot at as much."

My friend shrugged and said, "Maybe. Maybe not. I mean, this is LA."

I applied to several restaurants but the feedback I got said my English was still too unfinished. Waiters who did well, I was told, were native speakers who could easily parlay with customers. They could tell a restaurant's bartenders things like "No, really, give me a big boy pour" and "You call that a shot? That's more like an eyedropper. Give me more whiskey, please, or I'm not tipping you out tonight."

With doors closing all around me, I started looking for jobs a bit closer to home. Our apartment was located on a main strip where there were dozens of steady businesses. *Surely one of them will hire me*, I thought.

No.

I applied for the position of salesperson at an electronics store. The manager spoke to me all of three minutes before he decided that I didn't know anything about electronics and couldn't say as much in English. So I applied at a record shop. Same thing. And a shop that sold clothing. Yup. Same thing.

Next, I applied at a small grocery store/pharmacy called Thrifty Payless, which was a couple of blocks away from my family's apartment. The manager looked at my application for what felt like an insultingly long time before setting the clipboard down and making a point of not making eye contact. "What kind of a job were you thinking of getting?" she asked.

"Cashier," I said. I tried telling her how good I was at calculus and physics but wasn't sure if she understood. She asked me a few more questions, all of which I felt were designed to illuminate my command of the English language—or lack thereof. After which she told me to come back the following day. I had a job. I would start in the stockroom. I was thrilled.

My very first day on the job, I got one of the strongest lessons I've ever received about the importance of understanding American culture. I was in the stockroom, learning the ropes from three colleagues, each of whom was African-American, none of whom seemed to have any idea what to make of me. The man with seniority assigned me to tally some boxes of sanitary napkins a vendor had just delivered.

"You got it, boy!" I said.

I remember the stockroom falling deathly quiet. In my defense, I had just come from Israel where the word *yeled*—boy—is a term of affection. I hadn't the slightest notion that things would be different in America.

Fortunately, this particular worker was kind. Pulling me aside—read: away from his stunned friends—he brought me into a corner and sized me up. "Listen," he said. "I know you're an FOB an' all, right?"

"FOB?" I said.

"Fresh Off the Boat." He kept looking me over and now he was shaking his head. "Listen, FOB. I'm gonna save your life today, feel me? Here in America, see, white folks don't call black folks 'boy' unless they want to get popped."

"Popped?"

"Shot in the face, like. Or maybe the groin." He tapped the inseam of his pants and I cringed. "'Stead of 'boy,' you go, 'Hey, man!' or 'Whas' up?' Something like that. Keep it cool. You always got to keep cool now, feel me?"

"Yessir. Thank you," I said.

The man winced. "Nope. Let's do none of that neither. You don't call me 'sir'—"

"How about 'buddy'?" This was a term I'd heard white people using a lot with each other.

My new teacher shook his head. "Definitely not that. Not *sir*, not *buddy*, not *homie*, and never the N-word. You gonna hear black people calling each other that but that ain't for you, you get what I'm saying? Not unless you want to get dead."

"So. . . please to. . . what should I call you?" I said.

"Don't call me anything. Or, like, see. . . if it turns out you absolutely *got* to use something, use my name, but don't overdo it. Like, twice a day should be fine. More than that and you're probably pushing it."

"Great!" I had pulled out a paper and ballpoint pen and was taking notes. "So. . . please to tell me. . . what is your name?" I fumbled my paper and pen as I stuck out my hand. "My name is Ray!"

My new colleague stared at my hand like it was radioactive. When at last, I reeled it back in, he told me his name was Julius. Like the orange drink, he said. After which he appeared to be pondering something. "You ready for lesson number two, Ray?"

I told him I was.

Julius nodded. "Fine, then. Gonna teach you how to make money."

"But we're making money right now!" I said, very proud. "We have *jobs*!"

Again Julius looked at me like I was from another planet. Then he led me back to his two friends and spoke to them quietly for a moment in jargon I couldn't understand. After which, they showed me how to stack boxes of digital watches off in a corner behind some garbage bins toward the very back of the store.

"Why are we doing this?" I asked.

"Watch and learn," Julius said.

An hour later, the manager went off-shift and a new manager came to take over. During this interval, which kept everyone occupied with paperwork, Julius met some men who knocked on the back door of Thrifty Payless. Again, everyone spoke in low tones using that jargon which, to me, was utterly foreign. The newcomers accepted the boxes of digital watches in exchange for a Ziploc gallon freezer bag full of much smaller bags, which they passed to Julius. Then, very quickly, the newcomers left.

"What was that all about?" I asked Julius.

My new teacher grinned at me. "That was what we call bartering, FOB. Now then, you ready for lesson number three? Someday—someday soon, it turns out—you might get blamed for something you didn't do. But you don't say nothing about anything you saw or might have had something to do with. Feel me?"

I said that I did. I was naïve but I wasn't stupid. The very next day, I went to the manager and quit.

"What's the problem?" she asked me. "I thought you needed a job."

"I do," I said. And I did. But the more I thought about things, the job I really wanted wouldn't come with a criminal record. I had no choice. I had to keep looking.

All along, it had been my dream to study at the University of California, Los

Angeles. It was a great school with an international reputation and very afford-able if you were a California resident who qualified for in-state tuition. While in Israel, I had read books by Carlos Castaneda. His first three titles—*The Teachings of Don Juan: A Yaqui Way of Knowledge*, *A Separate Reality*, and *Journey to Ixtlan*—were written while he was an anthropology student at UCLA. So to me, it was the most famous school in America. But there was a problem.

While my SAT Math score was basically perfect, my Verbal grade, despite all my hard work at Pierce Community College, was only 350—about as low as the test measures. This made me ineligible to apply to UCLA. I began to deeply regret that the U.S. has no system like Israel's Ulpan where I could learn to speak like a native.

An acquaintance recommended that I start taking classes at Santa Monica College. My plan was to work hard at SMC, learn English, then transfer to UCLA by the end of the year. But things got hard right away. First, the college put me through a standard language placement test where again I scored really low. The administration stipulated that I start taking classes in English as a Second Language and College English. The full course of that would take about two years before I could reapply at UCLA, assuming everything went perfectly.

English, I discovered, is not an easy language to learn, particularly when you come at it from a base of Farsi and Hebrew, which have markedly different syntaxes. *No wonder my parents are having so much difficulty with the language,* I thought. There was also the fact that my teacher, Mrs. Castillo, didn't like me right from the start. She returned one of my first essays slathered in red ink and marked with a very low grade. This was especially bad because she had already told me I wasn't cutting the work and would have to take a more basic course that would further delay my plans.

Immediately, I rewrote the essay and gave it back to her the next class. She looked at it like I was holding a live snake. "What's this?" she said.

"My essay."

"I'm not changing your grade."

"I know," I said. "But could you read it, please, and see if I've learned anything from your comments?"

She shook her head at me, chuckling. "Ray, you're very interesting." This, I soon figured out, was her nice way of saying, "Ray, you are a real pain in the ass."

"Please!" I said. "I want to stay in your class." When she hesitated, I said,

"Look, Mrs. Castillo. If you're willing to read my essays, I'm willing to write them. And rewrite them."

If memory serves, I rewrote that paper four times. Mrs. Castillo never changed my grade but she let me stay in her class on condition that I double my homework assignments and write an essay for her every week, which I did. To make a long story short, Mrs. Castillo and I formed a partnership. I ended up taking all her classes and finished my ESL work by the end of that year. Every immigrant has a hero that gave him or her a chance. To me, Mrs. Castillo will always be one of my heroes.

Learning English wasn't the only challenge I faced. While taking a full slate of classes at college, I worked between forty and fifty hours a week doing various jobs in and around Santa Monica. I wasn't picky about what I did. I couldn't afford to be. The work I took was catch-as-catch-can. And since Santa Monica was twenty miles away from my parents' home, where I stayed (a journey that often took ninety minutes or more due to LA traffic), I woke up every day at 5:30 a.m. and sometimes didn't get home until two the next morning. At which point, after a couple hours' sleep, I'd do it all over again. And again. And again.

One of my favorite jobs was working as a patient transporter at St. Jude's Hospital on the corner of 20th Street and Santa Monica Boulevard. I basically rolled patients through the hallways on wheelchairs and gurneys. I didn't need to be all that proficient in English and the hours were perfectly flexible. I worked most nights after classes or sometimes I took the Saturday-Sunday shifts that no one else seemed to want. Maybe the biggest perk was that I got to see a lot of celebrities. Sometimes I handled them personally. I met Liz Taylor, Michael Jackson, and Ronald Reagan this way. That had certainly never happened back in Khorramshahr!

Like a lot of young immigrants, I was always looking for new and better gigs. One time, I met a Persian friend who worked as a male model. I thought he was lying when he told me how much money he made but he said no, he was telling the truth. All he'd done was get some pictures taken. On the back of these pictures, he'd listed his name, his physical measurements, and his phone number. The casting agents did the rest, he said.

"You should do it," he said. "Why not give it a shot?"

I got pictures taken and sent one to every casting director in the city but I never got a single call for work as a model. Not one. Another Persian friend laughed when I told him this. "Ray!" he said. "Uhm. . . seriously? What were you expecting? Have you looked at yourself in the mirror? That's a crazy competitive business. Casting directors must get ten thousand pictures every time they need to fill one job. But I have an idea. Come work with me. There's great tip money in it."

"What do you do?" I asked.

Just like that, I was introduced to the world of valet parking in glitzy Los Angeles. The job was amazingly interesting for a twenty-one-year-old kid. And my friend had been right. I made excellent tips. I also got to drive some really nice expensive cars, which, before that, I had only seen in the movies. Since there was no such thing as GPS back then, I had to buy a book of maps that allowed me to navigate LA. It was a small price to pay for a job that helped me move closer to my financial goals. At that point, my primary financial goal was keeping my head above water.

As my English got better, I followed in my mother's footsteps and got a job working as a technician at a UCLA research lab. This struck me as especially providential. More than anything else in the world, I wanted to study at UCLA. After shelling out funds for training, I got certified as an emergency medical technician and began riding in ambulances all over Santa Monica. This was my first real taste of being a hands-on healer, a Johnny-on-the-spot dispenser of vital first aid, and I loved it.

After only one year at Santa Monica College, I got a scholarship to UCLA. To me, this was two blessings in one. First, I was finally able to study at UCLA; I would earn my undergraduate degree there. Second, it took a great deal of the financial burden I'd been carrying off my shoulders. Studying at the college or university of your choice is always a great gift. Studying at the college or university of your choice for free, or very close to it, is an even greater gift.

I was still working hard, studying full-time while working multiple jobs, and sleeping, on average, five hours a night. But I had direction now. I was focused. For the first time, I realized I was on the path I'd always wanted to walk. And I realized that I would do anything to see that path through.

Ramin also went to UCLA but he chose a different trajectory. Building on his identification as an Iranian Jew, he founded Sigma Pi Beta, also known as the Persian Social Athletic Club (PSAC). It was established in 1993 as the first and only Persian fraternity in the United States, and probably the world. PSAC gave Ramin and his fraternity brothers a sense of identity and camaraderie that still exists today, some thirty-five years later.

It was good to see Ramin in his element, studying hard and working all angles but also embracing our new culture. He's always been more gifted than I am when dealing with people. Many times, I let him introduce me to new friends, thinking that no one could do the job better than my charismatic brother.

We were still as close as ever and we still fought, as brothers do. But the way we fought had changed. When we were kids eating Kit Kat bars under the blanket tent we had made in our room, every altercation ended in a wrestling match. Whoever won the match won the argument. I always won, of course. I was older and bigger. Later, when we were in college, we got in an argument. I pushed Ramin but he was so much bigger now, he didn't move but half an inch. He was like a rock. And when he pushed back, I moved several feet.

Realizing I had to change our old rules, and fast, I said, "Okay, look. We're in America now so we can't use physical force. We have to solve problems with words."

Ramin chuckled. He knew what I was doing. He also knew that he'd won because he's always been better at logic than me. "Sure, Ray," he said. "Whatever you like."

That was the last time we fought.

Ramin isn't very religious, though I would call him fairly traditional. His grades were so good, he could have studied practically anywhere, the same way he could have gone to the Boyar school in Israel. He chose to attend medical school at the University of San Diego mostly for the same reason he didn't attend Boyar. He wanted to stay close to family—to look after Mom, Dad, and Romina. His roommate at USD was another Iranian Jew, whose family has since become close with ours. Both families could not have been more ecstatic that their sons would have such a good friend while studying ninety miles away from home.

Ramin eventually did his cardiology fellowship in Seattle. For a while, he dated a woman with whom he grew close. Together, they traveled and explored the Pacific Northwest. She was willing to convert to Judaism and move to California with him once his fellowship ended. But Ramin decided he could not commit to a life with her. They had too many differences in their upbringings and life expectations.

A couple of years later he came to the same conclusion with a nice Iranian Jewish woman he was dating. One time, they went out for dinner at a sushi place. Ramin ordered the *unagi*—freshwater eel. When it arrived, the girl looked down at the plate, then up at Ramin in disgust. "Are you going to eat that?"

Ramin nodded. "That's why I ordered it. I love *unagi*."

"But it's not kosher."

"That's true."

"Okay." She took a deep breath and sat up straight. "I guess we can let that slide before we get married."

Ramin just smiled and ate his meal. Finished, he asked for the check and paid it, got up, drove this woman back to her home, and never saw her again.

"But why?" I asked him later. "I thought you two were hitting it off. She's Jewish, she's from a good Persian family, she seemed perfect. Mom would have loved her. What went wrong?"

"I draw the line at *unagi*," he said.

By this point, my mother's mother, Maman Bozorg, also had become a fixture in Tehrangeles. She lived with her daughters, who moved her from place to place each month until, finally, they got her a room in an assisted living facility on Melrose. Each weekend, my parents sent me out to get her in the Blank Page; I would pick up Maman Bozorg and bring her back to our place for Shabbat dinner. I always went a bit early to pay her a visit and see if she needed anything before we left. Many times, we sat out on her balcony, watching the traffic carve past under the golden beams of the Pacific sunset. Again and again, I heard her tell the tale about how, many decades ago, she and all the other Jewish women in Tehran flooded the synagogues and defeated the Nazis with their prayers.

"That's what did it," she told me. "The praying."

"Right," I said. "That's clearly what did it."

"God heard us!" she said proudly.

"Well, of course He did," I said.

"He really *did*!"

I looked at her. "Maman Bozorg," I said. "If God doesn't listen to you, I doubt very much he would listen to anyone."

One time, she was upset when I went to visit her.

"Maman Bozorg, what's wrong?" I asked.

"Just yesterday, I was sitting. Right here." She waved one spindly arm at a chair on the balcony. "I was having my tea in that chair and then I leaned over. I looked down there, at the street." She stiffened. "I saw two women kissing each other!"

I laughed. "Maman Bozorg, that's not so odd here. This is America."

She made the sign of *hamsa*, Arabic for "five," a gesture like a clawed hand intended to ward off evil spirits. "That's not the end of the story!" she snapped. "They stopped kissing and turned around and I saw they weren't women. They had *beards*! They were *men* with long hair."

Suffice it to say that she never really adapted to certain elements of Western culture.

A little while later, I walked her to the elevator and out through the lobby, to the Blank Page, which sat in the parking lot. The drive to my parents' place took about thirty minutes. That time, however, I noticed how quietly she sat in the passenger seat. The way she tilted her head up and looked at the nighttime sky as the streetlamps strobed past us on Santa Monica Boulevard.

"What are you looking at, Maman Bozorg?" I asked.

She was quiet a while. Then she said, "I miss my home. My house back in Iran."

I said nothing to that. There was nothing to say.

"I miss the sky," she went on. "It was so full of stars."

"Maman Bozorg, this is Los Angeles. All the stars are here," I joked.

She wasn't amused. "You know what I mean." Again, we drove in silence. Then, out of nowhere, she said. "Do you know why there are no stars in the sky here, Farzin?"

"Why, Maman Bozorg?"

"Because none of the people here fear God. They are all *kafar*."

Kafar means "unbeliever" in Farsi.

I drove in silence. The car windows were open and Maman Bozorg was gazing out at the sky. I wanted to tell her that everyone believes in something. That most people are basically good, or that's what I've always assumed. That I liked the people here in the U.S. They might not be like us but I thought they were good and that we could be friends. But instead, I just let her be and enjoyed the Persian music I'd dialed the radio to.

"Do you like the music, Maman Bozorg?"

That time it was her turn to say nothing.

We arrived at the house, where everyone was all smiles and hugs. They threw their arms out wide, squealing with delight while chattering in Farsi. That's how the older folks wanted it, just like home. But I saw a problem with that.

Like Maman Bozorg, my parents weren't adapting to life in America. Why should they bother? They had everything they needed—family, old friends, new friends, all of them Persian. It felt like everyone they'd ever known back in Iran now lived just a few blocks away. My mother even reconnected with old college friends she hadn't seen in decades.

The city's Persian community clung to the old ways. People watched TV shows dubbed in Farsi and shopped at Persian grocery stores. They bought cars, insurance products, and real estate from Persian professionals. Their neighborhood even had a Persian Yellow Pages. Perhaps most powerfully, everyone shared a deep nostalgia for a once-grand country that no longer existed.

In some sense, these crutches were all necessary and well deserved. We were part of a diaspora that had fought hard to get where we were. Why shouldn't we live as we pleased? But I noticed my parents used English less and less. They never got truly proficient in the language, and what little they learned was already starting to atrophy. They confined their business and social interactions to other Persians. And both had developed odd habits. My father was now very prone to reading newspapers written in Farsi and shaking his head, like everything going on in the world was amazingly stupid. My mother became a hoarder. She never threw anything out. Her kitchen cabinets were stuffed with plastic grocery bags.

"Someday we will need them!" she told me.

"For what?" I said. "Mom, you've got enough plastic here to kill every fish in the ocean if you dumped it into the water."

"We will need them, you will see!" she insisted.

I opened the door to a closet but stepped back quickly in case everything stuffed inside should tumble out and bury me alive. "What about this?" I said, pointing to the wall of books, shoeboxes, tennis racquets, old VCRs, loose clothing, and tchotchkes bought at garage sales. "I suppose we need all of this, too? Is that what you're saying?"

"Farzin!" she would shrill at me. "One never knows, so one must be careful!"

It was then—only then—that I started to see that each of us deals with our experiences in different ways. My father had chosen to scoff at the world while my mother, against all odds, was preparing for the next great catastrophe. Her response to years of deprivation was to collect everything. I, on the other hand, collected nothing. At that point in my life, I could count on two hands the number of objects I owned.

Ah, well, I thought. *At least my parents are happy. Thank God for that.*

They had never felt truly at home in Israel. Los Angeles was a different matter altogether. To them, LA was like heaven, a place where the weather was always gorgeous and they were safe, surrounded by people they loved. I realized then that my parents would never leave. Their wanderings had finally ceased. But I could not say the same.

Where is my home? I wondered. *Where does Ray feel at home? Or Farzin?*

I still hadn't quite figured out who I was and, on some deep level, this disturbed me.

Distracting myself from such thoughts, I knuckled down on my schoolwork. By taking extra courses, I was able to graduate UCLA in two years while working forty-hour weeks, mostly over the weekends, to make a living. But it didn't work. The distraction, I mean. Because I always found school and work less taxing than establishing an identity in my new American home.

I never knew who to hang out with. Over and over, I asked myself, *Who do I resonate the most with?* I met a lot of Iranians at UCLA. Our numbers were disproportionate there compared to other colleges and universities around the country. And yet I didn't quite fit with their vibe.

Maybe it's all that time I spent in Israel, I thought.

So I tried hanging out with Israelis but, back then, there weren't many of them at UCLA. Also, the ones I ended up meeting had a different set of experiences than I did. In many ways, they seemed as foreign to me as someone who'd grown up in China, Senegal, or a remote island in the Pacific. So who did that leave?

I met a few Arabs at UCLA. Many of them became good friends. Funny how, back in Iran and in Israel, we couldn't get along. But now, in a foreign land, we all gravitated to each other like long-lost cousins among strangers. Why not?

We had similar cultures, similar temperaments. I made a couple of Mexican friends who eventually came to grips with the fact that—my appearance to the contrary—I was not Mexican. But because I had so many Mexican friends, my first Christmas in America took place at the house of a Mexican friend's grandmother. Neither of us spoke a word of the other one's languages. Didn't matter. I genuinely loved her cooking and ended up eating a lot of it. There isn't a grandmother alive who doesn't adore someone who appreciates her food.

Of course, I was meeting Americans, too. Most were second and third generation. I remember being fascinated by this notion. How comfortable these students seemed in their role as Americans while their parents or grandparents had been. . . well, just like me.

How quickly time changes fate, I reflected. *Right now, I am filling the immigrant's role in the grand American plan. If the people who came before me could make a success of themselves, so can I.*

This notion inspired me to work very hard and make the biggest contribution to society I could. It still does to this day.

At UCLA, I struggled to pick a major. I saw this decision as tantamount to choosing the future course of my life and, at that point, I wasn't quite sure which direction I wanted my life to take. I thought about being a doctor, of course. I knew that my mother had wanted to study medicine. I guess part of me thought I could realize her unfulfilled wish by becoming one myself. I also knew that Mirza Agha had given me the name Raymond as a way of predestining me toward medicine. But I'd also grown up watching Dad work constantly at his practice. He rarely came home, he'd been a doctor in a war, and had now become a shell of himself. I didn't want to be like that, to live that way. I wanted to be different.

For a while, I considered being an engineer, a philosopher, mathematician. . . anything that would keep me away from studying medicine. Many immigrants gravitate toward the sciences because math is an international language. It doesn't rely on your grasp of English or cultural phenomena. Math exists in its own perfect universe that anyone can access once they study the way math works. To feed my natural inclinations, I took courses in math, physical chemistry, philosophy, and quantum physics. I did really well in those studies.

But the turning point came when I took an immunology class. I needed to take a biology course to graduate. Immunology was the closest biology class that seemed mathematical.

While studying immunology, I was reading a book about chaos theory. I remember being stunned by the butterfly effect, first proposed by the American meteorologist and mathematician Edward Norton Lorenz. In its briefest form, the butterfly effect proposes that major weather events, such as tornadoes, can be influenced by incredibly minor events, such as a butterfly flapping its wings many weeks earlier at some distant location. This phenomenon proposes a quantum interrelationship between apparently disparate elements and it can be extrapolated, meaning the butterfly effect isn't just about weather; it pertains to just about anything that happens in life.

The more I considered this, the more I began to question the empiricism of biology. Traditional theory states that logic dictates chemical interactions, which therefore dictate the states we call health and disease. But immunology wasn't so simple as that. The science of immunology seemed more or less susceptible to the butterfly effect, meaning it was inherently unpredictable. *How interesting*, I thought, *that—once you pop the hood on life and stare at its engine—nobody knows how it works.* And this was the tip of the iceberg.

The more I studied, the more I discovered that the human brain is ruled by similarly mysterious processes. Basically, no one I spoke to seemed certain of how the brain works. This struck me as odd since every human being carries a brain inside their skull. Our brains help produce what we call our "minds," which in turn produce our individual experiences of the world. *If we all have a brain and a spinal column*, I thought, *how can it be that no one has yet cracked the code on how these systems operate?*

Intrigued by this question, I spent a year working under Dr. Eli Sercarz. I also worked closely with Vipin Kumar, who was then in his postdoc work, studying the pathology of multiple sclerosis. MS is an autoimmune disease that prompts the human body to attack and disrupt its own nervous system. In particular, the body attacks its own myelin sheathing, the layer of fatty proteins we exude to insulate nerve axons so they can link more securely and convey information at greater speeds. The more I performed this work, the more I began to consider medical school. It occurred to me that I wouldn't have to be the kind of doctor my father had been, I could specialize in something that really interested me—immunology, neurology, or something equally fascinating. In the end, this all helped me select a major in molecular biology.

I suppose it helped that, during this period, I was also studying the Talmud, the primary source of Jewish theology and Jewish law. The approach I took was scholarly. I was less interested in the Talmud as a religious treatise, more as a wisdom book full of fascinating insights into ancient Judaic legalities. By this point in my life, I felt I was no longer a religious person in the classical sense. Even so, I maintained a strong cultural connection to Judaism. Famously, the Talmud states that a person who saves one life thereby saves the entire world. Everything I had lived through up to that point had borne this out. My parents had saved the lives of my brother, my sister, and me. Because of their sacrifices, we had been given our own worlds to live and develop however we chose.

Toward the end of my studies at UCLA, I applied to medical school. In my essay, I wrote about what I considered the interrelationship between Talmudic theory, chaos theory, and the fields of immunology and neurology. "This is where I want to make my contribution," I wrote. "By helping one patient, I can—in a very real sense—help the entire world. As the Talmud teaches, 'He who saves a single life, saves the world entire.'"

I got accepted at Harvard and the University of California, San Francisco. At that point, the schools were ranked number one and five in the country. UCSF offered an excellent scholarship package. In essence, they offered to pay me to get my medical degree from one of the best programs in the world. Excited, I gave my parents the news.

My mother frowned. "Which school are you leaning toward?"

"UCSF!" I said.

She shook her head. "Farzin, if you go to any village in any country all over the world, everyone's heard of Harvard Medical School. This other one. . . what do you call it again? UC-what? Nobody's ever heard of it."

"But they'll pay me," I said.

"If it's a matter of money, we can help you," Dad said. "Tell those other schools 'no thank you.' Tell Harvard you'll attend. Sign their contract. Then bring us the numbers you need."

I did as he told me and signed with Harvard, whose costs at that time, including living expenses, came to about $250,000. My parents took one look at the bill and shrugged. "This is too much," they said. "We can't help you."

"But you told me you would!"

"Farzin!" my father said. "What are you worried about? You'll be fine. You'll be a doctor from Harvard Medical School. You'll make tons of money. This bill will be nothing."

It only later occurred to me that my dad had done to me what his own family did to him when they lost his savings. Twice.

Ah, well, I thought. *At least the path forward for me is now clear. From Khorramshahr to Tehran, Tehran to Tel Aviv, Tel Aviv to Jerusalem, Jerusalem to Los Angeles, Los Angeles to Boston. . .*

I got to Boston by driving the Blank Page clear across country. Again, I had only one bag to my name. And though I was excited to begin this new experience, I discovered right away that Harvard only exacerbated my identity crisis.

My orientation for medical school remains memorable. My incoming class had about 160 students divided into five different societies, which the orientation committee split into smaller groups of six. Everyone took seats in a circle, facing each other. The facilitator asked us to introduce ourselves one at a time.

The first person in my group said, "Hi, my name is Geoff McDonough. I'm from Canada."

The second person said, "Hi, I'm Jeff Sullivan. I'm from Buffalo."

The third person said, "Hi, my name is Kelly Sullivan. I'm from. . ."

And so it went with the fourth and fifth classmates. Everyone had an Irish name.

Eventually, it was my turn. "Hi," I said. "I'm Ray Tabibiazar. Despite my name, I am Irish, too. So please accept me into your contingency."

Everyone had a good laugh over that, which was good; it dispelled any awkwardness, at least temporarily. But it didn't change certain facts. At UCLA, the student body had been so diverse. At least some of those students had been immigrants or the children of immigrants. A good number of them were attending school under less than hospitable circumstances, either politically or economically. But at Harvard Medical School, the majority of incoming students were well off and not so diverse. I met very few immigrants and almost no one with whom I could relate.

In this, I have some culpability. I had only been in America three years. During that time, I was either studying or working odd jobs to support myself.

I had very little time to socialize and learn the new culture. I was still working hard on my English and feeling more comfortable than ever using the language. But I still hadn't really adapted to American culture. My classmates listened to music I didn't understand, from artists like Aerosmith, Guns N' Roses, and Counting Crows. After class, they went out for beers and, occasionally, cigars. At the bars, they watched TV and rooted for teams playing sports I struggled to comprehend. Some liked to play golf while others enjoyed lifting weights. Neither activity appealed to me. Group outings were at Fenway Park to watch baseball, a game I'd never beheld before arriving in the U.S.

"Why are the guys in the gray jerseys climbing out of those bunkers?" I'd ask.

"It's the end of the inning," my friends would explain.

"The what?"

"The inning. The inning. You see? The gray team was just up at bat but they got three outs, so now it's the other team's turn up at bat."

"Aha," I said. "Yes, now I see. But where are the wickets?"

This question drew a number of curious looks, after which, very gently, I was taught the basic differences between baseball and cricket. My grasp of American football turned out to be even more precarious. In Israel, we'd played basketball and soccer. In Boston, I discovered that, while billions of people worldwide watch FIFA religiously, most Americans seemed barely aware of it. On top of all this, everyone I spoke to thought *Seinfeld* was the funniest TV show they had ever seen. It was all anyone seemed to be talking about.

"That George Costanza character is so funny!" people would roar. "He's so neurotic! I know someone just like him!"

I understood the clinical definition of neurosis but I just couldn't understand why everyone found it so funny. And what was wrong with the Kramer character? Had he been dropped on his head too many times as a child? He just didn't make sense to me.

Very quickly, I learned that I was one of the first Persian Jew UCLA grads to make it to Harvard Medical School. There was another guy who fit that profile named Siavash. We ended up hanging out together or with other Persian Jews who were students at Tufts and Boston University. It felt good to speak Farsi with someone and to share our experiences of UCLA. We went to movies together and talked about friends from "home." We drank a lot of tea, which we sweetened with nuggets of candied sugar in the classic Iranian style. Once in a while, we even mustered ourselves to hang out with our new American friends.

But try as we did—and we tried really hard—it became increasingly clear that our two groups shared too few cultural reference points to make a go of it.

Once you put the weather aside, my overall experience in Boston was wonderful. This was mostly due to my classmates. The Class of '97 was an excellent group of smart people committed to making big contributions with their talents. By and large, I was humbled and excited to find that most of my classmates were equal parts brilliant and super nice. Despite our cultural differences, we shared a passion for medical practice and studies that bonded us to this day. But I still felt like an outsider in their presence.

I'd arrived in America thinking the name my grandfather, Mirza Agha, had given me—Raymond—would finally open some doors. But it was undeniably true that Ray Tabibiazar looked different from everyone else he worked with. He certainly sounded different. I dreamed of a social landscape where I would no longer have to be Persian or Jewish, coming or going, an insider or an outsider. Somewhere I could just be me and I could prosper. But the more introspective I got about all this, the more I had to admit that I just didn't fit in.

Rather than let myself get distracted by this, I plowed ahead with my work. I angled my studies toward brain research. By that point, I was less interested in the philosophy behind consciousness, more enamored by its scientific underpinnings—how the subjective experience we tend to call consciousness is actually an expression of more traceable and predictable chemical, synaptic, and atomic phenomena. I felt that if I could understand these foundations, I could shed light on age-old problems, like why we dream, the origins of human creativity, and the curious phenomenon we now call neuroplasticity.

Thanks to my growing interest in understanding how the brain is wired, I decided to take a year off from Harvard and focus on neuroscience research at Boston Children's Hospital. My work exposed me to some of the best neurosurgeons in the world. It was during this period that I gravitated toward brain surgery.

In my last year of medical school, I did several months' worth of surgical and neurosurgical rotation. I even applied to a residency in Neurosurgery but I ultimately withdrew from it. While I loved the clinical practice of neurosurgery and was enamored with the prestige of the role, I also knew that to be a great neurosurgeon required a level of dedication I might not possess. Neurosurgeons must prioritize their craft over everything else in life, including their families. At the time, I was eager to pursue this path. But I could already look down the road and see that an older version of me would regret having chosen such a rigorous career. So I let neurosurgery go.

CHAPTER SIXTEEN

THE HOLY MAN ON
THE MOUNTAIN

Nepal, Los Angeles, Stanford | 1998–2001

NEARLY THIRTY-FIVE YEARS AFTER my father finished his medical school, I finished my own. It was April 1998. Stanford had accepted me for residency in internal medicine so it looked like I was headed back west for the next few years, at least. It also seemed I had a couple more years to figure out a subspecialty since I'd decided against neurosurgery. I was now, as my father had been before me, an M.D.: Dr. Tabibiazar, the latest Doctor Fire. One year later, my brother, Ramin, would also join this small but distinguished club.

It felt good to have so many great opportunities ahead of me. If I had any reservations, it was the feeling that something was missing, that I carried an emptiness inside me, a void or a maelstrom, silently churning, whose origins were unknown to me and whose effect could be deeply unsettling. But search my soul as I did, I still couldn't pinpoint what this emptiness was.

Hoping to gain some perspective, I did what so many young people have done since the dawn of time when looking for answers. I planned a trip. Trekking had been a big part of life for young people in Israel. Almost every Israeli I knew had traveled after performing their national service. The most common destinations were South America, India, or Nepal. I liked rock climbing and mountaineering so the Himalayas and Everest Base Camp beckoned. They seemed like a natural fit. After all, I'd had my own experience trekking high altitudes as a twelve-year-old while crossing the mountains from Iran to Turkey.

Stuffing some clothes in a backpack, I took off in late April 1998 with only $2,000 to cover two months of travel expenses. I used frequent flyer miles to buy myself a round-trip ticket to Katmandu. I brought minimal hiking gear but I figured I wouldn't need much in that department. Scaling Mount Everest required a $65,000 permit, so that was out of the question. I resolved to be satisfied if I climbed up to Everest Base Camp and some of the many surrounding peaks. The budget I worked out allowed me to spend about $20 a day. This might sound absurdly low but back then it was possible to live off such paltry sums while trekking Nepal with a sleeping bag and a tent. It's one of the other reasons I chose that trip. Nepal was one of the few destinations I could afford.

Whoever said travel is good for the soul knew the truth of the human spirit. I discovered that traveling solo can be particularly therapeutic. You learn to rely on yourself while meeting new people and encountering strange situations. While doing so, a part of you is always there, standing apart from yourself, observing how you handle things and reforming your sense of self. It's a powerful process, and one I highly recommend to anyone caught in the feedback loop of a personal doldrum.

On the first leg of my journey, I hiked the majestic Annapurna range that runs through north-central Nepal. If you've never believed in God, I urge you to watch the sun rise and set over the Annapurnas. It can change your mind about so many things. I know it changed mine. The terrain I hiked recalled to me the high mountainous desert my family and I had crossed while sneaking into Turkey more than a decade before. At night, the sky overhead loomed infinite black. Nestled deep in that void, shining brightly, even cheerfully, was the multitude of stars mankind has mostly forgotten are there.

I met a lot of trekkers while hiking the Khumbu Glacier east of Everest Base Camp. It was normal and pleasant to make new friends who came from all parts of the globe. At one point, I met a group that was heading back west. "You're American?" one of them said.

Persian? Israeli? American? By this point, I'd learned that full explanations just made introductions more complicated. I nodded. "Uh-huh."

"We just met another American at the camp up ahead of you. Look him up when you get there, maybe you'd like to say hi."

Intrigued, I pushed onward, arriving at camp around 8:00 p.m. The world had turned pitch black by then. The Himalayas at night are as dark as the bottom of the ocean. Once I got settled, I asked around for the American I'd heard was here. We met at the local tavern, which was really a plywood shack with a fire pit inside and food that wasn't worth writing about.

"Hi." This guy stuck out his hand. "Luis Alvarez."

We shook on it. "Where you are from?" I said.

He laughed. "Well, see, that's a hard one. My family and I are immigrants. We're political exiles from Cuba who settled in Los Angeles."

I smiled at him, relieved. "Me too. I mean, the hard one part. My family and I are exiles from Iran but we also settled in LA. I only left there for medical school."

Luis looked at me. "Me too."

"What did you specialize in?"

"Internal medicine."

"Get out of here! Me too! I'm starting my residency at Stanford and—"

"Are you kidding? Me too!"

We were astonished by all the connections we shared. The only disparity was that Luis's trek was ending while mine had just begun. Excited, we exchanged information. I promised to get in touch with Luis when I got back home to the States and we parted, already good friends.

I was in pretty good physical shape back then so I found the Annapurna range easy, even though I carried fifty-five pounds of equipment and food. The hike became more challenging once I turned my sights toward Everest's South Base Camp on the Nepalese side of the mountain. At that point, the journey became like the fabled uphill climb. Each step you make takes you into higher elevations. One moment, you're at 14,000 feet, then 16,000, then 17,000. The higher you climb, the slower you go. You have to stop often so your body can adjust to the lack of oxygen. Experienced hikers are a lot like deep-sea divers. They know the danger of changing pressures. They also know that you disrespect it at your own peril.

I remember being aghast at how tired I suddenly found myself. The equipment I was hauling seemed to double, then triple in weight. It probably didn't help matters much that, for days and days at a time, my diet consisted of *dal bhat*, a staple food local to India, Pakistan, and Nepal. Essentially red lentils mixed with rice, *dal bhat* is a nutritious meal that provides complex carbohydrates and proteins commensurate with those found in meat. But it gets really old really fast when you're eating *dal bhat*, day in and day out.

Now and then, I would spring for a Snickers bar, which the way stations sold infrequently. One time I even splurged on a yak steak, which, to this day, I associate closely with heaven.

Not long after that, I reached the temple.

About fifteen kilometers southeast of Everest, at the confluence of two rivers in the gorgeous Khumbu Valley, the Tengboche monastery huddles under banks of gauzy white clouds. From the hill on which it sits, you can take in the landscape in any direction. To call it breathtaking would be absurd. Imagine Mount Everest, Mount Lhoste, the long ridge called Tawache, Mount Nuptse, and dozens more features revealing themselves in splendor. Of all the places I've visited, few are as magical as this one.

The altitude at Tengboche is more than 12,500 feet above sea level. I had read it made a good pit stop for trekkers seeking to acclimate themselves to the altitude before moving on. I had also read that the monastery was the home of Ngawang Tenzin Jangpo Rinpoche, an abbot of the "red hat" school of Buddhism. Up until then, I'd no interest in Buddhism. Some instinct compelled me to stop at the monastery. I asked if I could meet the Rinpoche but was told he was not available.

Oh, well. No matter, I thought.

I settled in for what I assumed would be an uneventful couple of days. I was just getting used to the quiet when, later that evening, just before sunset, a helicopter landed in the middle of the trail. Its doors opened and a TV crew from Norway hopped out. The crew went into a little hut where travelers could buy a cup of hot tea and a plate of *dal bhat*. I was headed that way anyway so I went in and introduced myself.

The crew's director said his name was Peter Nomi. "What are you doing up here?" Peter asked.

I told him I was a Western doctor taking time off to explore. That I was Jewish and from Iran. How I'd gone to Israel and later America. Peter listened to everything, asking questions now and then to clarify his understanding. I could tell he was a seasoned storyteller and liked him immediately.

"So that's me," I finally said. "What about you? What are you doing here?"

Peter said that he and his crew had come to interview the Rinpoche.

"I tried to get in to see him," I said. "But his calendar was full. I guess I see why now. He'll be talking to you."

Peter shrugged and said, "You still want to meet him? Let me see what I can do."

I met Peter the next day. Smiling, he told me he'd arranged a private meeting between me and the abbot.

"You're kidding," I said.

His grin got bigger. "Not at all."

Later that afternoon, I went to the quiet monastery, where I was ushered into an even quieter back room. Ngawang Tenzin Jangpo turned out to be a small brown man sitting utterly still in the lotus position. His eyes were closed. He was barely breathing. Not knowing what else I should do, I sat before him in the same position.

Okay, I thought. *What's the protocol here? Do I speak? Do I wait for the Rinpoche to speak? If I speak first, what should I say?*

Fifteen or twenty minutes went by in total silence. The Rinpoche never moved. Finally, a monk came in and stood by the door. Taking that as my cue, I got up and bowed and said a quiet "Thank you" before leaving. On my way out, I felt like a fool.

Really? I thought. *You've come all this way to sit at the feet of one of the world's holiest people and you couldn't think of a single thing to ask him? Ridiculous.*

I found Peter back in the tea hut. "How did it go?" he asked.

"Not so well."

"Well, what did you talk about?"

"Nothing."

"Nothing?"

"We didn't say anything. Not one word."

Peter just looked at me. "Let me get this straight. You said nothing the whole time? And he said nothing?"

"Exactly."

He shook his head. "Well, he's a monk." As if that explained things.

"I was just nervous," I said. "But yeah. I guess he's a monk."

The next day, Peter and his crew took off in their helicopter. It was my time to go, as well. I started packing my things and had nearly finished when the monk who'd ushered me in to see the Rinpoche found me.

"Hello," I said.

The monk bowed. I bowed back.

"Please." The monk's English was broken but usable. "Please, the Rinpoche wants to see you again."

I thought he was kidding but the monk just stood there waiting. "Okay," I finally said. "I'll. . . uh. . . go see him? Is now good? When were you—"

The monk shook his head. "The Rinpoche says he will come to you."

The monk left and came back about an hour later with more monks and the Rinpoche. Outside my hostel, they set up two ordinary plastic chairs that faced one of the mountain ranges. The view was spectacular. The Rinpoche took a seat in one of the chairs and I sat beside him. For a long time, we looked at the mountains and said nothing.

This time, you have to say something, I thought. But what question do you ask one of the highest Buddhist monks there is?

Finally, I broke the silence. "Can you tell me, please. What is the meaning of life?"

Oh great. Yeah, that's just perfect, Ray. You just asked the corniest, most obvious question ever. Idiot!

But the Rinpoche didn't seem to find my question odd. "The meaning of life is to be happy," he said.

"Okay," I said. "So how do you get to be happy?"

"Through enlightenment."

"And how do you become enlightened?"

"This happens when you are content with what you have now," the Rinpoche said. "When you feel that this is enough, you are free."

I mulled this over and thought it made sense. It was so simple, how could I have missed it? I nodded and said, "Thank you."

For the next ten minutes, we lapsed into silence. Then, once again, the helper monk stepped forward in what was clearly a signal our time was up. I bowed to the Rinpoche and said thank you again, then watched as the holy man and his procession walked back toward the monastery. But they stopped.

The Rinpoche seemed to be saying something to the helper monk. The helper monk nodded and walked back toward me. Again, we bowed to each other.

"Is something wrong?" I asked.

"The Rinpoche asked me to tell you that he enjoyed speaking with you. He believes you have a pure heart. He believes you will do great things helping people through your medicine."

I had no idea how to respond. So I bowed and the monk bowed back.

"Please tell the Rinpoche it was my honor to meet him."

The monk smiled like I'd said the perfect thing. Then he turned and walked back to the Rinpoche and together they went back to the monastery.

Over the next few days, I walked closer and closer to Everest Base Camp. The going was hard now. The air had begun to feel heavy. Each footstep seemed to take three times the effort it had just days before.

Soon I arrived at a small town called Namche Bazar, where I hired a Sherpa to help bear my things and help me navigate the rest of the way. Together, we traveled east in a line toward Everest Base Camp. In a little town called Lobuche, we heard reports that a massive storm was coming. I was told, if I knew what was good for me, I'd get myself out of the region before the storm hit.

"I can't do that," I said. "I've made it this close to Base Camp. I've got to keep going."

Almost immediately after I said that, my Sherpa succumbed to altitude sickness. This was bizarre. It never happens. Sherpas are world renowned for their hardiness but mine couldn't get up, let alone walk or carry my pack.

"No problem," I said. "You stay here. Watch my stuff. I'll go forward to Base Camp. Be back in a couple of days."

"No." He tried to get up but fell back. "I am a Sherpa. This is my job. You must let me do it."

"Your job is to handle my equipment," I said. "My equipment is staying right here. I'll take a small pack. Be back in a couple of days."

I left him there in Lobuche with my things and went on. The only food I had with me was a Snickers bar but that was no problem, I thought. *Dal bhat* could be bought plentifully in those parts. But I'd also been forewarned that the trek to the Base Camp and back could be arduous. There were no stores to buy food at the camp itself and no one there would be inclined to share food with strangers. In another little wayside hut like the one where I'd run into Peter, I loaded up on *dal bhat*. I met some new friends and exchanged stories with them.

"Wait," one of them said. "You're Iranian? Did you know?"

"Know what?" I said.

"The Iranian Mountaineering Team is here. They've never been to Everest before and they're about to make their first summit. Do you want to meet them?"

Of course, I did!

A few hours later, I was in Base Camp. After taking some pictures, I began looking for the Iranian team's tent. I ended up meeting their entire organization. They were surprised to meet an Iranian in that part of the world. We became instant friends.

While talking, I learned that, as Muslims who couldn't eat non-halal meat, the team relied on deliveries of specialty food. Here again, luck was on my side. The previous day, a load of fresh supplies had been dropped off by helicopter. The team had an on-site cook who'd been hard at work preparing a feast, which I was invited to attend. They served *chelokabobi*, shish kabob, and lots of grilled vegetables, all of which were delicious. To this day, that might be the best meal I've ever eaten. Drinking Fanta was never as thirst quenching as the one I had at Everest Base Camp. I was also pleasantly surprised that they had *pofak namaki* with them, the Iranian equivalent of cheese doodles, a snack for schoolchildren. I hadn't eaten *pofak namaki* in more than a decade. I was surprised how nostalgic it made me.

The Iranians repeated that the oncoming storm was supposed to be awful. They filled my bag with provisions and said, "If you're going back to your camp, you had better go now." Their advice was both good and bad. Good because it acknowledged the oncoming weather. Bad because I heeded it. Alone, I started walking back to Lobuche, where my Sherpa was waiting.

Word to the wise. Never trek anywhere by yourself, especially when it's getting dark out and you're way up high on a glacier in Nepal. I was not careful. My foot slipped out from under me, then I went down, and then I was sliding, falling. I ended up stuck in a crevice that ran by the side of the road whose depth was twice my height.

Stuck like Dad would have been, I thought. If I had let go of him up in the mountains that time.

I had no idea what to do. The crampons strapped to my shoes weren't helping me find any purchase. It was dark out. The road was not frequently traveled. The storm was fast approaching. The possibility of someone finding me before I froze to death was slim.

It's all up to me, I thought.

Moving slowly, I tried digging steps in the ice but the ice was hard as stone and it took a long time for me to gain even minimal purchase. Hours passed. I worked inch over inch until, at long last, one of my hands slid over the lip of the chasm and found a hold. Shaking from fear and cold, my breath coming ragged, my heart pounding hard in my chest, I hauled myself back to the road, where I started berating myself for having done something so stupid. My self-flagellation didn't last long. I was thrilled to be alive. That emotion gained precedence after a while.

Before leaving Lobuche, I climbed Kala Patthar, the black peak that stands next to Everest and has no snow on it. Anyone can summit Kala Patthar. It requires no permit. Also, from a technical perspective, Kala Patthar is not a difficult climb. Once you hit the top, you get an excellent view of Everest's white-gray spike knifing up at the heavens, plus Everest Base Camp, like a tiny speckle below it.

I stood atop Kala Patthar, looking east, toward Bhutan, then west, past Nepal into India. Only then did it occur to me. I was on top of the world, both literally and metaphorically.

This is what I came for, I thought. *This view. This understanding. This feeling.*

Moving carefully so I wouldn't lose too much body heat, I unzipped my jacket and pulled out the Israeli flag I had brought with me from the States. Though there was no one around to see me, I waved the flag proudly.

Thank you, I thought. *Thank you for being my home when a home is what my family and I needed most.*

Once I got back to the States, I called Luis. We decided to room together at Stanford.

It was July 1998. We were both excited to start a new chapter of our lives but we knew it would be difficult. We were both set to intern at Stanford Hospital for one year after which we'd do two years of residency rotations in internal medicine at places like Stanford University Hospital, Santa Clara County Hospital, and the local Palo Alto veterans' hospital. On top of all that, I started moonlighting at a private clinic in the Bay Area plus a local private hospital. Palo Alto is one of the most expensive locales in the country. I needed the extra cash. Usually, I covered for doctors who called out of their shifts. It was good work. I learned a lot by repeatedly thrusting myself into situations where I had to think quickly and improvise.

Luis and I found that we shared the same values. We wanted to use our talents to give back to the broader community. Sometimes we traveled to Native American reservations in Arizona and Nevada, where we volunteered to work with underserved communities. Sometimes we traveled to South America to learn about non-Western medicines in places like Peru, Bolivia, Ecuador, and the Amazon.

It was only after our sixth or seventh trip that I realized the Rinpoche's words had come true. I was helping people through medicine. This gave me one of the greatest joys I have ever known.

CHAPTER SEVENTEEN

AN IMMIGRANT'S SECRET TO LIFE

Menlo Park, Portola Valley | 2001–2018

BY AND LARGE, IMMIGRANTS have no idea what will happen to them, but they're certain of three things. First, they trust themselves and their resourcefulness to figure things out as they go. Second, they are not afraid of failing. Rather, they are confident that, if they fail, they will simply try again and again until they succeed. Third, the immigrant knows that wherever they are now—no matter how challenging conditions might get—they're better off here, in their new home, than they were in the place they came from.

My father, having failed the medical tests a few times, was deeply embroiled in his jewelry business while my mother worked hard to keep our family's finances afloat.

In 2001, once we had finished our residencies, Luis became a kidney doctor while I accepted a cardiology fellowship at Stanford. Within the breadth of internal medicine, cardiology seemed like the closest surgical discipline to where I'd been heading. It was by far the most diverse specialty. As a cardiologist, I could see patients, use pharmacology, perform procedures, read radiological studies, and conduct a broad range of research. Luis and I knew we would both be knuckling down for another four years but that's how it is for young doctors. Seems like you're always knuckling down. I was still moonlighting to pay off Harvard Medical School. It would take me the full eight years to do that but long before I was finished, I saw it was worth it.

Little by little, more opportunities kept opening up for me, not only to practice medicine and see patients but to pursue interests beyond clinical practice. Between 2003 and 2005, I did clinical rotations while becoming board certified in internal medicine, imaging, and four related areas. I also conducted research with a great team at a fine laboratory. Our work kept getting awarded large grants, for which we were all very thankful.

After carefully studying the implications of this research, and working closely with a beloved professor, I co-founded a company in 2004. Our efforts were focused on developing drugs to treat vascular inflammation, which we believed was the root cause of heart disease. This was my official entree into the world of biotech and venture capital. With the same professor, I later co-founded another company that focused on diagnostics using inflammatory proteins that the vasculature secretes. These proteins, we discovered, can be used to identify patients at risk for near-term heart attacks.

In 2007, while still conducting research, still practicing medicine part-time, still moonlighting and volunteering at local hospitals, I joined a large venture capital firm in a role that's known as a venture partner. It was fortuitous timing. The Bay Area region was then a hotbed for VC firms. Still is. The partners at my firm were kind. They took me under their wings and taught me the business side of medicine. My role was to evaluate companies they were considering for investment from a scientific and clinical standpoint. Once I had reached my conclusion, I advised the firm on which companies showed the most potential to profit. But the most fulfilling role I had was learning how to create new companies based on innovative ideas that can make a real difference in medical practice.

I discovered rather quickly that my status as an immigrant prepared me well for entrepreneurship. Most immigrants feel they've been given a second chance by coming to America. Maybe their parents sacrificed everything to get them here or maybe they left their old country of their own volition and under their own steam. Either way, the immigrant feels poised to do something special. They also, by and large, possess certain personality traits that I find essential to successful entrepreneurship.

Both immigrants and entrepreneurs must feel comfortable with fear of the unknown. People who arrive in a new country might not speak the language or know the culture of their home. They might not have money. For certain they don't understand all the various gears that turn their new home's government, socio-economic, and political systems. So what? "No problem," the immigrant says. "I'll figure it out." At which point, they throw themselves into the challenge to see what impact they can make.

Yes, this involves a certain naïveté but I argue that's precisely why so many immigrants do well. Sophistication leads to stagnation. Without naïveté, a person might study a problem too much and not take the leap of faith required to lift a new goal off the ground. Paralysis by analysis is a luxury most immigrants cannot afford whereas a spirit of high adventure and a willingness to bet practically everything on a new campaign is what immigrants tend to excel at.

This is the outlook that fuels both immigrants and entrepreneurs. It's the zeal to ignore rationality, herd mentalities, and received wisdom while forging your own path forward. It's the ability to temporarily suspend disbelief long enough that the conditions once dreamed of become actualized. When the American West opened up back in the nineteenth century, people loaded their horse-drawn carts with everything they owned and hung painted signs from their tailgates that said, "California or Bust." They were stating a mindset that entrepreneurs and immigrants understand well. *This is our destination. We'll either make it or not. There is no in-between.*

For all these reasons and more, I view the immigrant mentality as perhaps the most American of all mindsets. Immigrants are resilient. They understand that it's not how many times you fail but how many times you rise from failure that matters. In many cases, they understand all too well how little there is to lose when you have already lost so much.

America and Israel are both countries built by immigrants. It makes me shake my head when I hear people in both nations railing against immigration. They say immigrants have no place here. Why? Because we often work harder than you? Because we're willing to do what others won't to succeed? Because we refuse to sit back on our laurels but rather insist on forging ahead? In the United States especially, it might be worth asking, "Who do you think built this country? Who created a vastly disproportionate amount of its innovation? Who risked everything so that the vast majority could live better lives?"

Consider the recent COVID-19 global pandemic. It rocked the entire world, grinding cultures and economies to a halt. Most industrialized countries weathered the storm and got back to normal or very close to it in under two years. Why? Biotech companies worked hard and fast to develop vaccines that would save many lives. Two companies in particular made critical contributions, Moderna and BioNTech. Both companies are led by immigrants.

BioNTech was founded by a Turkish immigrant now living in Germany with his wife and business partner, who is also an immigrant. Moderna's founder is an Armenian Lebanese whose family survived the Armenian genocide that took place during World War I. He was once quoted as saying, "One of the unfortunate advantages Armenians have had by having gone through a genocide and spread around the world is that we do have an experience of escaping and of immigrating and of constantly restarting." These are just two of the companies that prove the contributions immigrants make to bettering the world we live in.

An immigrant arrives in a new country knowing nothing about what the future will hold. In the same way, an entrepreneur starts every new project with no guarantees of success. Both will work hard. Perhaps one will sink while the other will swim. Maybe one will be broken and have to crawl home, defeated, while the other will take off and fly and it suddenly becomes clear that all their sacrifices were worth it.

In my experience, most people run from this level of uncertainty. It feels safer to them to walk the same road as the rest of the world. Ask these people why they prefer the safe path, they often say things like, "Oh, I could never go out on my own, I'm too scared of what might happen!" I have always found this reaction odd since, to me, the scariest thing imaginable is trading your prospects in for a locked routine. People who do this lead a life where they don't ever fly too low. But of course they also never fly high. Again, most people are comfortable making this trade-off. Immigrants and entrepreneurs are not. They must be willing to confront their fears. If they can't, their plans fall flat.

I once asked my father, "How did you and Mom deal with your fear?"

"My fear?" he said.

"You know what I mean. All through the revolution, the war, our escape. You must have been terrified."

Dad shrugged. "You'd have been a fool *not* to be terrified."

"Right. So how did you get through it?"

His answer surprised me. "What choice did we have? Fear is a big part of life. You can't let it fester. You have to move forward and live."

"So you're saying you conquered your fears by not paying attention to them?"

"I'm saying I *never* conquered my fears," he said. "In every situation I can remember, I chose the path I was least afraid of. To be honest, many times, I was more afraid of your mother than anything else. You know what a force of nature she is. She never felt fear that I ever saw. Not once. She was the brave one, not me."

I will always cheer for the immigrant story because, though its details may change, it is nonetheless my story. The story of my family.

Lest I forget to mention, there are some downsides to having an immigrant mentality. For instance, many immigrants don't like to be told what to do. This outlook that makes them formidable workers and entrepreneurs can make them lone wolves. Many aren't "team players." They don't go along to get along. Their attitude can boil down to "We've suffered to get here. Who the hell are you to tell me what I can and cannot do?"

This attitude often strikes natural-born Americans as arrogance. It isn't. It's the byproduct of laughing in the face of fear. When you start from nothing, it's hard to be afraid of risking everything. Of investing in yourself rather than a socially vetted hierarchy. It's the ability to look someone else in the eye—often a person in higher positions than you—and say, "No. I will not do that. I do not believe that's in my best interests. There are better uses for my talents and I will find them. Thank you. Good day."

Ultimately, being an immigrant and entrepreneur is about doing what you believe in. If more people did that, what a world this would be.

In 2001, during my cardiology fellowship, I met my future wife, Kelly. Like me, she was a clinical cardiology fellow at Stanford. Our cohort was not very large so everyone in it got to know each other pretty well. Though she was two years younger than me, Kelly was smarter, already ahead of me in training. She did her residency at Harvard and serendipitously became friends with some of my medical school colleagues. When she got to Stanford, they told her to look up their old friend Ray Tabibiazar.

Kelly and I didn't hit it off right away. She had a southern accent, which I found hard to understand. I felt certain she couldn't understand my accent either. But as we interacted more with each other at work, we got to know one another. We were both a bit surprised to learn that, despite our different upbringings, we shared a number of common interests plus similar views about life, community, and family.

In 2003, I realized that Kelly and I had what it takes to make a good life with each other. I thought she felt the same way but the more I considered a marriage proposal, the more I saw our religions as a problem. Kelly's family is devoutly Episcopalian and I, of course, was a Jew. The Tabibiazar family history testified that Jews who marry outside our religion suffer heartbreak and loss. Consider what happened to my uncles Mouis and Jahangir. They'd done well for themselves in so many ways but their marriage to goys had also brought about difficult family lives. And while they suffered certain losses, the rest of my family shook their heads. "We told them so!" they would say. Or: "If they'd only married a Jew, they'd have had the cultural support to get through situations X, Y, and Z!"

Still, I knew I loved Kelly and I felt certain that she loved me. Tentatively, I called my parents to sound them out on the idea of marrying a Christian. To my surprise, they accepted the notion, albeit with resignation.

"What are you asking *us* for?" Mom sighed. "Do whatever you want. Nasser, do you agree?"

On the other end of the line, my father was silent a moment. "Your mother is right," he finally said. "Be happy. That is the purpose of life, is it not?"

I remember hanging the phone up thinking that something had just gone terribly wrong with the universe. Either that or something had gone very right indeed and I was just too gobsmacked to understand it. Were my parents just happy I'd finally found someone? Or had the spirit of the Rinpoche swooped down from the Nepalese mountains and somehow worked its way into their hearts?

Maybe there's a third option, I thought. *Maybe my parents are adapting to American culture after all. Maybe they're able to see Kelly for who she really is, a family-loving and caring individual who holds similar values dear despite that she comes from a different religion.*

Whatever had happened, my dilemma wasn't yet solved. The rites of *khastegāri* aren't often practiced as part of American life. Still, I felt it was important to make a formal bid for Kelly's hand. Her father's name is Joe. I got his number and sat down to call him during a relatively free moment at the lab. Everyone I worked with knew what I was doing. They were all pulling for me.

"Go in there and do it!" one colleague said.

"We'll be waiting right here!" said another, pushing me into my office. "It'll just take a couple of minutes. Her dad will say yes and then we can celebrate!"

Of course, I was nervous. Looking back, I'd built up a negative mental paradigm about what I was about to do. Joe, I knew, was a smart man, educated, generous, and kind. *Still*, I thought, *what the hell will he think when this Persian Jew calls him up out of the blue and asks to marry his daughter? And not just a Persian Jew but—to use a more modern term—an Iranian Jew.*

I had already learned the hard way how many Americans carry a stigma against Iranians. This is mostly because they are clueless about the close and complex relationship between the two countries. *Will Joe assume I'm some kind of terrorist?* I wondered. *Will he think that I'll drag Kelly off to the Middle East and he'll never see her again or any children we might produce?*

For a while, I sat staring at the phone as these fears raced through my brain. But I knew my feelings for Kelly. I also had five or six eager faces pressing themselves to the windows of my office. Hands that kept flashing me thumbs-up signs. Taking a deep breath, I punched in Joe's number. Moments later, I heard myself say timidly, "Joe, I've called to ask your permission to marry Kelly."

There was a pause, then Joe said in his gravelly voice, "Why are you asking me? What does *she* say about it?"

"Well, I wanted to ask you first."

"But why?"

"Because you're her father."

"So?"

"Well, as her father, you have the right to—"

"No, I do not."

"But. . ."

"Look, Ray. This is America. Here the woman gets to choose."

"But I thought it important to ask your permission."

"Alright." He paused to consider this. "What if I say no?"

By this point, I was sweating. "You're saying no?"

"I'm asking a hypothetical question. *Suppose* I say no. Would you give up on her?"

"Of course not."

"Then why bother asking me in the first place?"

It had escaped me that Joe was a lawyer, and a damn good one.

For two hours, we went back and forth like this. My colleagues were waiting outside the whole time. Whenever I turned in my chair, I could tell by the looks on their faces, they felt that something was wrong. Maybe it was. At that point, I wasn't sure. I just stuck with the program while Joe kept drilling me over different lines of thought I'd unknowingly assumed, then gently instructing me on how to replace them with more Americanized ideals.

"So you're saying it's all up to her."

"That's right."

"But I think she'll say yes."

The poor man must have been rolling his eyes and shaking his head. "And so?" he finally said.

". . .I guess I'd better ask her."

"That's the spirit," Joe said. "Good luck, Ray. Thanks for calling. And congratulations."

We hung up.

I turned and saw everyone still peeking in at me. Waiting.

Wiping sweat off my forehead, I flashed them the thumbs-up sign. "I think we're good."

The lab erupted in cheers.

After we got engaged, Kelly and I thought it only right that our parents meet. We knew there would be obstacles, mostly related to communication. Mom and Dad's English was still very poor and their accents were thick. I would translate for them, of course, but this still begged the question: What venue is best suited for them to relax in?

Kelly and I settled on flying both couples in to meet us in Palo Alto. Having them sit down together for a quiet home-cooked meal seemed a bit too intense. We took them instead to a fun restaurant called Asia SF where the food is exquisite, the drinks are well poured, and the servers are all gorgeous women—except they're not women at all. They're female impersonators. Drag queens. I can tell you that, during that dinner, religion was the last thing on anyone's mind.

Joe and my dad didn't get it at first. Asia SF is known for its raucous shows. My dad in particular had no idea why these women kept plopping themselves in his lap and fondling his bald head. My mom got what was going on right away and she thought it was hilarious. She kept nudging my father, saying, "The *khanoom* is not a *khanoom*! You see?" Try as she did, and she tried very hard, she couldn't convince my father that the women doting on him weren't actual women. That was a very good night.

Apart from the hilarity of their performances, the drag queens kept conversation from venturing into uncomfortable territories . Questions like "So. . . how did you come to America?" or "How will you raise your kids both Jewish or Christian?" never came up, for which I was thankful. It would have been kind of a downer, I think, to describe the conditions we'd weathered in Iran during the revolution, how we got to Israel penniless, or how we'd arrived in the U.S. with almost as little. Far better to let a *khanoom* who was not a *khanoom* dance for us, telling jokes. It made such a remarkable spectacle, no one cared to discuss much else.

Kelly and I got married two years later in May 2005. It was a very happy occasion. I was thirty-five years old and Kelly was thirty-three. She'd always wanted to get married on a beach so we chose a spot beside the ocean in West Palm Beach, Florida. Our families were so scattered around the country, we thought a destination wedding seemed fair. Also, it was close enough to her parents' home in Chattanooga that her mom could come out and help Kelly with preparations as the day drew close.

About two hundred guests attended the ceremony. Since neither Kelly nor I wanted to convert from our birth religions, we decided to combine our faiths in a hybrid ceremony. A rabbi officiated alongside Kelly's childhood pastor. Kelly took the Hebrew name Kelilah. Before the ceremony, she and I signed a *ketubah*, the traditional Jewish wedding contract. Then, while the rabbi and pastor held hands, Kelly and I passed under a *chuppah* dripping with flowers. My family was gathered on the right side while Kelly's was on the left. There was a bit of dissonance here because we Persians make a lot of noise during weddings. My side of the family kept cheering like it was the Super Bowl while Kelly's relatives stayed more or less smiling, somber, and upright, except for her uncle who, at one point, lifted everyone's spirits with his wild rebel yell. "Yee Haw!"

With everyone watching, I stomped my foot on a piece of glass wrapped in a cloth. This ancient rite symbolizes, among other things, the destruction of the first Jewish temple as well as the old life Kelly and I had lived without one another. We said prayers and heard readings from both traditions. I remember looking at Kelly and seeing again, as if for the first time, how beautiful she is, her strength, her compassion, her drive—all the many things I admire. The cheer that went up when we kissed was like a trumpet call out of my past.

Now you have truly arrived, it seemed to be saying. *Despite everything you and your family have been through and all the trials you've weathered, you have reached happiness. Savor it. Share it. For this is what life, at its best, is about.*

When all was said and done, we got married three times. The first time was in Tennessee where we did sort of a pre-wedding with about two hundred guests attending. The second time was the official ceremony in Florida. The third was back in California where about four hundred people attended, a great many of them from the Persian community in Tehrangeles. It wasn't uncommon, this sort of multiple ceremony. My mother's mother, Sara—my Maman Bozorg—passed away a few months before my wedding. Twelve hundred people flooded the synagogue where we held her funeral. We had to hold three services in a row because we couldn't accommodate everyone.

As I said, community is deeply important to both Kelly's family and mine. We are now each other's people. Our friends are our families and our families are our lives, the reason we work as hard as we do and build in time to love one another. Here again, I think the Rinpoche was right. Happiness comes from enlightenment. And enlightenment comes from wanting what you have right now, in this moment. Everything else is just smoke in your mind.

After the wedding, Kelly and I moved into a house we'd bought across the street from Luis and his wife, in Menlo Park. I'm still thankful that Kelly had so many things to fill our house with—furniture, cookware, flatware. Despite having been in America fifteen years, I still had very few belongings, only the futon I had been sleeping on plus the car I had bought years before to replace the cantankerous but heroic Blank Page.

Two years after our marriage, Kelly and I started our family. Eliana was born in 2007, followed by Addison in 2009 and Liam in 2011. Our first two kids were born at roughly the same time that Luis and his wife, Winona, were starting their own family. Our kids were constantly running to and fro across the street to play with each other. It was a heavenly situation but as our family continued to grow, we saw that we needed a bigger place. In 2011, we moved about three miles south to Portola Valley, a little community nestled on the eastern slopes of the Santa Cruz Mountains overlooking San Francisco Bay. This was the right move since it gave us the space we needed plus a more quiet environment to enjoy when we weren't working, which wasn't that often.

Sometimes my parents would fly up to visit us. Whenever this happened, I'd talk to my father, whose simpler way of looking at the world grounded me in what I was actually doing amidst the madcap waves of my life and career.

One time, we were sitting on my back deck overlooking the hills rolling down to the Windy Hill Open Space Preserve. "How are things?" he asked me in Farsi.

"Not so bad." I waved a hand that was meant to encompass our house, which we all adored, the land around it, the broad blue sky overhead. Then I frowned. "It's just. . ."

"Yes?" He watched me closely.

"I guess, sometimes I don't really know who I am," I confessed. "Am I Farzin or am I Ray? Am I Persian, Israeli, or American? Am I a doctor or am I a businessman?"

He shrugged. "Does it have to be one or the other?"

I tried on a half-smile. "I don't know, Baba. I guess I wish things were simpler, that's all."

In his typical way, he fell silent again. When again he finally spoke, he said, "You're solving problems. That's all anyone ever does, you know."

We went to bed after that but I couldn't sleep. I stayed up a long time pondering what he'd said. *Is it true?* I wondered. *Is that all we're really doing on Earth, solving problems day in and day out, month after month and year after year?* It seemed too simple an explanation but the more I thought about it, the more I saw Dad was right.

When you're a doctor, patients come to you, ill. Very often you have no clue what's troubling them; that's the problem you have to solve, so you run some tests to diagnose what's ailing them. You treat what you think is the issue, then watch very closely to see if the treatment takes. If it doesn't, that's another problem you have to solve. Repeat, repeat. That's medicine in a nutshell.

The process is really no different than being an immigrant. When my family arrived in this country, we had no money, no prospects, and no foundation from which to start building a better life. That was the problem. We solved that by sticking together and making new friends. By helping each other while working as hard as we could. Was it any different when we fled Iran? Or that time my father got left at the hospital and had to walk, alone, through a demilitarized zone full of corpses and burning cars? Was it different when I was that toddler who hit his head on the metal steps of Dad's clinic and started foaming at the mouth? Or when my teacher took me to see a man get executed in the Korramshahr town square?

Not at all. Each of those instances was a problem begging an answer. And so we created one.

The more I thought this through, the more I realized my father was far wiser than I'd given him credit for. And I'd given him lots of credit.

The very next day, he astonished me again. We were out driving through our area when someone zoomed passed us in a bright red Ferrari. Offhandedly, I remarked, "Wouldn't that be nice?"

Dad was sitting across from me in the passenger seat. He lifted one eyebrow, encouraging me to say more.

"Look at that car, Baba. Didn't you see it?"

He'd seen it. He shrugged like, So what?

"It can go really fast," I said.

He glanced at my speedometer. "How much faster do we need to go?"

"It's really expensive, that car," I said. "I bet that guy lives in a great big house."

"You can have the biggest house in the world," he said. "But you only need one bed to sleep in each night."

These folksy answers of his were beginning to wear on me. I wanted more out of him. More validation. More affection, I guess. I posed a new question. "Look," I said. "I get that money isn't everything, any fool knows that. But it still can be useful, right? Think, Baba. If you'd had a little more money during the revolution, we could have used it to flee the country before everything turned crazy."

My father gave my comment serious consideration. "If we'd had more money, we'd have ended up like Habib Elghanian and plenty of other rich people," he finally said. "We'd be dead."

I conceded this point, with a caveat. "But some things would have been easier."

Dad shook his head. "We are where we are because of everything we have experienced, son. And not just the good things. The bad things also played a role in our coming to America. The way I see it, we are all blessed. Look at you. Kelly is a fine and beautiful wife. Your children are also fine and beautiful. You have a family that adores you. Isn't that what matters?"

I pushed back on this. The timing felt right. "Why don't you talk much about what happened to you in the war?"

"What is there to talk about?"

"Are you kidding? After everything you saw?"

He waved one hand as though he was brushing aside a mosquito. "There's no point festering over challenges life may give you."

"But I've always wondered," I said. "How could you possibly move on to a normal life after everything that happened?"

"What choice did I have?" He looked out the window. "Farzin, when you boil things down, what choice does anyone have? And anyway, what is a *normal life*? That term means nothing to me. Life just is, and wise people take life as it is—the good and the bad, the ups and downs, for better or worse. It's all the same thing."

I shook my head.

"What?" my father said.

"I wish you could just speak clearly for once."

My dad chuckled. "*Zendegi hamineh,*" he said. In Farsi: "Life is as it is."

Money had never meant anything to my father. Our safety and happiness were all he'd ever cared about; he knew that money can't buy those things. Only a passion and a commitment to family can. Somehow he was able to harness that passion and commitment, to move on and not fester on the past.

I began adopting this perspective in my own life and was soon astonished at how worthwhile it is.

CHAPTER EIGHTEEN

A NEW HOME

Chattanooga | 2018–present

IN 2018, KELLY'S MOM fell and broke her hip. We were worried about her, of course. So worried that we started looking for opportunities to be closer to her parents in Chattanooga. As often happens with big shifts like this, the entire world seemed to conspire to make things happen. Finding a house was less of a problem than we first suspected and Kelly found a job that paid more than what she was currently getting while also giving her a half day off each week. I confess I had reservations about leaving the West Coast. My own parents were getting older plus we loved our house in Portola Valley. But I also love Kelly's parents. I understood Kelly's desire to have our kids spend time with their grandparents. And at that point, my job had become very accommodating. We just had to make sure that the kids were on board.

We went to each of them separately, sounding them out on what we'd planned. Eliana was eleven at that point. Addie was nine and Liam was seven.

Eliana was very mature about it. "I have mixed feelings, Pappy," she told me. "I'll miss my friends but I look forward to making new friends. If we do this, I'll have friends in both places!" It was hard to argue with that kind of logic.

Addie's attitude was likewise impressive. "Well," she said. "I don't like moving so far from Baba and Fafa in LA. That will make me sad. But we'll be in Chattanooga so that means we'll be near JJ and Ish." These are the nicknames we use for Kelly's parents. "And being close to them makes me happy so I'm excited about that!"

Finally, Kelly and I spoke to Liam. He was the most excited of anyone.

"I love Chattanooga! Let's do this!" he said. "We must have a house with an elevator and a view of the river, like JJ and Ish. When are we going?" I hadn't expected such enthusiasm from him but I thought, *Don't look a gift horse in the mouth.*

A few days later, we picked Liam up from school. He rode in back while Kelly and I were up front. He got very quiet, which was unusual for him. Finally, I asked, "Liam, is everything okay?"

"Pappy," he said. "I've been thinking about the move."

"Yes?"

"I know when we move to Chattanooga, we're going to live in the house Mama got us."

"That's right."

"So what I'm confused about. . . where is Gibson going to live? And Spencer? And Riley?" Quickly, he rattled off a list of his ten closest friends. "Where will *they* live in Chattanooga?"

Kelly and I shot looks at each other. Then Kelly explained, "Liam, they're not coming with us. They're staying here."

The poor little guy started bawling. That's when we understood he hadn't had any real concept of what was happening.

"But what about the rock mining company?" he shouted.

He and his friends had started this company, digging for rocks in his friend's backyard. Liam was the CEO and one of his friends was the CFO. They paid their sisters to help them paint the rocks and then sold them in a local store. I was proud of him for that. Eventually, we brought him around to the idea of remote work. He and his friends could keep up the business by talking to each other over videoconferencing, if that's what they wanted to do. Liam gave the matter serious consideration. It calmed him down and just like that we were right back on track.

In the summer of 2018, we started our journey toward Chattanooga packed into our 2011 Toyota minivan. It was a fine trip that took us five or six days. We didn't make a beeline but stopped at many different places, making a party out of it. In Arizona, we stopped at Lake Havasu after which we went rafting in the Grand Canyon. From there, we continued to Santa Fe and showed the kids the precise spot where I'd proposed to their mother. Then we pushed on through Oklahoma and Arkansas, into Tennessee, stopping in Memphis first, then Nashville until, finally, we arrived in Chattanooga.

It was a great bonding experience but I was worried. Somewhere along the way, while I was driving and everyone snoozed in their seats, I began to have doubts. From Khorramshahr to Tehran. Tehran to Tel Aviv. Tel Aviv to Jerusalem. Then LA, Boston, San Francisco. . . hadn't I already moved enough? I was used to big cities. What was I going to do in Chattanooga? How many Persian Jews would I find there? How many synagogues are in Chattanooga?

What the hell am I doing? I wondered. *This is insane. I don't belong where we're going.*

I thought about the kids' enthusiasm for Chattanooga. Wasn't it the same sort of excitement that Ramin, Romina, and I had felt leaving Iran? I thought of the circumstances we'd fled. Weren't things better now? Weren't they different? We didn't have guns pointed at us, we had toll booths and highway rest stops brimming with hamburgers, milkshakes, and French fries. The kids weren't riding ghost horses, weren't in peril of plummeting to their deaths down a narrow mountain gorge. They had Wi-Fi. They were texting their friends, watching YouTube, playing games, and solving puzzles on their computers.

I was forty-eight years old as I made that drive across country. About the same age Dad had been when we fled Iran and he led us over the mountains. Would I want to be back in his shoes? Would I want to face the same trials he had? Would I want to arrive someplace where I didn't speak the language, had no money, no prospects, and had to abandon my livelihood?

No way.

Admit it, I thought. *Things are much better now, here in America. You have a wife and kids who adore you. You're successful in business. You have a house waiting for you and loved ones to fill it. Is there anything better than this?*

I told myself: *Ray, don't worry. You've got this. Home is where your family is. That's not a cliche, it's a law of life. So don't worry. Whatever happens next, you'll figure it out.*

So that's what we did.

In fact, in a very real way—now that I think about it—it's all that anyone ever does.

My parents' health changed almost the moment we got settled into our new home. In August 2019, my mom called my cell phone. "Farzin?" she said.

I was traveling at the time. My hands were filled with reports I'd printed out to read on the plane. I had the phone cranked between my ear and my shoulder and I was barely concentrating on her. "Yeah, Mom. Hi? How are you?" I said.

"I don't mean to worry you."

Which of course got me worried. "What is it?"

"It's your father. He's very depressed."

This was unusual. "Okay," I said. "Why is he depressed, Mom?"

"I don't know," she said.

"Well, can you describe this depression?"

"He's not eating or drinking much. He sleeps late in the morning and he's stopped doing his exercises."

Uh oh, I thought.

Ever since he'd been in the military, my father has woken up early each day, climbed out of bed, and done a round of jumping jacks before taking himself for a walk. This was a running joke in our family. We ribbed him ceaselessly about it. An eighty-year-old man doing jumping jacks? He looked ridiculous and he knew it. But he always brushed our japing aside. "They keep me healthy," he said. "As long as I can exercise, I know I'm physically fit."

"Has he lost weight?" I said.

"Yes," my mom said.

"About how much weight has he lost?"

She thought for a moment. "I would say twenty or twenty-five pounds."

Okay, that didn't sound right. Not right at all. "Mom, listen. I want you to take him to the emergency room."

"Why?" she said. "What's wrong?"

"That's what I want to figure out. You take him, okay?"

"When?"

"Right now."

"Right now?"

"Have the doctor call me after he sees him."

"But Farzin—"

"Mom, just do it. Okay? Please. I'm traveling on a business trip, I'll call you as soon as I land."

I remember touching down in Michigan and hearing over the loudspeakers that my next flight was delayed. I checked my phone. I had voicemail. A doctor was calling from UCLA Medical. I called him back, introducing myself. "This is Dr. Tabibiazar," I said. "I'm calling about Nasser Tabibiazar? He's my father."

"I see." The doctor's voice sounded heavy. "I have some news. Are you sitting down?"

I found an empty seat in the terminal, heaved myself into it. "Yes. Go ahead."

"We did a CT scan on your father. It shows a mass in his left lung. A big one."

"How big?"

"Ten-point-five centimeters."

I thought I couldn't have heard that right. He must have meant 10.5 millimeters. That would have been more normal, more believable. I asked the doctor to repeat what he'd said but no, he got it right the first time. I couldn't believe it. A 10.5-centimeter mass in the lung of an eighty-two-year-old? Technically speaking, that's huge and most likely a death sentence. I started to cry.

The doctor understood my feelings at once. "I wish I had much better news."

The moment I got off the phone, I cancelled my business meeting and changed the last leg of my destination to Los Angeles. Ramin met me at the terminal when I landed. We hugged, then got in his car and drove to the hospital.

"What do we do?" I said.

Ramin shrugged in a way that was eerily similar to the way Dad always had. "You know the drill as well as I do. First, we do tests."

"We should do the full workup," I said.

Ramin nodded. "If the cancer's metastatic, we see where it's spread, maybe try to do chemo. If it's not metastatic, try surgery. Take the thing out. The problem with that, the thing's huge."

"But I think we should try it," I said. "I mean, this is Dad we're talking about. He survived everything else."

Ramin said nothing for a moment. "A mass that big, we have to be honest. The chances are good that it's spread."

"Don't go there yet. Let's wait for the tests."

Ramin was a clinical professor of cardiology at UCLA so Dad was able to get all his tests done fast. Days later, the oncologist called me with the biopsy results. "It's a clear case of non-small cell lung cancer, the same kind we see in smokers. Your father's lungs are full of tar. Has he ever smoked cigarettes?"

"No," I said. "Well, there was that time when he was a kid. He was doing his Humphrey Bogart thing."

"Excuse me?"

"Nothing," I said. "No, he never really smoked. But he lived for a long time in Abadan, near the oil refineries."

"Sorry. Where's that? Abadan?"

"It's in Iran. They had oil refineries there and the air always smelled sharp with the fumes."

"That could have done it," the doctor agreed. "Or maybe he was around other people who used cigarettes. Secondhand smoke could have caused it. Or maybe just living in Los Angeles with all the smog we have here."

Amazingly, the tests showed Dad's cancer was localized. This was a very good sign but we still had to deal with the mass in his lung. After discussing it with Dad's doctors, we decided the entire left lobe should be excised. Dad went through the surgery well. Then, as a precaution, we started him on rounds of chemotherapy but Dad's system couldn't tolerate the drugs so we stopped doing that two rounds into the course.

"Now what?" I said.

"Now," Ramin said, "we wait and see if it worked."

Those next few months were some of the longest of my life but our patience was rewarded. In August 2021, Dad's doctors declared him cancer free. We were overjoyed. After talking it over, Kelly and I decided to host everyone in Chattanooga to celebrate my father's good health. Two weeks before the reunion, my phone rang again. It was Ramin.

"Are you sitting down?" he said.

"Good God, not again. How's Dad?"

"It's not Dad. It's Mom," Ramin said. "She wasn't feeling so hot so we took her for tests and a biopsy. Ray, she has the exact same cancer that Dad had. The exact same mutation."

I remember rubbing my eyes, feeling weary. "What do we do?"

The answer was obvious. We'd pursue the same process Dad had, hoping it worked out as well for our mother. Cancelling the reunion, we set our sights on helping Mom through what appeared to be an uphill climb.

When I spoke to her over the phone, she asked, "But where did I get this thing? You think I contracted it from your father? Can I give it to anyone else, like Romina? What about my grandkids?"

"Maman, you know cancer isn't contagious. Look, I'm coming out there, okay? I'll explain it all to you then."

"But that's what I'm saying," she said. "If this is the same mutation, maybe you shouldn't come out. I don't want to give it to you."

I tried again and again to explain this was not how cancer worked. For all her training in microbiology, chemistry, medicine, all of it, for some reason, this wasn't getting through to her.

Business needs took me back to Boston in the days leading up to Mom's surgery. Three days before her appointment, my phone rang while I was in a meeting. It was Ramin. Excusing myself, I left the room and took the call.

"Okay?" I said.

"Are you sitting down?"

"Enough with this sitting down bullshit. Just tell me what's going on," I snapped. "Is Mom okay?"

"It's Dad again this time. Yesterday, we noticed he was having trouble walking."

I held my breath. "Okay?"

"We took him back to the hospital. They did an MRI." Ramin inhaled. "His cancer is back. It's gone to his brain."

My mind was whirling faster than I ever imagined it could. "Who knows?"

"I haven't told anyone else yet. Not even Baba knows."

"Keep it that way. I'll be there the first thing tomorrow."

I flew to LA the next morning and took a car to Ramin's house. We hugged each other, then sat down to tea, which we both drank automatically, barely tasting it.

"What do we do?" Ramin said.

"We can't tell Mom," I said. "She's about to go under the knife. She has to stay focused. She needs her strength. If she knows about Dad. . ."

Ramin understood. "But what about Dad?"

"Does he know his results yet?"

Ramin shook his head.

"Then here's what we do. We take them out to dinner. Get Mom pumped up that she'll come through her surgery. Tell her all will be well."

"And Dad?"

"After dinner, you and I take Dad for a walk. Tell Mom we're just checking his balance but really we tell him his tests came back. We tell him the options and ask what he wants us to do."

Ramin concurred so that's what we did.

When we broke the news to my father, he said nothing. A long moment passed. The first words he used to break the silence were "Don't tell your mother. You understand me? Not under any circumstances."

"We know, Dad," Ramin said. "We won't."

"Dad, what do you want us to do?" I said. "What course of treatment?"

He shrugged. By then he had lost so much weight, he was difficult to recognize. He looked like a lawn gnome version of the man I'd grown up with. "I'll do whatever you think should be done. You're the doctors," he said. "Work out the treatment that gives me the best chance. I'll follow it. We will fight this thing again and see what happens."

Ramin and I traded looks.

Dad caught our glances and smiled. "Listen," he said. "If it doesn't work, I've had a good life. Take care of your sister. Take care of your mom."

"Don't worry, Dad," said Ramin. "We're going to win this."

Again, my dad smiled. "As far as I see it, I've already won. I'm so proud of you all."

Mom's surgery went well. She had almost the same procedure my father had, a total lobectomy, very invasive but also remarkably comprehensive. Her doctors told us she wouldn't require chemo but her recovery would last about three weeks. We took advantage of her downtime to book Dad immediately for courses of radiation and chemo. And while I'd like to report that my mother had no idea what was going on, sadly this wasn't the case.

"Where is your father?" she would ask us. "Why isn't he coming to visit me?"

"He was here yesterday, Mom," we told her. "But you were asleep."

"So you say."

"Well, it's true."

"And the day before that? You said the same thing."

Eventually, she found out what had happened. By that point, however, any upset our deceit might have caused was forgotten. We had bigger issues to contend with. Dad's health was touch and go for a while but it looked like he would pull through. Then, around Christmas in 2021, I got another phone call. It was Mom.

"Hello?" I said.

Mom's voice: "Farzin?"

"How is he?"

"Not well." Mom's silence tells me how bad things are. "He says the Nazis are coming."

"The what?"

"The Nazis. Your father says they are on the way now. We must hide, he says. They're coming to take all of us to the ovens. He isn't speaking Farsi, he's speaking in Turkish."

"He's hallucinating," I say.

Encephalitis, I thought. Given everything Dad had been through with his cancers, the chemo, radiation—encephalitis made sense.

"Mom, have you called Ramin? Does he know about this?"

"No," she said.

"Call 911. Take Dad to the emergency room right now. I'll fly out tomorrow."

"And that's what happened today?" Eliana says. "Before we got here? Fafa called to tell you this?"

"Yes." Pulling my cell phone out, I rose from the table. "So we'll have to leave things there, okay? I need to book a flight to LA. I'll go there tomorrow and see what I can do."

"Can we help you in any way?" Kelly asks.

Her question halts me dead in my tracks. "To be honest. . . guys, I could really use a hug right now."

Moments later, I find myself enfolded in four sets of arms.

There is no place else I'd rather be.

Encephalitis is a serious disease that lacks a definitive diagnosis. In medicine, we consider it a diagnosis by exclusion. It's one of the frustrating aspects of treating it. How do you decide to proceed? But proceed you must because, without treatment, encephalitis can be devastating. On top of all this, Dad was in the hospital at the height of the COVID pandemic. Precaution protocols were off the charts and he wasn't allowed many visitors.

Ramin and I hold daily conversations with his doctors. In the absence of a definitive diagnosis, we decide to treat dad empirically, not entirely sure what he has but willing to bet our suspicions are right. Dad's medical team begins giving him high-dose steroids and intravenous immunoglobulin: antibody mixtures shunted directly into the bloodstream to treat any number of health conditions, including severe inflammatory diseases.

Encephalitis cooks the brain like a cake in an oven. People who have it lose their higher functions until the inflammation dies down. By the time I arrive in LA, Dad is still caught fast in the grip of powerful visual and auditory hallucinations. When somebody goes in to see him, he thinks they're Nazis or Pasdaran operatives coming to get him and he reacts violently. Or sometimes he pretends to be dead. One time I'm in his room, swaddled in protective gear—plastic gown, rubber gloves, plastic visor. I watch Dad's medical team try to measure his level of consciousness by pricking his fingers and toes. When he doesn't respond, they write him off as catatonic. Possibly he's had a stroke, they say. So sorry. There's nothing more we can do.

Once they leave and the door closes behind them, Dad opens one eye and stares up at me. "Farzin! Are they gone?"

"They're gone, Dad. Yeah."

"Quick! They'll be back! It's not safe here. They're tapping the phones. Get your mother, Ramin, and Romina and get them all out of here. Hurry!"

How does he remember our names? I think. *He doesn't know where he is so how does he even recognize me?* Even now, bereft of a fully functioning brain, my father's primary thoughts are for the safety of his family.

It takes several weeks of patient, diligent treatment. With Ramin's guidance, the hospital staff finally brings Dad's inflammation under control. This becomes an especially busy time for me. Each month I spend about one week in Chattanooga with my wife and kids, two weeks up in Boston pursuing new business opportunities, and one week out in LA to check on my father and help my mother. I'm booking so many flights for myself, I consider opening my own travel agency. If only I could afford a private jet.

At one point in all this, Dad's health dips again. He loses most of his fine motor skills and can no longer feed himself. Fearing the worst, I fly Kelly and the kids out to say their good-byes. COVID protocols are still in full effect so Dad can't see his grandkids face-to-face. Undaunted, I take a video camera into his room and set it up on a tripod.

Weak and thin as Dad is, he regards this process with clinical interest. "What are you doing?" he asks.

"Making a video so you can talk to your grandkids."

He purses his lips, looking comically upset before shaking his head. "Not like this. Get me out of these scrubs. I want to wear a nice shirt."

Mom helps get him get out of bed and gets him dressed. She sits him in a chair so he can look comfortable. Somewhat normal.

I hit the record button. "Baba, do you have anything you want to say to your grandkids?"

My father grows suddenly cagey. "What do you want me to say?"

"Whatever you want."

He thinks this through. "Stay healthy," he finally says.

"That's it? What about if they get sick? How should they get over their sickness? How did you overcome your illness?"

Dad thinks about this a bit more. "Be supportive. Be together," he says. "Give strength to each other and help one another. Be blessed. If you're healthy, I'm healthy. Be happy. Your happiness is my happiness. That is the best gift."

I then go through each grandchild—my kids, Ramin's, and Romina's. Dad offers them words of advice in response to my specific questions.

Do you want Liam to be Jewish? "Doesn't matter what your religion is," Dad says. "Everyone is the same. We all have the same God so don't worry about labels. Just be pure in your heart and be good to your parents."

Addie is worried about her size. My dad shakes his head. "Addie dear, greatness is not measured in body size, it's measured in what you do."

Which sport should Eliana pursue? And what should she study in college? "That's not for me to say," Dad responds. "Do whatever makes you happy and a better person. Find your passion."

We all feel tremendous relief when, once again, Dad pulls himself out of a nosedive. His recovery is nothing short of miraculous. After all the things he's survived up to now, I suppose we might have expected this. By March 2022, he is feeling much better. So good, in fact, that we renew our commitment to hold a family reunion. Ramin flies everyone out to Chattanooga to visit in August 2022.

I will always remember that visit as one of the highlights of my life. I think my parents will, too. There are challenges, of course. Dad has trouble moving around. Due to his illness, he has to learn to walk all over again, like a toddler taking his first steps. This would be difficult for a young person. For a man in his mid-eighties who's nearly died more times than any of us can count, it is nothing short of heroic, as was my mother's constant care for him.

During the reunion, neither of my parents let their infirmities get in the way of the family's good time. Dad sits in whatever chair we put him in with a smile on his face while he holds Mom's hand. I watch him enjoying the ruckus, the laughter, the jokes, shared memories, and all the many tales of trials undergone in years now past.

One day, we take him out on our boat and motor along the Tennessee River. I let him take the wheel. He seems deeply impressed by the power I've put in his hands, how the gentlest nudge in one direction or another causes the sleek craft to bank and carom over the waves like a flat stone skipping across a brook. *Like life*, I think. *All directions are open at every moment. But the trajectory, the velocity, the angle you launch yourself with. . . that's all up to us. Intention is everything. Outcomes are there from the start if we choose to think in this manner.*

"What do you think, Dad?" I have to holler a bit to be heard above the seethe and roar of the engines. "Doesn't this remind you of Khorramshahr? The Karun River?"

His hearing isn't as sharp as it was. I repeat the question a few times before he understands. Then he laughs. "This river is cleaner," he tells me in Farsi. Then he turns to my mother. Of course, he does. Even now, perhaps especially now, the two are bonded, inseparable. They are nothing without each other. "Flora, what do you think?" he calls.

My mother looks around and calls back, "This place is prettier than Khorramshahr ever was."

Something about this moves me to tears. I lift my phone and snap a picture of Dad standing at the steering wheel, holding it tight in his old man's tendon-y grip. The summer sun bounces off his bald dome, hurling heliographs at the lens, and an eerie feeling strikes me, familiar but unrecognizable, too. It confuses me until, later, I find myself flicking through family photos and find the picture again.

There. I knew that I had seen it. Just hadn't had words at the time to describe it. The grinning old man in the photo I took of Dad at the wheel of the boat is smaller, for sure. All his hair has been shed. Time and age have worked on him, folding and carving his skin into layers of wrinkles. Thinner, he looks more vulnerable and frail. Still, I recognize this man at once. The same man in the faded old photograph of young Dr. Nasser Tabibiazar sitting behind the wheel of the green Volkswagen Beetle of which he was once so fiercely proud.

Isn't it odd? I think. *We start out as one thing in life. But the years, our crazy experiences, our goals, our dreams, our relationships. . . they end up sculpting our spirits like clay. In the end, we are always much different but also the same as the very first day we began. How is this possible? What links these versions of self? What strands interweave in the web of our lives and shape it into a whole?*

The very next day, my father answers these questions.

It is the last day that my parents, Ramin, Romina, and their families will be in Tennessee. Everyone is packed. Cars stand waiting to take them to the airport. Given my parents' ages and given the issues they've recently faced, I know we all feel this might be the last time we gather, complete as a family.

This makes the occasion poignant enough on its own. But at one point, my mother pokes my father in his slat ribs with her bony elbow. "Nasser," she tells him in Farsi. "Do it now if you're going to do it!"

Ramin, Romina, and I trade glances.

"Do what, Mom?" Romina says.

Mom fixes us with her most serious look. "Baba has something he wants to tell all of you." She turns to my father and waits.

Dad sits in his chair wearing a look of tremendous reluctance. Then he screws up his wrinkled old face and worms his lips to shape words in English. "I. . . love. . . you," he says.

It feels like a lightning bolt has struck me. The hair on my arms stands up and I realize distantly I've stopped breathing. All my life, I have never heard Dad utter these words.

"I. . . love you," he repeats. A bit stronger this time. More sure of himself. "I love you."

Ramin, Romina, and I are speechless.

Our children, however, respond as children everywhere do when these words are spoken. Crowding around my father, they wrap their smooth, pink arms round his neck in a hug like a human safety net. Tears spring into his old man's eyes but he quickly blinks them away. He mutters something in Farsi and Liam turns toward me. "What did he say?"

It's hard to speak. My throat has gone tight. I can barely believe what I've heard. "Baba would like each of his grandkids to come forward. He wants to hug you all, one at a time."

And so this is done. With my mother hovering over him like some angel, as she always has, my father takes each child in his arms and kisses them, murmuring words in his broken English: "I love you. You are my family. I am so proud of you."

I notice that, each time he does this, he finds some deeper level of peace.

When it's his turn, Liam moves forward, wrapping my father in his embrace. After whispering something in his Baba's ear, he moves to his Fafa and hugs her, too, before stepping aside so his sisters can have their moments. Eliana and Addie move in. Liam looks up. Our eyes meet. And somehow, in that fraction of a second, the odyssey our ancestors made over countless generations, spanning continents, hardships lost and forgotten. . . it all finds a home in my son's youthful gaze.

I move to a quiet place in the house. As if drawn by powerful magnets, Liam moves toward me, then we, too, are hugging. My eyes have turned wet and I dab at them.

"Pappy, are you alright?"

The words pour out of me. "Now do you understand?"

Liam looks up at me, not really sure what I mean.

"I told you the story of our family," I say. "It's peppered with secrets throughout for why and how ordinary people do extraordinary things. Things that turn them into heroes. Do you know what I mean?"

Liam thinks about that for a moment, then nods. "These things are. . . like dealing with fear and danger and sacrifice. Right? And that family comes first."

"Exactly," I say. "Real heroes don't wear capes. And now you know all the secrets of being a hero for your own family."

Liam smiles.

"Everything Baba and Fafa—my aunts, uncles, and grandparents—sacrificed over and over again. Why did we do it? It was so all of us— you, your sisters, your uncle, your aunt, your cousins, your mother and I. . . so we could all be here in this moment. Together. To me, this is the best, the only success that is ever worth having. The only reason for being a hero."

Liam looks at his grandparents, thinking. "If there's one big secret to being a hero, it's love," he says. "Love for your family."

In this moment, I am proud of him. Proud of us all. "You are correct," I say. "There is no more powerful force in life. Remember that."

Liam looks at me, grinning. "Yes, Pappy. I will."

ACKNOWLEDGMENTS

This book could not have been written without the contributions and encouragements of many people. While I cannot thank all of them properly, I feel compelled to name a special few.

First thanks go to my wife, Kelly, a wonderful mother, loving daughter, and dedicated doctor who's also my hero and angel. And our three children, Eliana, Addie, and Liam, who inspired and keep inspiring me to write.

Next thanks go to my brother, Ramin, my best friend and lifelong companion. Words can't express how much you've done for our family, Ramin. Thanks also go to my sister, Romina, the secret glue holding our family together through all our crazy adventures. Romina, you never stopped encouraging me to tell our family's story. This book is steeped in your spirit.

To my nephew Zach, who took such tender care of me when I needed it most during my father's illness and who never tired of hearing stories about his father and grandfather. Thanks also go to my nephew Noah, who taught me that love for our families begins at a very young age. Noah, the image I have of you rushing to hold my father's hand, then helping him shuffle, sick from his chemo, across the street, is forever etched in my heart. May this book acquaint you with all the stories of why it's important that we keep looking out for each other.

Thanks also go to Saeed and Sima, whose friendship acts as a pillar within my parents' lives. As do all my many aunts, uncles, and cousins, whose love is the force of life itself. In fact, the more I kept writing this book, the more I began to see that the real ordinary heroes I was hoping to identify—and the secrets of their heroism—were each and every one of us. Your stories are mine. My stories are yours. May they build and support one another as time marches forward.

In that regard, I must also thank the many fond memories I have of Sarah, Tavooz, Mirza, Ahron, Rabi, Zarbabel, Mouis, Jahangir, Elyas, Helen, Lotfalla,

Rahel, Manoocher, and Parviz. I also thank Farideh for the very important role she played in our family's evolution.

Damon, Amanda, and Steve were the best editors any writer could ever wish for. This book would be unreadable had it not been for their uncompromising commitment and dedication. Thank you all for that. Thanks also to Virginia and Ian for keeping the road to this book's successful completion as clear as it possibly could be.

Last but not least, I'd like to thank all the other storytellers who, over the years, have bravely shared their lives in the pages of their books. You are my role models. I take courage from you. And I wish to pay that forward.

It is my fondest wish that someone reading this book will be inspired to tell their own tale. Perhaps you're doing it to respect your parents. Perhaps to undergo your own catharsis. Or perhaps you're writing to inform your own children and grandchildren of where they came from.

Each of these reasons is fine. In fact, no specific reason is needed. But do it. Write down everything that you know and give it to people you love.

Each time somebody does that, I can't help but think we all win.

Dr. Ray Tabibiazar
Chattanooga, Tennessee
May 2023

ABOUT THE AUTHOR

Dr. Ray Tabibiazar is a physician-scientist and an entrepreneur. He trained as a medical doctor at Harvard Medical School and as a cardiologist at Stanford University.

He is the founder of a handful of biotechnology companies, including, most recently, a company that pioneered a new class of medicine that adds a healthy genetic code to a patient's genome to treat their genetic diseases.

When not working, Ray spends time with his wife and their three children while enjoying art, hiking, diving, and traveling around the world. The family lives in Chattanooga.

This is Ray's first book.

More about the book: **www.SecretsofOrdinaryHeroes.com**
More about publisher: **www.KeralPublishing.com**

www.ingramcontent.com/pod-product-compliance
Lightning Source LLC
Chambersburg PA
CBHW020440130626
46549CB00001B/223